W9-AFL-294

SCIENCE FICTION: TEN EXPLORATIONS

Also by C. N. Manlove

MODERN FANTASY: FIVE STUDIES

LITERATURE AND REALITY, 1600–1800

THE GAP IN SHAKESPEARE: THE MOTIF OF
DIVISION FROM *RICHARD II* TO *THE TEMPEST*

THE IMPULSE OF FANTASY LITERATURE

SCIENCE FICTION: TEN EXPLORATIONS

C. N. Manlove

The Kent State University Press

MIDDLEBURY COLLEGE LIBRARY

AAZ 4203

1/1987

© C. N. Manlove 1986
All rights reserved. No reproduction, copy or
transmission of this publication may be made without
written permission.

Published in the United States by
THE KENT STATE UNIVERSITY PRESS
Kent, Ohio 44242

Printed in Hong Kong

Library of Congress Catalog Card No. 85–14738
ISBN 0–87338–326–5

PS
374
.S35
M36
1986

Library of Congress Cataloging-in-Publication Data

Manlove, C. N. (Colin Nicholas)
   Science fiction.

   Bibliography: p.
   Includes index.
   1. Science fiction, American–History and criticism.
2. Science fiction, English–History and criticism.
I. Title.
PS374.S35M36   1986   813'.0876'09   85–14738
ISBN 0–87338–326–5

To the Memory of My Father

We are not going to end with a bang.
We are not going to end with a whimper.
We are not going to end.
That's all.

Donald Wollheim, The Universe Makers

Contents

Preface

This book began from a feeling which must be common to many readers of science fiction. With the story read and a whole new world of images lived in and explored, there is a sense of mystery and power about these works which no mere dismissal in terms of 'well thought-out story', 'interesting twist', 'subtle intellectual argument' or 'superb imagination' will suffice. All these phrases are true, in their place, yet one feels that what has been explored by the minds that made these works needs for adequate response an exploration on the part of the reader also. We have to try to find out why these strange worlds and events are as they are. We have to journey into the interior of the text and discover in the end that actually all the details can be part of patterns and the whole work become rich with unity and unsuspected significance. This has been one of the primary pleasures of writing this book; and the communication of that pleasure is its first object.

Most of the chapter on Gene Wolfe's *The Book of the New Sun* originally appeared as an article in *Kansas Quarterly* for summer 1984. I am grateful to the editors for permission to reprint.

I owe a considerable debt to Edinburgh University Library for its ready acquisition of large numbers of books making possible essential research into current criticism of science fiction. My thanks also to my colleague Ian Campbell for kindly lending me his collection of journals on science fiction. And I am grateful once more to Sheila Campbell for typing the manuscript so well: no-one could ask for more care and diligence than she has given. To the dedicatee of this book I have felt perhaps less a sense of obligation than of renewed kinship with a mind which while sternly scientific also liked to speculate among the interstellar spaces.

C.N.M.

Acknowledgements

The author and publishers wish to thank the following who have kindly given permission for the use of copyright material: the Hutchinson Publishing Group Ltd and Simon & Schuster, for the extract from Gene Wolfe, *The Claw of the Conciliator*; and Laurence Pollinger Ltd and Kirby McCauley, for the extract from Clifford D. Sinak, *Shakespeare's Planet*.

1 Introduction

Science fiction, for long spurned as the sub-literary product of cranks and escapists, and read and ardently defended only by cultists of the genre, has over the past decade in America at least established for itself a wider acceptance in academic circles and certainly a much larger world-wide readership, to the point where some see it as taking over the role of the realistic novel. The reason for the expansion of the readership is doubtless the increased vogue for the fantastic generally, together with a heightened awarenes of the dynamic process of scientific discovery and the contingency of our frail and threatened world. But the reasons for science fiction's having become academically respectable are rather different. It has done so largely by being seen as a metaphor, myth or projection of our world.

It was always the case that the literary establishment was just willing to give a place to such works as Mary Shelley's *Frankenstein*, or Wells's *Time Machine* or Huxley's *Brave New World*, because these were seen to be visions of dangerous features of our own society and selves, whether in the dangers of unfettered science, the repression of the unconscious or the destruction of individuality. But now this stance is hardening into dogma. Science fiction we find is only really worth considering when it tells us something about ourselves. Even some science fiction writers, eager to break out of the *laager* of the genre, maintain that their fantastic worlds are really heightened pictures of our own.[1] The 'New Wave' science fiction in the 1960s was in large part an attempt to escape from adventure-yarn science fiction to a more complex and referential literature, which among other benefits would bring the genre in from the cold of the disreputable. In this it has certainly succeeded. But if one looks at the writers and works repeatedly put at the forefront of consideration, one finds that they are generally the most extrapolative and satiric, and certainly the most evidently intellectual and sophisticated – writers such as Olaf Stapledon, Stanislaw Lem, Samuel Delany, Thomas Disch,

Ursula Le Guin, Philip K. Dick; particularly 'meaningful' works by other authors, such as Clarke's *Childhood's End*, James Blish's *A Case of Conscience*, Pohl's *The Space Merchants*. And one finds that the science fiction medium, the images of other worlds and beings, the strange narratives and laws, are often either ignored or reduced to being carriers – albeit commendable – of some deep meaning that tells us more about our condition.[2]

There can be no wish finally to disparage this form of reading. It is good that science fiction should be able to carry this power, that it should be able to hold its own in literary potency with other more hallowed genres. But it does seem the case that the 'fictional' element, the element of invention, is receiving less than its due. And it is worth recalling that science fiction's readership enjoys the medium of fantastic worlds as much as – perhaps more than – any burden of 'significance' the works may carry. The very existence of the science fiction creation supposes that our world is only one among many: why should we so obstinately seek to haul it back to our world alone? This book is directed to restoring attention to the fictional element in science fiction. We need to get back to the creative impulse behind much science fiction and to the strangeness of the worlds it puts before us. We need to recognize that such themes as it may generate within itself can have more immediately to do with the reality of its *own* world than with that of ours. This is in effect a plea for a renewed awareness of the alien in science fiction, the alien as the indestructible this-ness of the worlds it makes, rather than as a projection only of our fears or hopes.[3]

The book has another if perhaps lesser aim. All too often criticism of science fiction has devoted itself either to talking about science fiction in general terms only, or has considered individual works only briefly as they relate to a single motif pursued across the entire genre. When it comes to actual literary analysis many commentators falter, give plot summaries with occasional comment, talk at length about the meaning of a text rather than the way that meaning is carried, or turn to the more evidently discussible sorts of text already mentioned to provide often arcane readings. In short, and to be very blunt, there is precious little in the way of extended and plain literary criticism of science fiction, certainly not of book length since David Samuelson's *Visions of Tomorrow* (1974). And this is actually parallel to the larger concern of this book: just as critics refuse to attend to the individuality of science fiction's worlds and look away from them to ours, so they find it hard really to talk about the books as literature. It is not easy to do either of these things, it is true: but they must be done if science fiction is to be given its full due as literature.

The authors we shall be considering are most of them household names in science fiction – Isaac Asimov, Frederik Pohl, Brian Aldiss, Frank Herbert, Robert Silverberg, Philip José Farmer, Arthur C. Clarke, Clifford Simak; and of the books themselves all but three have won science fiction awards, and several of them – Asimov's *Foundation* trilogy, Herbert's *Dune*, Farmer's 'Riverworld' series and Wolfe's *The Book of the New Sun* – are among the modern giants of the genre. Only a few of them have been extensively analysed before. With most of them we shall be exploring what is often a fairly resistant surface, finding a way of both appreciating and understanding the peculiar idiom of each work. For each is peculiar, each world sheerly different from that of the others. Together they could be said to form a cross section of science fiction: some are intellectual, some fantastic; some quite near in terms of possibility, others very remote; some scientific, some semi-mystical.

All of the books discussed here grew out of quite prodigious jumps of the imagination, as large if not as portentous as those of a scientist discovering a new way of looking at something. It would be wrong to say they are all 'original' in the sense of totally novel: one can trace indebtednesses and ancestries. But all delight in exploration of the new and strange: the desert planet Arrakis in *Dune*, the mysteries of the world happened on in Simak's *Shakespeare's Planet*, the afterlife world of Farmer's Riverworld series, the bizarre, jungled Earth of Aldiss's *Hothouse*, the huge, cylindrical spaceship explored in Clarke's *Rendezvous with Rama*, the nature of future history in Asimov's *Foundation* books, the changed Earth in Attanasio's *Radix*, Silverberg's *Nightwings*, Pohl's *Alternating Currents* and Wolfe's *Book of the New Sun*. Apart from Pohl's *Alternating Currents*, which is often a satiric, if fantastic, extension of present-day trends, or Clarke's *Rendezvous with Rama*, which poses contact with a 'UFO', none of them is given any direct link with our world, whether as prediction, warning or metaphoric portrayal of what we are; though this is not to say that analogies cannot be drawn.[4] Like Wells's *The Time Machine*, Aldiss's *Hothouse* and Wolfe's *Book of the New Sun* are about Earth in the far future: but unlike Wells they do not link the human condition then to tendencies at work in the present; and this is also true of the temporally nearer but still islanded futures portrayed by Silverberg and Attanasio. Asimov's *Foundation* trilogy is conducted in a galactic context with no reference to Earth; and the same could be said of Herbert's *Dune*, Farmer's Riverworld books, even of Simak's *Shakespeare's Planet*, which though it mentions Earth, deals with human problems in confronting empty space which have no direct reference to us.

All the works centre on imagery: one or more images, whether of a hollow cylinder kilometres long and wide, or of endless rows of bodies stacked in a void, or planets at the opposite ends of a spiral galaxy. Because they are so founded they are guaranteed irreducible power: no matter how much they work things out or become explicit, the image is still there like some dark sun breeding energy. In science fiction these images are usually quite novel, where in fantasy they tend to be more traditional: Tolkien's Middle-earth is as he says a 'recovery' of the old, and Peake's Gormenghast is a huge castle. The object in science fiction is the discovery of the new rather than of what we have somewhere already been aware: no one has ever thought of a giant cruciform war machine whirling through the air with people shooting from turrets on each of its arms; no one has imagined let alone created so solidly as Clarke has done a five-kilometre long spike sur- rounded by lesser spikes as part of a possible propulsion unit of an alien space-craft; no one has had as a character in a book a walking pond that is the offspring of a far, watery planet. In Farmer's Riverworld series the creation of the images of the afterlife that start the first book alone generates enough energy to drive us through four books in search of an answer.

Anything so radically new and exciting as this deserves credit simply for having been brought into being. Certainly it is where this book starts from – the sense of the creativity of these works. Just as they explore, the mind of the reader is drawn in, fascinated, to explore them. Because they have given pleasure, one wants to communicate some of it. We really do need to have some way of talking about the power of such creations. This book is an attempt to find such a language. It sets out to celebrate the originality of the images and worlds created, both in themselves, and in the way that they further the significances of the works in which they appear. In this way the science fictional element of the books will retain its own value without becoming justified solely in terms of the extent to which it is amenable to the methods of criticism applied to 'mainstream' literature. This approach must be set against some understanding of what science fiction is – how it developed, and what are some of its distinguishing features. For its beginnings one can go back as far as Plato, but its real development starts with the time of the industrial and scientific revolution itself, in the late eighteenth and early nineteenth centuries, and with Mary Shelley's *Frankenstein* (1818), which reflects the new scientific powers given to man.[5] In this work man has the god-like power to make life; but he is repelled by his own creation. The work contains both progressivist and sceptical tendencies, and these tendencies are to be seen in much science fiction of the nineteenth century – indeed it is possible to see them as part of the heritage of all British science fiction, including the work of Wyndham, Clarke, Aldiss and Brian Stableford (writers such as Huxley, Orwell and Ballard being more exclusively satiric and sceptical). In Poe's 'The Facts in the Case of M. Valdemar' (1845), a life-extending drug fails, with sordid results; in Lytton's *The Coming Race* (1871), the scientific advances of the Vril-ya beneath Earth will finally destroy man, in something like an eruption of the suppressed unconscious. *The Strange Case of Doctor Jekyll and Mr Hyde* (1886) portrays both the convention-breaking power given to Jekyll through the drug he discovers, and also the disaster caused when those powers no longer keep to their allotted province. The same Faustian ambiguity – praise of man's mind together with condemnation of its unfettered menace – is seen in H. G. Wells's *The Island of Dr Moreau* (1896) and *The Invisible Man* (1897), where scientific brilliance is shown as dangerously amoral in its manipulations of life. In many nineteenth-century works, too, the brilliance of scientific mind is set beside a seemingly correspondent degradation of body: the ugliness of Frankenstein's monster beside the pure intellect of his maker, the loathsome decay of Valdemar, the deformity of Hyde, the huge Martian intellects of *The War of the Worlds* (1898) locked in their gross and helpless bodies, the perversions of human and animal form shaped by Dr Moreau. Science fiction continues to the present to show a sense of the dualism of mind and body, if not in quite this form. The genre, inasmuch as it is centrally concerned with the works of science, often registers the alienation of modern man from his environment: mind from the body it inhabits, cities and machines from the country and the life on which they ultimately depend.

Nineteenth and early twentieth-century science fiction could still often locate the pursuit of science in the individual, the manic inventor with his lonely and often dangerous insight, his forbidden knowledge. But over the course of this century, and particularly since the last war, the advance of science has ceased either to be a peculiarity or the creation only of a single mind. Science has become an arm of the state and a product of the collective, and to that extent responsibility for its doings lies no longer with readily identifiable personages but with nations or the human race as a whole. In the nineteenth century the individual inventor in a science fiction narrative – whether a Frankenstein or a Captain Nemo – might pay for his indifference to humanity; but modern 'dystopian' fiction, from Huxley's *Brave New World* to Thomas Disch's *Camp Concentration*, registers the sense that science is now a juggernaut before which the individual man, perhaps even society itself, is now helpless. Increasingly one finds in modern science fiction an element of determinism, of stress on fate or chance, whether for the good or ill of humanity; and the heroes of science fiction have often ceased to be eccentrics or outsiders and have become representatives or even carriers of a wider collective, often the entire human race, devoted to the same ends as themselves.

Modern science fiction has become far wider or 'epic' in its purview. The action in nineteenth-century science fiction (unlike the fantasy) is often fairly circumscribed – a mountain setting, a few rooms and streets, caverns underground, a house; there may be visits to utopias or dystopias, sometimes on other planets, but it is not the journey or the distance that counts, but what is found there and how it contrasts with our world. *Frankenstein* ends with the magnificent chase over the far northern ice, true: it shows the urge that is there in science fiction to push the mind and the environment to its furthest limits: but it is only with Verne, in such works as *A Journey to the Centre of the Earth* (1864), or *Twenty Thousand Leagues Under the Sea* (1870), that the sense of a gigantic new dimension and backcloth is opened up. What Verne initiated in space, Wells continued, though also giving, in *The Time Machine*, a sense of the epic vastness of time. The quest for sheer wonder at the vast is continued in the so-called 'space operas' of the 1930s, such as those of E. E. 'Doc' Smith in his celebrated 'Skylark' and 'Lensman' series, .where heroes act out spy stories and western shoot-outs against a galactic and temporally enormous backcloth;

the novels of Jack Williamson (for example *The Legion of Space* (1934) and *The Legion of Time* (1938)); and A. E. van Vogt's wonder-gobbling *Voyage of the Space Beagle* (1950) is a late example. But these large contexts began to take on more substance when they became part of a cosmological vision, in the work of Olaf Stapledon, particularly in *Last and First Men* (1930) and *Star Maker* (1937). In *Last and First Men* Stapledon rises to an imaginative projection of billenia of human evolution out into the solar system. *Star Maker* is more teleological in concern, describing the journey of a human mind out from the Earth to contact the minds of other intelligent races and thence further outwards to communal minds, interstellar and intergalactic minds, until reaching a final transcendent awareness of the infinite spirit which forever contemplates the multitude of universes it has actualised, with 'all pity and all love, but mastered by a frosty ecstasy'.

Stapledon's view is Olympian and essentially boundless in those novels (not so in the more 'local' *Odd John* and *Sirius*). In a sense what he did could be done well once only: he captured the essential lust for infinity of the mind. But he gave to later writers a world view with which to shape the stubborn universe; even a new teleology. Wells had tended to see the scheme of things as either indifferent to or hostile to man: Stapledon accepted the indifference and made a higher purpose beyond it. It is to him in large part at least that science fiction owes its later recurrent concern with the meaning of existence. And he gave back a contemplative side to the genre, putting the universe and the stars and man's simultaneous significance and insignificance beside them at the centre of his effect, rather than as the stimulating backgrounds of 'space opera'. After him it was for Asimov in his *Foundation* series to use a galactic perspective which is more bounded by human purpose, and in which more individual human characters played a part: he gave to Stapledon's vision a relatively local habitation and a name.[6] This fusion has played a crucial part in the evolution of subsequent science fiction. Increasingly science fiction writers have evolved their own worlds, stellar systems or universes and put them and wonder at them at the centre of their work.

Unlike its sister 'kind' of fantasy, science fiction was early established as a genre, at least so far as an audience was concerned. This process was initiated through magazines of what was first called 'scientifiction': the pioneering editor was Hugo Gernsback, who began *Amazing Stories* in 1926. Gernsback's aim –

if he soon found it only partly capable of realization – was to teach the possibilities of science through the medium of fiction. The other side of what has been called this 'physical science' period of science fiction was the vogue of 'space opera', of heroes in physical combat against a galactic background; space opera was recklessly insouciant of scientific plausibility, and was in effect a release for the imagination, otherwise tied down to technical 'exactitudes'. The next vehicle of definition was *Astounding Stories*, begun in 1933, which under the highly influential editorship of John W. Campbell became *Astounding Science Fiction* in 1938, and continued thus till 1953 when it developed through further titles. This, one of the longest-lived of science-fiction magazines, served to develop the talents of many of the giants of the field, including Asimov, Pohl and Simak. Campbell looked for stories with a strong technical basis, though not with technology at the centre: he looked too for more predictive stories, and his concern was with 'social science fiction', with the influence of science on man in general rather than on individuals or by itself. Under his aegis science fiction became more capable of vision. In the same period and partly through his influence one finds increasing use of mental as much as physical science in science fiction – thus telepathy, communal minds (John Wyndham) or psychohistory (Asimov).[7]

The final magazine development of science fiction went one stage further: the writers of the 'New Wave' in the 1960s and contributors to the British magazine *New Worlds* under the editorship of Michael Moorcock aimed to break down the 'genre' fence of science fiction, and, while still retaining its imaginative and technical licence with 'reality', make it capable of effects which would give it authority as literature in its own right. Even this level of control has now gone, and science fiction is now developing in myriad directions under its own momentum, as can be seen already from the range of the invited stories submitted to Harlan Ellison by science fiction writers for his *Dangerous Visions* series (1967–72). Over the whole period it can be said that the development of science fiction has been steadily away from hard scientific content and towards the creation of more fantastic worlds – though there are continual exceptions, such as Hal Clement's *Mission of Gravity* (1954), Stanislaw Lem's *Solaris* (1961), Frank Herbert's *Destination: Void* (1966) or Frederik Pohl's *Man Plus* (1976). At the same time, if one excludes 'space opera' from consideration, there has been something of a development outwards, from the individual to the collective and from this world to less plausible and finally fantastic ones. Thus science fiction has in a sense been fighting its way out of its own corner for the last fifty years, to the point where many science fiction writers can now write semi-supernaturalist works of magical realms (even if the magic often turns out in the end to be scientifically based) – Brian Aldiss's *The Malacia Tapestry* (1976), Ian Watson's *The Gardens of Delight* (1980), Robert Silverberg's *Lord Valentine's Castle* (1980) or his *Majipoor Chronicles* (1982), Clifford Simak's *Special Deliverance* (1982).

Given such mutation, it might seem no easy task to find distinctive features in science fiction, let alone define it. Surprisingly enough, however, there are a number of recurrent characteristics. Even if the level of science in science fiction is not a constant, the genre could generally be said to be concerned with technology, or at least with the area of mind responsible for technological advance – the intellectual, conscious self. Herbert, Aldiss, Ballard, in their different ways stress the frailties of the conscious mind, and show the devouring force of the primitive and unconscious when they have been shut away: in one way Herbert's planet Dune, with the engulfing worms and spice beneath the arid desert is an image of the layered mind. Others such as Pohl or Philip K. Dick warn of the dangers of advances in communication and mass control. Still others value technical development and increasing control over nature – Asimov, Larry Niven. A side of science fiction which makes the word 'science' accidentally opposite is the concern in many such works with knowing, with finding something out – the location of the Second Foundation, who made Riverworld, how to escape from a closed planet, what has made the world as it is, what is the nature of an alien space-craft. Fantasy, by contrast, looks more directly to the unconscious or 'spiritual' as the source of behaviour; and the concern is not so much with finding things out: in Morris's *The Well at the World's End* Ralph knows in advance what his objective is, as does Frodo in *The Lord of the Rings*, and in neither case is it to find anything out; Anodos in George MacDonald's *Phantastes* and Maskull in David Lindsay's *A Voyage to Arcturus* do not plan at all but take experience as it comes.

Almost all science fiction is orientated towards the future; fantasy, by contrast, looks most often to the past, and to past values.[8] All the works we shall be considering, for instance, have

the future as their concern. It is there that most of them are set –
Pohl's stories not far from now, Clarke's *Rendezvous with Rama* in
A.D. 2130, Farmer's 'Riverworld' series from A.D. 2246 onwards,
Attanasio's *Radix* in the thirty-third century, Simak's *Shakespeare's
Planet* a millenium beyond the early years of interstellar travel,
Silverberg's *Nightwings* in the Third Cycle of humanity after the
ending of man's domination over not only the galaxy but his own
destiny, Asimov's *Foundation* trilogy and Herbert's *Dune*
thousands of years beyond human colonisation of the galaxy,
Aldiss's *Hothouse* and Wolfe's *The Book of the New Sun* millions of
years into the future near the death of the sun. There are of course
future inventions that enable one to travel into the past, as in
Aldiss's *An Age* (1967), but even in these stories it is a future
development that is the source of such travel; and Aldiss's book is
striking in that it presents a world in which the apparent past
turns out in fact to be the future state of life. In keeping with this
future orientation is the emphasis on exploration one often finds in
science fiction, the charting of unknown regions. It is a modern
form of the voyage of the Argonauts – but where the Argonauts
explored some of the surface of the Earth, now it may be the
abysses of limitless space and time that are faced. Because of this
stress on exploration the science fiction genre is necessarily
concerned often with adventure purely for its own sake: it is a kind
of devourer of experience. It is interesting to see fantasy turning
into science fiction when it takes on the exploratory instinct:
Kingsley's Tom in *The Water Babies* becomes, in his insatiable
desire to see all the world, an extension of Kingsley the scientist,
and the book ends with his future as an ineventor; as soon as
Mervyn Peake's Titus wants to find out what lies beyond the
horizon bounding Gormenghast, he encounters (in *Titus Alone*) a
world founded on scientific invention.

Nearly all science fiction is founded on a sense of the
contingency of our reality. Science fiction writers seem imbued
with a sense of the frailty of existing conditions: they write of
invasions, disasters, alternative times or places, galactic societies,
human evolution, technological change. Lytton and Verne show
us new worlds beneath the earth; Wells gives us travel to the
remote future, invisibility, invasion by Martians, threat from a
star; Pohl has a future Earth run by ants, and Simak by dogs.
Curiously, for all their supposed empiricism, science fiction

writers are almost the least enslaved by fact. They refuse to accept finalities: even death itself is a mere interruption in Farmer's Riverworld. Science fiction contrasts with fantasy in its presentation of alternative worlds. The new world in fantasy – whether Middle-earth, Earthsea, Gramarye, Perelandra or Fairyland – is either more desirable or more real than our own: Tolkien and T. H. White see the modern world in terms of a loss of contact between man and nature which it is the business of the fantastic world to counter; George MacDonald feels that the realm of the imagination is the true and divine one beneath the shadow that is this world. But for the science fiction writer, everything is contingent and all worlds merely possible: 'reality' is constantly subject to alteration without notice.

The idiom of science fiction, as has often been said, is change. If one has a strong sense of the contingency of the actual, then the 'actual' will be constantly shifting, because it only has identity in its shifts, its self-destruction, its nonentity. Fantasy, on the other hand, often seeks to keep things as they are – to preserve worlds, to contemplate phenomena for themselves, to maintain past values. There is no single emotional drive behind this sense of contingency in science fiction: it can come as much from a sense of wonder at the infinity of creative possibilities as from awareness of the frailty of the world-order we take for granted: it can be born in delight as in fear, and often in a mixture of both. But always it will not let us stay still for a moment, from the billions of years of future human development imagined in Stapledon's *Last and First Men*, to the metamorphoses of environment in Moorcock's *Dancers at the End of Time* or the ethic of unceasing dialectic in Herbert's *Dune* series. The narrative of science fiction, the 'exciting story', here subserves this idiom. Such narratives often have no end: the voyagers in Verne's *Journey to the Centre of the Earth* do not reach their objective; Wells's time traveller returns to the future; the triffids at the end of Wyndham's *The Day of the Triffids* are as yet undestroyed; even beyond the end of time there is possibly some further existence in Brian Stableford's *The Walking Shadow* (1979); more alien craft may be on their way in Clarke's *Rendezvous with Rama*; at the close of Wolfe's *The Book of the New Sun* the Autarch Severian is about to make his journey to the stars; Asimov, Herbert and Farmer have extended their epics into new books. Fantasy, by contrast, usually comes full circle, with all ends tied

up, the hero often returning to his place of origin, and all things
back 'as they were': it does not have the expansive linearity of
science fiction.

On the whole the urge of science fiction is for more life. Survival
is one of its common motives. The hero, whether it be an
individual or the whole human race, must live on. In Henry
Kuttner's *Fury* (1947), man is freed from the Venusian deeps to go
out to the stars. Each of the protagonists through death creates a
new personalized universe at the end of James Blish's *Cities in
Flight* (1955–62) – the book ends, 'Creation began'. Humanity is
saved from destruction by aliens in Samuel Delany's *Babel-17*
(1966). Hell Tanner in Roger Zelazny's *Damnation Alley* (1969)
brings a plague serum across a ravaged post-holocaust America to
rescue an isolated human community at Boston. As the universe
nears its end in Moorcock's *The Dancers at the End of Time*
(1972–76), the remaining humans discover means of survival.
Even in works much more satiric of man, such as Karel Čapek's
War with the Newts (1936), or Walter Miller's *A Canticle for Leibowitz*
(1959), man survives disaster at the last. In fantasy by contrast
dying and loss of self are more the rule. In *Lilith*, George
MacDonald shows his longing for death as a means of becoming
one with God. Tolkien's Frodo is mortally wounded in saving
Middle-earth, as is Lewis's Ransom, or T. H. White's Arthur in
his last battle. The children in Lewis's *The Last Battle* are killed in a
railway crash and enter heaven. David Lindsay's Maskull in *A
Voyage to Arcturus* learns renunciation of the world to the point
where he can die. The science fiction writer may allow that the
future may involve decline or the present may be disrupted by
disaster, but not often does he permit the extinction of the human
germ plasm.[9] Even in Stableford's *The Walking Shadow*, which ends
with no humanity left in the universe, the two human protagonists (male and female) have gone on to another continuum, and
the novel ends, 'Meanwhile . . .'.

These are some of the ways in which we may describe or define
science fiction: and there are more that will arise in the conclusion.
There is also the issue of science fiction's use of possible worlds
(however remote the possibility) as against supernatural ones:
science fiction will almost always go for the technical or rational
rather than the mystical explanation, even if that only comes long
after we may have taken the particular book for a fantasy (Simak's
The Enchanted Pilgrimage, Silverberg's *Lord Valentine's Castle*, for

example). Doubtless all these characteristics can serve to plot science fiction's position in relation to other genres on some literary diagram. But the point here must be not which pigeon-hole science fiction fits, but whether we come away with any single 'feel' about it. As we saw, its diversity is vast and its character has changed considerably since its beginnings, and this does complicate the issue. It is possible to produce a reductive formula from the various features outlined so far, such as 'Science fiction is a literature concerned with the possibilities of the future and with the survival of the race through change,' or even, 'Science fiction is a picture of the germ plasm's drive to change and survive, under whatever conditions,' but the first sounds too ethical, the second too instinctual, and both too abstract. The definition may provide a fence around the various books, but it does not get close enough for us to catch a central pulse.

And there is such a central pulse. It is one that makes the term 'science fiction' perhaps finally peripheral. It is the one this book is about. For this is imaginative literature, where the most basic urge is to make a new construct or world that will be self-consistent. It is not any sense of the contingency of reality that stimulates Pohl, but the desire to make logically-turned universes. Asimov's *Foundation* trilogy does not start only from the science of 'psychohistory': it is a throwing open of the mind to imagine a galaxy of innumerable worlds with two of opposite character at either end. Futurity is only the background, not the concern, in Farmer's *To Your Scattered Bodies Go*, where the main interest is in the creation of an entirely new world inhabited by all the people that ever were. The struggle for survival may be the condition of being in Aldiss's *Hothouse* (though the hero rejects it at the end), but creative variety is the central effect. The energy that goes into invention makes each world radically different from others, and often sheerly divided form our own; indeed the same author can often create worlds so diverse that we would not know they came from the one mind.

It is this making that interests us here: the novelty of the imagination and the strangely apposite purposes its constructs can be found to subserve. Little has been written on this subject: The usual preference as we said has been for more 'discussible' or evidently 'relevant' science fiction, and for 'meaning' rather than 'vehicle'. The creation of a finely imagined world with no direct relation to our own has seemed to be something which, though it may be very fine, we can only admire, say how much it gives a sense of 'wonder' to the texts, and pass on. We need to find terms in which to talk about the imaginative energy behind science fiction, and make admiration at least partially articulate. We need to go out to texts in which the imagination is at its freest and and most dominant, and yet, if we read it aright, also at its most disciplined and directed. Above all we need to get as close as we can to the life of the literature, to recreate it as fully as we may: like science fiction itself criticism must be written as a series of explorations, rather than as the construction of a motorway through variegated scenery. This book is an attempt to do just that; and the reader can be assured that it has at least been an adventure to write.

2 Isaac Asimov, the *Foundation* Trilogy (1951– 53; serialized 1942–49)

For many readers of science fiction, Isaac Asimov is the presiding genius of the genre, the old master who revolutionized the form and provided the basis of many of its present characteristics. The primary work through which he did this is his award-winning *Foundation* trilogy – *Foundation* (1951), *Foundation and Empire* (1952) and *Second Foundation* (1953).[1] This trilogy is a foundation in more ways than one: it is the basis of the development of the modern science-fiction epic,[2] from James Blish's *Cities in Flight* to Herbert's *Dune* series, and from Piers Anthony's 'Cluster' series to Julian May's *Saga of the Exiles*. Indeed Herbert's *Dune* novels are in some ways the 'Foundation' trilogy rewritten.[3] What Asimov succeeded in doing in this work was the combining of the Olympian overview of the human future that we have in Olaf Stapledon's *Last and First Men* (1930) with the adventures of individuals that had previously been the basic character of much science fiction, from Mary Shelley to Wells and from Burroughs to Van Vogt. In this he was not the first, but he was certainly the most distinguished. From the time of his work, science fiction gains a fully epic dimension.

The *Foundation* trilogy begins with a psycho-historian Hari Seldon, living on the planet Trantor at the centre of a galaxy and a galactic empire far in the future. Seldon foresees the imminent collapse of the Empire and sets up a Foundation to survive the collapse, so arranging things that the Foundation will be exiled by the Empire to the planet Terminus on the galactic rim, and thus escape the ruin. His apparent object is that the existence of the Foundation civilization should ensure the reduction of the barbarism that will follow the collapse of the Empire from thirty thousand to one thousand years. But he has also set up another

Foundation, at the 'opposite end' of the galaxy, at Star's End, the location of which he does not reveal. The Terminus Foundation is based on physical science; but this other Foundation has mental scientists: the two Foundations form a dualism.[4] The Terminus Foundation lives through a variety of threats, and eventually, under the genius of a mutant called the Mule, expands outwards to absorb the galaxy under its influence. But the expansionist urge increasingly has another object: the discovery of the other Foundation, of which neither we nor the characters for long hear anything, and its destruction. At the end, the location of the Second Foundation is still undiscovered by the First. But we learn its position – on Trantor. As the galaxy is a spiral, then one end of the spiral is at its centre, and the other at the extreme periphery. It was partly because the scientists of the First Foundation were physical scientists that they failed to see this: they failed to perceive that as a social scientist Hari Seldon would think of opposite ends in social rather than physical terms, in terms of the centre of civilized existence versus the extreme circumference, where civilization turned to barbarism, and barbarism trailed off into the night of intergalactic space.[5] What Seldon set up was a kind of social dialectic.

In Olaf Stapledon's *Last and First Men* is portrayed the often futile attempts of men to escape the annihilating forces of planetary environments in the solar system. The external world applies the stimulus to which man can most successfully respond by slow physical adaptation, as in the development of the Sixth Men in the heat and storms of Venus. But in Asimov's *Foundation* series the environment is largely out of the reckoning. No one is frozen or burnt on a planet, no landscapes or cosmic phenomena cause racial disasters. Man is entirely in control. The galaxy is conceived of almost as a megalopolis. The central image, almost the only landscape Asimov gives us, is of Trantor:

> He could not see the ground. It was lost in the ever increasing complexity of man-made structures. He could see no horizon other than that of metal against sky, stretching out to almost uniform greyness, and he knew it was so over all the land-surface of the planet. There was scarcely any motion to be seen – a few pleasure-craft lazed against the sky – but all the busy traffic of billions of men were [sic] going on, he knew, beneath the metal skin of the world.

There was no green to be seen; no green, no soil, no life other than man. Somewhere on the world, he realized vaguely, was the Emperor's palace, set amid one hundred square miles of natural soil, green with trees, rainbowed with flowers. It was a small island amid an ocean of steel, but it wasn't visible from where he stood. It might be ten thousand miles away. He did not know.[6]

The dangers in space are from enemy space-ships, the rigours on planets are being out-manoeuvred in politics. In a sense Asimov's entire galaxy is a larger city, with the periphery the forgettable slums and the centre the hub of administration.

The whole basis of the story is the alteration of blind unpurposive nature by man – in this case blind unpurposive human nature. The plan of Hari Seldon is the reduction of history to science. Left to itself history is, so some would have us believe, aimlessly and often miserably cyclic. Seldon's history is also partly cyclic: the collapse of the old Empire will eventually result in the rise of a new one, and all his scheme aims to do (so he says) is shorten the hiatus of barbarism. But inasmuch as Empire, at least at its height, represents man supremely in control of his fate, and barbarism does not, the reduction of the gap represents an increase of human mastery over destiny. Furthermore the mental scientists of the Second Foundation, who, it is briefly claimed late in the trilogy, are eventually to assume leadership of the galaxy, will bring about a positive evolution in civilization: progress will in fact no longer be circular but spiral, like the galaxy itself. It is the switch from circular or closed modes of thinking to more open ones that constitutes the substance and end of Seldon's plan. Nevertheless the content of Seldon's scheme involves prediction of and provision for the events likely to occur in the barbarian period itself. From the nature and position of Terminus, Seldon knows to within 98.4 per cent certainty that within fifty years it will be under threat from or actual occupation by the forces of the nearby planet Anacreon; and he has near-certainty too that the group of scientists originally set as rulers over Terminus while they compiled an encyclopaedia of galactic knowledge will now have been overthrown by a more dynamic, less bookish leader. Seldon has arranged that at varying intervals a projection of him as he once was on Trantor will be scientifically manifested in a special capsule on Terminus, when he can sum up the likely historical progress to date and focus his listeners on their real problem – without letting them know exactly how to deal with it. At his first appearance, after fifty years, he announces that the Encyclopaedia project under Dr Lewis Pirenne has been a sham designed to produce enough energy to start off society on Terminus, and that the true issue is not preservation of the Encyclopaedia at all costs – and hence the current misguided attempts to placate the Anacreonian enemy – but survival, and immediate thought as to how it may be most practically engineered. This gives the new leader, Salvor Hardin, his head, and by a piece of skilful diplomacy he is able to persuade the three other planetary powers apart from Anacreon near to Terminus that it is in their interest to issue an ultimatum to Anacreon which will otherwise use the unique atomic power resources (actually scant) of Terminus against them.

Thus Seldon the social and psycho-historian is able to cage within his mind the likely progress of Terminus over several hundred years. His stated objective in setting up the Foundations may have been the reduction of the barbarous interregnum: but we can also see that as a scientist what he is doing is attempting to pattern the random, to show that under certain conditions, and given a number of laws of mass behaviour, human conduct can be developed over hundreds of years to produce a given objective. And there is another aim, which becomes apparent only in the third volume – the development of the human mind and its powers further. Seldon's Second Foundation is composed of only a small band of people: but all of them are psychologists. They develop to perfection what the mutant Mule shows in *Foundation and Empire*, the ability to alter people's minds and emotions, so that a potential antagonist may be overcome simply by filling him and his people with fear or despair. The Second Foundation eventually become able to exert secret control over people, so that their apparently independent actions and responses are conditioned and predetermined. They, for example, arrange matters so that a giant Kalganian fleet that attacks the First Foundation will lose purpose and collapse; they too insert the belief that Terminus is the real home of the Second Foundation in the mind of a key character; and fifty of their number operate as martyrs whose eventual 'confessions' will further persuade the First Foundation that it has located and overcome the Second. It is because Seldon has so divided physical from mental science in the beginning that this prodigious advance in mental power has been possible. In the end all is circumscribed. True, Seldon had left the calamitous advent of the Mule out of his calculations, calculations which depended on the assumption of human, not mutant powers, at work in history: and that after the Mule the original 'plan' seemed to have diverged beyond recognition. But at the other end of the galaxy the Second Foundation, with its powers not simply to predict but now to *adjust* history to a scheme, was eventually able to absorb and contain the apparent aberrations of the other, so that, ' "It was here that . . . the train of events [was] begun that led to the great return to the Seldon Plan" ' (III, 186). Thus Seldon arranged for his own psychological 'long-stop':[7] his actual predictions might eventually diverge from historical fact, but the facts could themselves be manipulated to conform to his plan. In other words, even if by itself the experiment went awry, the obstreperous data could still – at least when the Second Foundation had fully developed its powers of mental control – be adjusted to produce the right outcome. (Though as we shall see at one point both the Seldon Plan and the Second Foundation were saved from the Mule only by good fortune.) When at the end the First Speaker of the Second Foundation says, ' "All roads lead to Trantor", says the old proverb, "and that is where all stars end" ' (III, 187), he is right in more than one sense: Trantor keeps hold on the stars like a magnet; it is the centre not only of force but of influence. At first sight it might appear that the need for such manipulations exposes the failure of the Seldon Plan and the whole experiment: but the answer to that is that the Second Foundation was also part of the plan from the beginning, and hence so were the adjustments of which it would be capable. Of course, this proves that, left to itself, the events and outcomes of history are not very predictable: but then history itself is not some given collection of events, but events added to by fresh data in every moment: and such data here are the two Foundations that Seldon has also set up and made a part of that one thousand years of prediction, so that what may go wrong for the one can be corrected by the other. And here we see something of that paradoxical interplay of free will and determinism which is one of the basic themes of the book.

The book is, as we have said, founded on duality: Seldon has so arranged things that one Foundation of one character is at the

opposite end of the galaxy from the other of opposite character –
the one at the periphery, the other at the centre. Because of this the
people of the First Foundation, quite apart from the knowledge
that they are able to take with them, are in a place of maximum
energy. As men of physical science they eventually quest outwards; the men of the Second Foundation, as mental scientists,
are more inward-looking and their primary aim is to remain
concealed. It is a case of positive and negative poles: between the
two energy is struck and progress is immensely speeded.[8] And
things are turned upside-down. The world of the periphery,
barbarous as the Empire collapses, becomes the focus of new
civilization, while Trantor, the centre of all, becomes a rusting
wreck from being sacked. In a sense the centre thus becomes
peripheral; though in another sense it is still central as the home of
the Second Foundation.

The mode of the narrative itself of the book is significant here.
Each critical point in the history of the First Foundation is told
through the doings of one central figure: Salvor Hardin, who
overcomes the threat from Anacreon; Hober Mallow, who defeats
the attempts of the Empire to back the Korellian republic against
the Foundation; Lathan Devers the trader, who tries to thwart the
skilful military campaign of the imperial general Bel Riose; the
young Bayta and Toran Darell, who witness the overthrow of the
Foundation and of the Traders by the Mule: and so on. While we
read the stories of each of these individuals, their thoughts and
doings seem crucial, yet even while they are so, they are not. We
are with each and his or her contribution for maybe fifty or a
hundred pages, and then they are gone, and the next story takes
up tens or perhaps hundreds of years further on, often in another
planetary system, by which time the individual who has just
loomed so large in our experience has shrivelled to the point of
being unknown, and the great event to which he has contributed is
a mere distant ripple on the vast historical ocean. And yet the
significance these characters had was real enough. The process
can be seen more largely in the triology as a whole. At first we see
all events from the point of view of the First Foundation: but by
the third volume the lens has shifted and we view that Foundation
through the controlling eyes of the Second Foundation. And even
Seldon himself becomes less important, his appearances no longer
mentioned after the first volume, his plan sometimes forgotten
even though still in operation.

We thus move between the two poles of significance and insignificance. Sometimes this is seen within single stories. The trilogy begins by putting us squarely with one Gaal Dornick as he comes – from the periphery – to see Trantor for the first time and help, as he supposes, the work of Hari Seldon. In fact the young Gaal is used somewhat as a gull, and by Seldon himself, who arranges to have a conversation with him which he knows will be overheard by the police, and in which he makes several statements concerning the future doom of the Empire to force the hand of the Empire against him and ensure the speedy exile of the Foundation to safe obscurity. Or there is the story of the subtle trader Lathan Devers (compare 'Devious') who seeks to overthrow the imperial general Bel Riose by taking back to the Emperor on Trantor a captured message sent by his fellow-officer Brodrig to Bel Riose which can be construed as a plot to overthrow the Emperor. On Trantor itself a number of factors frustrate Devers's plans, which makes them appear to matter even more: but in fact his entire effort proves quite unnecessary, as the Emperor has already decided of his own volition that Bel Riose's successes constitute a potential threat to himself, and has him recalled and killed.

Throughout the story threads the theme of the interplay between choice and necessity. At first Hari Seldon's Plan is dominant because the future is near enough to it to be either manipulated or precisely predicted: Seldon himself on his second 'visit' says ' "my figures show a 98.4 per cent probability there is to be no deviation from the Plan in the first eighty years" ' (I, 111). But too great a trust in the Plan leads to a fatal complacency, as in the case of Pirenne and the Encyclopaedists, or later under Mayor Indbur before the advent of the Mule. In a sense Seldon has forced a measure of complacency on all who trust to the Plan: for he has so arranged his human experiment that every initial crisis that faces the Foundation will force one line of action –

'We have placed you on such a planet and at such a time that in fifty years you were manoeuvred to the point where you no longer have freedom of action. From now on, and into the centuries, the path you must take is inevitable. You will be faced with a series of crises, as you are now faced with the first, and in each case your freedom of action will become similarly circumscribed so that you will be forced along one, and only one, path.' (I, 64)

This supposed predicament is bound to lead to passivity in those – at this point all – who believe it. Thus, as the second crisis with Anacreon approaches, Hardin ' "let[s] things drift" ' (I, 80) so long as more than one course of action remains open. In this case it works: but it works because there is a Hardin present to see what must be done and to do it. And the same can be said of Hober Mallow or Lathan Devers, the trader-heroes. Each is perceptive enough to recognize a Seldon crisis, to see what must be done, and courageous and adaptable enough to carry it out in the teeth of opposition – Hardin from Pirenne and from Sef Sermak's 'Action Party', Mallow from Jorane Sutt, secretary to the Mayor of Foundation. Mallow may say that ' "Seldon crises are not solved by individuals but by historic forces" ' (I, 184), but it is he who sees how the threat from Korell can be lifted. He has sold the Korellians all sorts of atomic devices, particularly for household use, with the result that Korellian life is dependent on them. When the planet of Korell declares war on Foundation, he sees that they can be defeated simply by not servicing or replacing these gadgets, which will quickly break down and cause a domestic revolt in the Korellian economy. Certainly we may accept that Mallow and the Traders could not have known in advance the use to which the atomics could be put (unlike the earlier Salvor Hardin, who made sure that the atomics on Anacreon were controlled by a group of scientist-priests with a mystic reverence for atomics and for Terminus as the source of them). Mallow has only to manipulate a situation given to him; but it took Mallow to see the point.

As is already being realised early in the second volume, ' "Seldon's rules of psycho-history on which it is so comforting to rely probably have as one of the contributing variables, a certain normal initiative on the part of the people of the Foundation themselves. Seldon's laws help those who help themselves" ' (II, 18; see also pp. 77–8). Helping oneself does not mean great or heroic acts of will or the bringing to bear of large forces: the forces are already given and all one has to do is utter a few words or turn a switch to harness them to one's own purposes. (Here too one sees the simultaneous centrality and peripherality of the individual in the trilogy.) What succeeds is always originality of thought, the mental jump that escapes from passivity and reverses the direction of phenomena in parallel with its own shift. The last originality of thought is the one by which Hari Seldon's Plan out-thinks its own First Foundation by the subtle riddle of the location of the Second. But no amount of thinking would help unless the conditions – known as 'Seldon crises' – were right.[9]

The advent of the Mule, not without significance a mutant, since he is a mutation, something not catered for in the Plan, is however the advent of total freewill and indeterminacy. Nothing explains the Mule: the Second Foundationers are entirely baffled by the sudden, isolated emergence of his mental powers of control, far greater even than theirs. The Mule's past exists almost entirely in negatives: he is ' "apparently a man of neither birth nor standing. His father, unknown. His mother, dead in childbirth. His upbringing, that of a vagabond. His education, that of the tramp worlds, and the backwash alleys of space. He has no name other than that of the Mule" ' (II, 76). He is renegade, his only motives the satisfaction of an inferiority complex in the swallowing of an entire galaxy under his control. True, he becomes the spearhead of Foundation, but it is a Foundation which (for the time) is quite other than that envisaged by Seldon. The gigantic orders of power that Hardin or Mallow were able to turn to their own use were external – the religion of atomics, the economic underpinning of a planet: but the Mule has this sort of power in himself alone. By himself he can remove the will to fight of whole armies, and cast planets into despairing surrender, all without more than a motion of his mind. With him, all use of external materials, all determinism, seems to go. Nearly all the chief figures of Foundation are 'Converted' by him – that is, he has altered their minds so that they are totally loyal servants to him. This image of interstellar passivity before this one active mind throws the mind's nature into relief. And he nearly discovers and overthrows the Second Foundation, which would finally have wrecked Seldon's Plan. With his advent, the Plan can never work on its own any more – it has to be altered and adjusted if its aims are to be realized; especially since to counter him the Second Foundation was forced temporarily to reveal its existence (III, 90). Equally, though, the Mule is kept from total power and the Seldon Plan saved by the free choice of an individual over whom he indulgently chose not to exercise mind-control – the girl Bayta Darell, who kills the Foundation psychologist Ebling Mis when in the library of Trantor he is on the point of telling the Mule in disguise of the true home of the Second Foundation: there is a sort of balance of acts of free will on both sides of the equation. Either way, however, the survival of the Seldon Plan was, so far as the Second Foundation was concerned, quite fortuitous (III, 22–3).[10] Thus psycho-historical determinism and acts of free choice are here again necessary to the Plan's continuance.

There are other oppositions basic to the book. Conflict itself, so far as the First Foundation is concerned, is of the essence. That Foundation was created by Seldon to form the basis of a new empire. It was given enough members to colonise a planet and thus became noticed by its neighbours. It had to struggle to survive. It could not remain static or it would be overrun: that is why the head-in-the-sand Encyclopaedists who originally ran it were overthrown to meet the first threat from Anacreon. Then it had to expand its influence, first by the atomic religion, then by the Traders who were its economic extension and by whose means an attack from the planet Korell was foiled. With the overthrow of the last great general of the Empire, Bel Riose, the Foundation then sank into stagnation and bureaucracy, and it was at this point that it was defeated by the mutant, the Mule. But now the Mule became the Foundation, and he began the spread over the rest of the galaxy. But there is still further conflict, of a different kind, to follow between the First and Second Foundations, a conflict which the Second wins but the First does not lose: for it becomes increasingly the objective of the Mule to discover and destroy the Second Foundation, and of the latter to escape detection finally. At the end of the trilogy, the two very different Foundations continue to exist, the one concerned largely with physical science and conquest, the other with mental science and preservation, preservation in particular of the Seldon Plan; neither is any longer in conflict with the other, but the continued existence of the duality that together they represent sufficiently shows that duality is in this work of the essential character of existence. (Asimov may suggest the eventual leadership of the Second Foundation (III, 89), but he chooses not to portray it.) The progress of the trilogy is almost Hegelian: the thesis of the Foundation against the antithesis of the Empire leading to the synthesis in duality of both Foundations. What at first was dynamism against stasis, Foundation against the rigidities of an Empire in decay, becomes eventually that which moves in uneasy

equilibrium with that which sits still, the expansive First Foundation that swallows whole areas of the galaxy, the Second and
unknown Foundation that remains at rest on its little patch of a
single planet. Just as the book is full of the interplay of opposites, so too it is
imbued with paradox. Those who succeed in the early stages of
Foundation do so by using the very powers that are directed
against them – Salvor Hardin setting three planets on Anacreon
by a trick, Hober Mallow turning the economic base of Korell in
on itself. The power of the Mule is entirely invisible. A striking
image of this is the approach to his 'palace' on Kalgan:

> Pritcher left his air car at the old vice-regal hangars and entered
> the palace grounds on foot as was required. He walked one mile
> along the arrowed highway – which was empty and silent.
> Pritcher knew that over the square miles of palace grounds,
> there was not one guard, not one soldier, not one armed man.
> The Mule had no need of protection.
> The Mule was his own best, all-powerful protector. (III, 12)

True power is often to be found in the least likely candidates and
places. Salvor Hardin, the mild-seeming mayor of Terminus,
'insignificantly dressed and uninteresting-looking' (I, 97), even
while held captive by the Anacreon Wienis at the moment of the
latter's apparent triumph, actually has the power of all Anacreon
in his grasp. Hober Mallow exerts power over the threat from
Korell through the household washing-machines and other
gadgets that maintain domestic life on the planet. The imperial
General Bel Riose is overthrown not in battle but by the jealousy
of his master. The Mule himself first appears as an inconsequen-
tial clown. The First Speaker of the mighty Second Foundation is
the apparently bumbling, uxorious farmer Preem Palver. The
central paradox of the book is the power greater than that of the
huge First Foundation wielded by the Second, which turns out to
comprise no more than a few farmer-inhabitants of the wrecked
planet Trantor, yet is able by mind control to destroy the
battlefleet of Kalgan and thus set the First Foundation on course
for Empire. As for Terminus, as Bel Riose at one point says, ' "It is
a world the size of a handkerchief, of a fingernail; with resources so
petty, power so minute, a population so microscopic as would
never suffice the most backward worlds of the dusty prefects of the

Dark Stars. Yet with that, a people so proud and ambitious as to dream quietly and methodically of Galactic rule. . . . And they succeed. There is no one to stop them" ' (II, 20–1). The paradoxical mode comes down to names. Terminus is at the end of the galaxy but it is the beginning of the Foundation. Stars' End is not at the periphery as from its name the first Foundationers keep thinking, but at the centre of the galaxy.

The dialectical character of the book is part of an ethic of forward movement that runs through it all. Movement is the idiom of the work – movements of minds as they try to decide how to act or where a hidden force or planet is, movements of individuals across the galaxy: the characters are continually journeying from one star system to another, and the point of vantage shifts from Trantor to Terminus, from Terminus to Anacreon, to Korell, to Haven, to Kalgan, to Siwenna, to Tazenda. There is constant action away from modes of thought that have gone static – the Empire, the habits that from time to time beset the Foundation itself. Seldon's Plan is a pushing outwards in the face of sterile thinking: ' "It was a sign of decaying culture, of course, that dams had been built against the further development of ideas. It was his revolt against these dams that made Seldon famous" ' (III, 60). The Empire thought it was in a state of immense power: Seldon perceived and dared to say that it was on the verge of collapse. The essence of Seldon's Plan is evolutionary. It is future-oriented, and so is the book. Each crisis in Foundation's history is a step forward to a goal, and each involves different mental strategies to deal with it. And the Plan itself is not fixed: ' "*He* [Seldon] never created a finished product. Finished products are for decadent minds. His was an evolving mechanism and the Second Foundation was the instrument of that evolution" ' (III, 60). Hence perhaps the irony of the name Terminus: there are no ends.[11] This insistence on the unfixed may explain why the identities of central figures become progressively more uncertain as the book proceeds – from the simulacrum of Hari Seldon, the anonymity of Salvor Hardin or the obscurity of the Outlander Hober Mallow, to the unknown character and shifting identity of the Mule, to the totally hidden, apparently cancelled, identities of the Second Foundationers.

Plasticity is of the essence. Each predicted crisis in the Plan is in a way designed to shake the Foundation out of settled habits of thought, as when the threat from Anacreon brings about the overthrow of the conservative Encyclopaedists, or Jorane Sutt's inability to see how the Korellian threat may be removed ensures his downfall, or the attack by the Mule overthrows the inert bureaucracy that the Foundation has become. The past is seen as the road to sterility. No lessons are learnt from it, because the conditions of each crisis are wholly new, and no guidance has been given as to how to meet them. This position could only arise by having the curious situation that prevails in the trilogy, whereby Foundation is seen as not self-evolving, but only as changing under the impact of external stimuli. In safe isolation, Asimov seems to believe, the human mind and spirit do not develop but grow stagnant: tension is essential to progress (III, 101). That is why Foundation is never considered on its own, but only in relation to other powers and stimulating threats from them – whether Anacreon, the Mule or the Second Foundation. Movement in itself is of no value, of course: only the relatively directed and purposive movement supposed through the operation of the Plan. It is between, or rather above, the two extremes of imperial rigidity and meaningless barbarian flux that the career of Foundation towards Second Empire moves.

And our minds too are moved as we read. The widening of mental perspective goes in parallel with the expansion outwards from Terminus. At first we think that the purpose of Terminus is simply to preserve knowledge so that the period of chaos between the fall of one empire and the rise of another will be reduced to a minimum. But then, with the overthrow of the Encyclopaedists, we see that the preservation of anything static is out of court, and that it is the preservation of Terminus itself, helped by the head-start of technology (applied science) that it has, that is the central issue. Then we see that the Plan involves not mere preservation at all but active conquest of others by the Foundation and the beginings of a new empire centred on Terminus. When Foundation falls to the Mule we think that Seldon's Plan is finished. At this point our minds are opened further to awareness of the existence of the Second Foundation. What this is, and what purpose it serves we do not know, and only come slowly to realize. For the time we may think that the Second Foundation, because it is called the Second, is meant to supersede the First. Now we see that beneath the apparent wreck of the Plan lies a deeper Plan. We begin to see too that Seldon's thinking is the reverse of provincial. He has not been concerned simply with the speedy return of a new

Empire; he has tried to achieve a final solution to history, the removal of the cycle of endless rise and fall for a constantly developing civilization fuelled by dynamic tension. That 'dynamic tension' itself has been partly experienced by us in reading, through the use of suspense and uncertainty to pull us through the book: the very act of reading is analogous to the directional character of the history proposed by Seldon. The totality of the form of the trilogy is in this sense fused to its meaning.

This work is more accurately to be called science fiction than many that have the name because its mode is that of a scientific experiment, albeit with people. Seldon's Plan is an 'experiment' conducted by mixing different human elements over a definite period in a galactic flask to make a new stable compound. The Second Foundation is eventually a catalyst, changing others while remaining unchanged itself. The inert medium is space. The variables are time, human choice, and the humans making the choices. It is a closed system, designed to generate perpetual motion from within itself. As a scientific process, all that is irrelevant to the interaction it supposes is excluded. The sole motives operative on all the peoples are the desire to survive, and the desire to dominate. No account is taken of morals, except perhaps in the case of the martyrs who give themselves for the Second Foundation. Perhaps, on Asimov's reading of history, he felt moral impulses to be ephemeral or subsumed in the other impulses. We hear very little of the personalities of the characters, and where we do, as in the case of the girl Arcadia Darell, this is purely to explain her motives; in any case she is unknowingly conditioned by the Second Foundation. The most memorable picture of the Mule we have is of a clown on a beach: and that is a front. So too with the 'Brooklynite' Preem Palver, in reality First Speaker of the Second Foundation. Persons are usually seen as typical rather than special, even as clichés:[12] the ascetic pedant Pirenne, the fat bureaucrat Indbur, the dashing but corrupt Bel Riose. The exception to this, since he is the exception, the variant, is the mutant Mule, but he is not given a personality, he is merely a powerful anomaly, the mysterious figure that does not fit. Nor do we hear much of landscapes, apart from Trantor and one sea-scape (one of the features distinguishing the Foundation trilogy from its successor *Dune*). We do not know how one planet differs from another, as, say, Ursula Le Guin differentiates the desert Anarres from the lush twin Urras in her *The Dispossessed*.

Nor are we given details of battles, lingering accounts of love, different customs of civilizations. There are no animals, only man. Doubtless these things 'were there', but since they are not seen as vital to the experiment, they are ignored. Thought-processes and conversations largely fill the trilogy, and nearly all these are concerned with finding things out and with gaining power. If this is scientific experiment, it has to be said that it is experiment conducted in isolation from many of the facts of human existence. And curiously, isolation, both from the facts and from the reader, is one of the less happy features of this brilliant work. If Seldon's Plan addresses itself to history, it must, arguably, take account of every datum injected into history, and that includes all those personalities, landscapes, moods, animals and weathers that the trilogy excludes. The trilogy does allow for the random in the form of the Mule, certainly (though actually the introduction of the Mule was forced on Asimov by John Campbell[13]): but in the end all is circumscribed and brought back to the predicted path by the Second Foundation. We must question whether the law supposed by the Plan that a strong Emperor will always owe his strength to having no strong subjects, as with the Emperor Cleon II and his general Bel Riose (II, 62–3), is universally or necessarily the case: yet this is axiomatic for Seldon's scheme. The more we ask questions like this, the more the scheme of the book is seen to depend on a limited or contingent reality, and the more of a 'game' world it inhabits.[14] It is here that Asimov's work goes against its own tenets: for in the world-view that informs it, nothing is finally contingent; everything is made part of a scientific plan. The result of what can best be described as an inveterately law-making habit of mind is a passage such as this:

If, from a distance of seven thousand parsecs, the fall of Kalgan to the armies of the Mule had produced reverberations that had excited the curiosity of an old Trader, the apprehension of a dogged captain, and the annoyance of a meticulous mayor – to those on Kalgan itself, it produced nothing and excited no one.

It is the invariable lesson to humanity that distance in time, and in space as well, lends focus. It is not recorded, incidentally, that the lesson has ever been permanently learned.

Kalgan was – Kalgan. It alone of all that quadrant of the Galaxy seemed not to know that the Empire had fallen, that the

Stannells no longer ruled, that greatness had departed, that peace had disappeared. (II, 79)

We may resist the application of the law of the second paragraph to the first: is it true, let alone an 'invariable lesson', that reverberations are always the greater as distance increases? The tone itself, rather pompous and condescending, reveals an unease: maybe the lesson has never been learned, not only because it is not a 'lesson' but only a piece of useless information, but also because it never was a lesson or law of any sort. And in the next paragraphs we are to learn, à la Gertrude Stein, that 'Kalgan was – Kalgan': or, to put it in other words, that it is the individuality and peculiarity of Kalgan itself, not its non-conformity to any supposed psychic law, that has produced its unruffled acceptance of events. It has been untroubled because it has been unaltered, unlike other planets near it: it is a luxury world able to buy off any would-be conqueror.

The book moves towards a notion of inclusiveness: the powers of physical and mental science are eventually in the far future to work together; all the forces of the mind and of the material world are to cooperate. And its orientation is to open-endedness. The cyclic movement of history is to be replaced by steady expansion. Yet in the end there is an effect of enclosure. The total movement of the trilogy is inwards: inwards from the edge of the galaxy at Terminus, towards the centre. The expansion outwards from Terminus is in another sense an expansion inwards to Trantor, with which the trilogy begins and ends. And this seems symptomatic of the isolation of the book, not only from the full randomness of reality but from the reader himself. Certainly the reader is drawn in by the brilliantly-handled narrative, whereby he is kept in a state of suspense throughout: not knowing how the Foundation will become the basis of a new empire but seeing a pattern form; knowing that there is a Second Foundation but not knowing where it is till the end. Yet Seldon's humanitarian but impersonal desire to save civilization puts us at a remove from the basic impulse of the work, as we are not when sharing the feelings of individuals in other works of science fiction: Paul in *Dune* grappling with his peculiar destiny to save a world, Severian in Wolfe's *Book of the New Sun* describing his journey through Urth, Attanasio's Summer Kagan in *Radix* growing towards 'godmind'. There is a coolness about Asimov's work: it is detached, planetary. It gives us a universe quite different from ours, one largely amenable to reason and science, one whose relative metaphysical comfort it may be a pleasure to contemplate,[15] but one which lacks full force because it is not opened to the whole character of reality. (Here again Herbert's *Dune* is in marked contrast.) Its world is also devoid of moral and spiritual issues: though Seldon has made the universe conform to scientific and historical laws, he has evacuated it of further significance. The benefit to be derived from shortening the period of strife after the fall of the Empire seems not so much the moral one of limiting human suffering as the practical one of avoiding an enormous waste of time. For all the analysis that goes on throughout the trilogy into the right lines of action to be followed or the location of the Second Foundation, no analysis is applied to the end itself. We hear little of what the Second Empire will be like, except that in some way it will be 'better' because guided by 'mental powers', though the most evident application of those powers will be to ensure its lasting survival rather than to make a greater civilization. In the end, it seems, the restoration of civilization itself is a sufficient object, because civilization represents order, and 'order', in the form of Seldon's Plan, is what solely concerns Asimov in the trilogy.[16] It is enough for him that it is established: what is done with it seems to be of less moment.

POSTSCRIPT – *FOUNDATION'S EDGE* (1982)

This book, which has received a Hugo Award and a fair number of sour reviews, is essentially a fine continuation of the three books just considered, particularly in its portrayal of relationships, whether hostile or sympathetic, among characters, and in its handling of suspense. It seems unfair to dismiss the book as an anachronism in the current development of science fiction when the author's aim has been to integrate it with the character of novels written thirty years before.[17] Generally the job has been done brilliantly, and the book has the same texture and feel to it as the others, if it is twice as long as any one of them. But there are differences. We follow just one plot and group of characters throughout, instead of having a series of adventures and actors often widely separate from one another in time. And there is a stronger sense of individuality, from the aspects of space-ships or

planets to the very physical situation in which Speaker Gendibal
of the Second Foundation is one day suddenly set upon by the
normally placid Hamish farmers of Trantor, and from the gentle
contours of Sura Novi's psychic landscape even to the twin-tufts of
the beard of the customs official Jogoroth Sobhaddartha on
Sayshell Union. Indeed the novel is often ontological in its
concern, questioning the peculiar make-up of this particular
universe, and eventually receiving an answer of possible validity.
Foundation's Edge adds a further dimension to our understanding
of the Seldon Plan. By the end of the trilogy we could feel that the
Second Foundation, with its mental power, could perhaps
outmatch the First. In this next book, five hundred years towards
the projected new empire, the Seldon Plan is again under threat.
The First Foundation has developed considerable powers of
resistance to mental force: in other words it has begun to develop
mental science alongside its advanced physical technology. We
learn too that, via the energetic Speaker Gendibal, the Second
Foundation will set about acquiring proficiency in physical
science. Thus the difference between the two Foundations is in
the process of being eroded. Yet by the end the Second Foundation is again concealed from the First, and each has lost its urge for
contrary powers, so that the dialectic on which the Plan was
founded remains. But it was not any factor catered for by the Plan
that saved it: it was protected partly by an outside agency of which
Seldon could have known nothing, and partly by a simple act of
human choice.

   In this book representatives of the First and Second Foundation
encounter a source of mental power greater than anything yet
known. It is located on a secret planet Gaia in the Sayshell Sector
of the galaxy. Gaia itself is the source, being a collective mind
composed of all the humans, creatures and material of that world.
(Actually the humans may be robotic, enormously sophisticated
developments of the robots that originally served man on
Earth.) The Gaians have foreseen the approach of a Seldon Crisis
in which the two Foundations will meet and one will be victorious.
The object of Gaia is actually to bring to the environs of the planet
leading representatives of the First and Second Foundations, and
to have an impartial human Trevize, uniquely capable of lucid
choice, select whether he will opt for the victory of the First or the
Second Foundation or for the continuation of the Seldon Plan for
its projected further five hundred years towards empire. Trevize

chooses the Plan, as Gaia had hoped. Had he chosen either of the other two the empire it would subsequently have established in the galaxy would have been of the same transient nature as the First Empire. After his choice the memories of the First and Second Foundationers who have met are altered, as is the urge of each Foundation to develop the skills of the other.[18]

The Plan has survived, it would seem, by the skin of its teeth, just as it did when the progress of the Mule (in fact a renegade who escaped from Gaia) was hindered by the free choice of Bayta Darell, allowing the Second Foundation time to develop the power to stop him. Yet Seldon had never supposed that his plan would work by determinism – his laws would help those who helped themselves, his predictions would decrease in accuracy over time. His plan needed the support of others to make it work: and that is what both Golan Trevize and the benign Gaians bring about. But that free choice depends on the essential 'rightness' of the Plan as well as there being individuals with the perception to see it and power to effect it. Why do the Gaians wish it to continue? The simple answer is that, insofar as they are robots, the 'First law of Robotics' decrees that the welfare of human beings shall be their first priority. But then they must have seen that only the Seldon Plan guaranteed that welfare. And that perhaps leads us in this novel to speculate a bit more about the nature of the empire-to-come than we did in the trilogy. Will the mental and physical sciences of the two Foundations be married, and if so, how? What sort of a new creative dialectic will remain, if at all? Having seen the power of the First Foundation in this book, can we be so sure that it will be a case of leadership by the Second Foundationers in the new Empire?

As if to underwrite this new interest in 'ends' more than in 'means', *Foundation's Edge* draws on the cosmogony first used in Asimov's *The End of Eternity* (1955), which predicates a group of Eternals, who chose from a myriad of possibles (also actualised) one universe in which man would be the sole intelligent lifeform – and in which, no doubt, a man called Hari Seldon would eventually arise to make all events in that universe no longer random but rational. There, indeed, is a larger Plan, a wheel governing wheels within wheels. It mirrors the process of expanding discovery that the novel follows – an expansion which widens out not to an infinite, but curiously to a benign 'enclosure', a circumscribing, that folds the universe back on itself; and back on its centre in the Seldon Plan. In parallel with this, one may note, Asimov himself has reached out to incorporate much of his literary output in the history of this galaxy, placing his novels *The Stars, Like Dust, The Currents of Space* and *Pebble in the Sky* during the period of the growth of the First Empire, and his 'robotic' novels and short stories during a period in which the galaxy was colonised by robots. His own separate works, like the temporally separated acts within the trilogy, are thus caught up in a larger Plan, devoured as it were by the very fiction they create. Nothing could more surely testify to the dominant urge behind Asimov's work being the need to make life coherent. Yet as we have seen, he does not enforce coherence in any desperate way: he lets it find itself almost by chance and certainly as much by choice as by imposition.

3   Frederik Pohl, *Alternating Currents* (1956)

While Asimov was composing his ever-widening epic of the future, devouring more and more of his own work in a huge fictive universe, Frederik Pohl was laying the ground for his terser, more satiric works. Pohl began his trade with conventional short stories of travel to far planets,[1] but in the early 1950s discovered that his *métier* lay as much in this planet, in the portrayal, via fantastic metaphors, of men caught up in social and technical changes beyond their control. Pohl did continue to write (in collaboration with Jack Williamson) plain adventure stories in the form of the *Undersea* novels (1954, 1956, 1958), but the central thrust of his work became less 'escapist', more committed to visions at once comic and nightmarish, of disasters man might bring upon himself.[2] Pohl's primary output, and the one for which he is remembered, during the 1950s and 1960s is the short and satiric story; only thereafter did he turn to the writing of longer novels of vision. With his penchant for clarity, logic and neat plotting, Pohl is probably the most witty of the authors considered here. His warnings are real, and yet their science-fictional guise enables him to escape identification; no one yet has pinned Pohl down to a philosophy. He prefers to see himself as just one of the race of science fiction writers, whom he characterises as imbued with 'an unwillingness to accept conventional wisdom, Arnold's "divine discontent" '.[3] Of all his fourteen collections of short stories,[4] *Alternating Currents* is arguably the finest and most integrated.[5]

The stories in *Alternating Currents* seem at first sight very diverse. In 'The Tunnel Under the World' (1954), a whole town which has been accidentally destroyed by an explosion is recreated in miniature with human simulacra by an advertising company so that the company can test methods of selling their products. In 'Target One' (1955), the earth has been largely destroyed in atomic warfare, and one of the few remaining scientists has

35

assembled a mode of time travel by killer atomic particles, which will make possible the murder in his youth of Albert Einstein, whose later theories were put to use in the construction of fission bombs: but the different world thus brought into being by the protagonists turns out to be vastly over-populated and itself on the verge of discovery of nuclear fission by another route. In 'The Ghost-Maker' (1953), a scientific fellow of a museum is sacked for publishing his belief in the efficacy of magic, and employs what is close to black magic to take revenge on the superior who sacked him, by bringing to phantom life numbers of the human and animal exhibits in the museum.[6] 'The Mapmakers' (1955) describes how a space ship becomes lost when the steersman who could guide it through hyperspace is blinded: in the end the steersman finds that though he is totally sightless he can chart a way through space far more effectively than before, and thus brings the ship home. In 'Let the Ants Try' (1949), we start, as in 'Target One', with an atomically-devastated earth and a scientist with a time machine, but this time the scientist actually travels in the machine, forty million years into the past with eight mutant queen ants which he leaves there to develop; when he returns to his own time it is to find the world filled not with a society of ants and men together as he had hoped, but with highly-developed giant ants alone.[7] 'Pythias' (1955) presents a man with powers of 'psychokinesis', or the ability of the mind to alter the external world directly, who can wall off the power of an exploding grenade from his body or fly across the Atlantic; when he reveals his powers to a friend the latter murders him, ostensibly to save humanity from the dangers of such power. In 'Rafferty's Reasons' (1955) a man with a lowly job in a futuristic society plots the murder of his repulsive boss. The central character in 'What To Do Until the Analyst Comes' (1955) has discovered a revolutionary substitute for cigarettes and drink that is both harmless and non-addictive. 'Grandy Devil' (1955), a less satisfying story, tells of a young man's discovery that his family is enormously prolific and each member immortal, so that things are set fair for them to overrun the world; and all of them are the progeny of a devil.

For all their diversity, the stories have a remarkable similarity of theme and outlook. There are numbers of recurrent motifs, which are less evident in Pohl's later writings. One of these is enclosure. The protagonist of 'The Ghost-Maker', Ehrlich, can release the wraiths of dead creatures when he touches their bodies with a magic ring: but if he so touches any living being it becomes dead and its ghost is released. As he wanders through the museum, aware that the task of frightening Brandon his superior is failing, and becoming addicted to bringing creatures to life purely for amusement, he casually puts his ring hand without looking against the skeletal tail of a tyrannosaurus rex to demonstrate his skill to Brandon, only to see his own dead body drop at his feet. He has touched his ring to a part of the tyrannosaurus skeleton that had been reconstructed from plaster by the museum staff, and the magic action, failing on the dinosaur, has rebounded on its wearer. Now he is shut in the ghost world, with only one or two of the human exhibits his ring released to talk to, and the growing dread of the carnivorous phantoms, harmless to humans, but real enough to ghosts, that he has made his companions in this twilight world; there is only the hope that the magician from whom he got the ring originally will be prevailed upon to release him. 'Grandy Devil' too, ends with one of the protagonists shut in, battering at the hatch of a cess pit in which he has been confined.

'Rafferty's Reasons' (a Pohl version of *Nineteen Eighty-Four*) is a portrait of psychic enclosure. Rafferty is so consumed with hatred for his boss, 'dirty' Girty, that fantasy takes over reality and the knife with which in the end he thinks he is stabbing Girty turns out to be merely a cigar butt. Throughout the story Rafferty keeps uttering hate-filled curses at every passer-by who annoys him, but the curses are actually soundless: 'Wherever he was, Rafferty talked to himself. No one heard him, no one was meant to hear him.'[8] The result is that we repeatedly think Rafferty has really spoken, only to realise that he has not; with a consequently more powerful sense of his enclosure:

A man jostled him and scalding pain ran up Rafferty's wrist as the hot drink slopped over.

Rafferty turned to him slowly. 'You are a filthy pig,' he said voicelessly, smiling. 'Your mother walked the streets.'

The man muttered, 'Sorry,' over his shoulder.

Rafferty sat down at another table with a party of three young Project girls who never looked at him, but talked loudly among themselves.

'I'll kill you, Girty,' Rafferty said, as he stirred the coffee-beverage and drank it.

'I'll kill you, Girty,' he said, and went home to his dormitory bed. (p. 86)

And at the end, with the hapless Rafferty dragged away to prison for his feeble assault on Girty, no one will know Rafferty's Reasons. When Girty asks why Rafferty did it, 'Girty's friend could not give him the answer, though he might have had suspicions. Mudgins [the leader of the state] could have answered him, and a few others around Mudgins or elsewhere. . . . But only a few. The others, the many, many millions, they could never say what the reasons were; because some of them had never known them, and some had had to forget' (p. 96). In this sense it is symbolic that Rafferty is shut off from reality, as his society is cut off from truth. But even then we wonder, after this story and the rage portrayed in it, whether Rafferty's reasons, and the very emphasis on them in the title begs the question, could properly be classified as reasons at all.

'What To Do Until the Analyst Comes' explores a situation of unwillingness rather than inability to make contact with the world. The Cheery-Gum in the story is chemically non-addictive, but people do become addicted to the happiness that comes through it, with the result that all humanity apart from the narrator, who sponsored its use, is soon enclosed within the drug, out of touch with previous reality:

I tried to lay in on the line with the Chief. I opened the door of the Plans room, and there he was with Baggott and Wayber, from Mason-Dixon. They were sitting there whittling out model ships, and so intent on what they were doing that they hardly noticed me. After a while the Chief said idly, 'Bankrupt yet?' And moments passed, and Wayber finally replied, in an absent-minded tone:

'Guess so. Have to file some papers or something.' And they went on with their whittling. (p. 154)

The enclosure is demonstrated in the mental re-ordering of the psychoanalyst Dr Yust who admits that he himself once felt worried about the effects of Cheery-Gum on the world and on the ability of society to keep working; but says that his fears proved

groundless, as people still work, if slowly, and better still, he has
no more mentally disturbed clients to deal with:

'And what's more, they weren't morons. Give them a stimulus,
they respond. Interest them, they react. I played bridge the
other night with a woman who was catatonic last month; we
had to put the first stick of gum in her mouth. She beat the hell
out of me, Mr McGory. It had a mathematician coming here
who – well, never mind. It was bad. He's happy as a clam, and
the last time I saw him he had finished a paper he began ten
years ago, and couldn't touch. Stimulate them – they respond.
When things are dull – Cheery-Gum. What could be better?'
(p. 153)

The question invites us into the charmed circle also. The neatest
touch perhaps is in the narrator's plight: his alienation from the
gum-takers and their bovine contentment is shown to depend not
on any high moral insight or principle, but on the fact that he is
allergic to the drug, and whenever he takes it, it gives him hives.
He is outside not because he chooses but because he cannot get in;
his sole escapes are through psychoanalysis or death. By removing
the narrator as a norm with whom to identify, Pohl makes his
story reach out to pull us in: if there is no good reason against,
what is there to stop us being 'for'?

'The Tunnel Under the World' is a fantastic vision of the
enclosure of consumers by producers. Time and space are shut in
to one day in the life of the town of Tylerton. It is always 15 June,
and only the two malfunctioning robot humans begin to sense
what is wrong. There is no escape from the town, for it is merely a
model on a table-top, surrounded by what is for its mostly
unknowing 'inhabitants' a huge drop; and beyond that, spot-
lights, and advertising personnel manipulating events. Ironically
– and here the story is reminiscent of 'What To Do . . .',
Burckhardt's rebellious consciousness makes him aware of his
own helplessness and enclosure as continued ignorance would
never have done: he does not break out into freedom, but into
knowledge of a tighter constriction. And the reader, shut in his
assumption that Burckhardt is a full-sized human being and the
town a real town, suffers a further form of enclosure himself as he
finds out the limiting truth.

'The Mapmakers' plays with the 'Tiresias' idea that to be blind may be to see more truly: though here the issue is physical rather than spiritual. Groden the space ship navigator, though cut off by his blindness from the normal external world, is able without eyes to 'see' the configurations of stars within hyperspace as he never could when sighted; as he puts it to the others, ' "I'm blind in normal space; you're blind in hyperspace" ' (p. 82).

The protagonists of 'Let the Ants Try' and 'Target One' find that manipulation of the past does not produce escape from a miserable present. In the former the ruthless ants are no more satisfactory an outcome to evolution's labours than were human beings. The story ends in a circular manner too. While the time-travelling scientists Dr Gordy is planting his mutated ants in the soil of the Carboniferous past, he hears what at the time he takes to be a raucous animal cry from the Coal Measure forest. On his return to 'the present' he finds himself in a strange city of ants, who first make him show them how his time machine works and is put together before preparing to kill him. With a violent struggle Gordy regains his machine and sets it once more for forty million years in the past, determined to reverse his experiment. But there is no escape from it, just as there was no real escape from grimness in the present. He finds, like Wells's time-traveller, that his time machine, having been moved by the ants, has arrived at a slightly different position in the primeval forest. He emerges, and a little way on sees his time machine and himself from his previous visit. But there is also another machine of strange design, closer to him. As he watches, a door opens in it, and a horde of giant ants races out of it towards him. Having learnt from Gordy how to make a time machine, the ants had 'infinite time' to make one of their own and realize what they had to do to prevent the destruction of their race. The story ends, 'As his panicky lungs filled with air for the last time, Gordy knew what animal had screamed in the depths of the Coal Measure forest' (p .45).

In 'Pythias' the narrator kills the inventor Connaught (which ironically means 'know nothing') to prevent the secret of psycho-kinesis becoming known to man; and just as he has tried to shut in this dangerous knowledge so, as he wished, he is shut in jail for murder. His intention is to reach the final safe enclosure of death through his own execution; yet his closing assertion that Connaught could not be trusted to look after the secret 'But I can', comes over as rather sinister, suggesting that he may use his powers to defy the executioner at the last. But if the narrator may thus break the enclosure and become the path by which this knowledge is made known to the world, a different kind of enclosure is entered: that by which there is no escape from knowledge. That enclosure was also present in 'Target One' where the destruction of Albert Einstein did not prevent the discovery of atomic fission by another route.

There are enclosure motifs in some of Pohl's later stories, several of them in the collection *Day Million* (1970). The title story (1966) in *Day Million* describes what seems a bizarre love relation between two physically transformed humans remote from us in time, only to turn and ask how we might look to them. The narrator of 'Making Love' (1966) in the same collection prides himself on the fact that as one of the privileged classes he has a mistress who is a real human being and not a robot – or is she? The humans in 'The Snowmen' (1958; *The Frederik Pohl Omnibus*, 1966) are cold predators shut in their houses and indifferent to the steady freezing of the Earth caused by their rapacious consumption of energy, and about to experience the consequences. 'Speed Trap' (1967; *Day Million*) is the story of a man who discovers a means of immensely reducing bureaucratic inefficiency and thus of hastening social and economic change: he finds that one of his associates commits suicide and that he is shunted into a job where he is rendered ineffectual: the implication is that it is in Someone's interest for things to stay as they are. But most of these stories differ from those in *Alternating Currents* in that the enclosures have a moral base in human pride and self-delusion: the stories in *Alternating Currents* deal much more with people trapped in situations beyond their control; and it is perhaps in keeping with this that they contain much more in the way of imagery relating to enclosure, signifying that the environment is its source rather than the self. *Alternating Currents* has much less sense of personal responsibility than later collections: it is shot through with Pohl's sense, perhaps heightened by contrast with wartime victory, of man's powerlessness before his own creations, the atom bomb, the consumer society, conformism, drugs, advertising, and thus has a darker, more tragic vision than many of his other stories,[9] which generally end happily or at least justly.[10] This is highlit by the anomalous stories with happy endings (among their other different features) which were added to the US and British first editions of *Alternating Currents* – respectively 'Happy Birthday, Dear Jesus' (1956: written by Pohl for the collection) and 'The Children of Night' (1964).

Much of Pohl's later fiction could be said to deal with exposure rather than enclosure. In 'I Plinglot, Who You?' (1958)[11] and 'The Day The Icicle Works Closed' (1959),[12] the evil schemes of an alien and a human are unmasked. In *Drunkard's Walk* (1960) and *A Plague of Pythons* (1965), the source of human destruction in a group of power-crazy mind-rulers is discovered and destroyed. In *The Age of the Pussyfoot* (1969), the hero exposes an alien plot against Earth. *The Cool War* (1979) ends with the exposure to the world of the covert international warfare being carried on by unscrupulous politicians. Much of Pohl's fiction of the 1970s has left its previous confines of Earth, and visits other planets or roams the galaxy. In *Man Plus* (1976) the protagonist has his self and body totally altered, torn away from human identity, so that he may survive as a cyborg in the harsh environment of the Martian surface. 'The Merchants of Venus' (1972),[13] *Gateway* (1977), *Beyond the Blue Event Horizon* (1980) and *Heechee Rendezvous* (1984) are about a civilization of aliens nicknamed 'Heechees' who have left tunnels containing some of their artifacts on Venus and tunnels plus Heechee space ships on an asteroid; initially the urge is to open ('expose') the tunnels, but increasingly through exposure to risk (*Gateway*), the purpose becomes to discover the nature of the Heechee themselves. *Syzygy* (1981) ends with man realising that he is no longer alone in the universe. In *Starburst* (1982) a group of people is sent ostensibly to colonise a planet near Alpha Centauri, but actually to develop their minds prodigiously in the controlled environment of their space ship and give Earth the benefit. The plot is exposed, Earth punished and a new and higher human civilization actually established in Alpha Centauri.[14] In 'The Five Hells of Orion' (1962)[15] captive humans are brought into increasing contact with an alien race, and as they do so their environment becomes progressively less enclosed: first the darkness with which one of them is surrounded is lightened, then doors are opened till he makes contact with another, then each is made one with the consciousness of the aliens, brought up to a planetary surface and all journey from thence to perceive the lurking threat in the far centre of the galaxy.

A second theme behind most of the stories in *Alternating Currents* is the idea that attempts at changing 'the given state of things' somehow will not work – a peculiar message for science fiction, and again one that does not occur in Pohl's later work, such as *Man Plus, Syzygy* or *Jem: The Making of a Utopia* (1979). Despite the efforts of the time-manipulators, the present stays stridently the same in degree of misery in 'Target One' and 'Let the Ants Try'. In 'What To Do Until the Analyst Comes', nothing its sponsor can do can reverse the universal use of Cheery-Gum or its social and economic effects. In 'The Tunnel Under the World', we think that the intrepid narrator, having discovered something odd about Tylerton, will be able in the end to right matters, but in fact his efforts only result in the revelation of his true helplessness. The same reversal of hoped-for change comes at the end of 'Let the Ants Try', when the narrator rushes back to the past to try to reverse his experiment. The paradox of this story is that the narrative constantly changes, the bottom falling out of it, as it were, in constant reversals, to show that there can be no change. In 'The Tunnel Under the World', the bottom literally falls out of Burckhardt's world when he suddenly realises that beyond Tylerton there is only an abyss. Gideon Upshur in 'Grandy Devil' fails to halt the spread of the Orville family. Rafferty in 'Rafferty's Reasons' fails to kill Girty. While releasing the wraiths of the museum creatures, Ehrlich in 'The Ghost-Maker' becomes a ghost himself.

Another, related motif of these stories is the benefits of losing the separate self. If 'The Mapmakers' is anything to go by, it is only when man is helpless, lost in space and blinded, that he can begin to see aright; for only then is he no longer separate from, but in tune with the larger patterns of the universe. The very assertion of the narrator at the end of 'Pythias' of his mastery over his own fate poses its absence; indeed his very intended death is a paradox, since he proposes by it to destroy the mastery over fate given by Connaught's invention. It seems that peace only comes when one submerges one's mind with the collective, when one becomes in a sense unconscious. It is Rafferty's sharp sense of injustice that marks him out and dooms him to his tormented life and fate. McGory in 'What To Do Until the Analyst Comes' longs to be part of the society taking Cheery-Gum and becoming literally unconscious of the external world, but is forced to be separate and judging. In a sense inventions prove a 'Bad Idea' – Cheery-Gum, time machines, psychokinesis. Partly this is because they are aimed at changing humanity. Pohl, in an almost eighteenth-century manner, seems to insist on the limits of the human purview. Looked at one way his stories sometimes appear to propose that we should submit, and that 'whatever' – and the whatever is often hard to take – 'whatever is, is right'. Seen thus, it is 'better' that one should put up with the disasters of atomic warfare that the collective wisdom of mankind has brought about than that one man should seek to reverse them. 'Better' that one's mind should not be so abnormal, so awake, as to permit realization of the horror of one's predicament: thus with Burck-hardt. 'Right' that Grandy Orville wins against Gideon Upshur, because he is part of the family and the latter an intruder. 'In Pride, in reas'ning Pride, our error lies': Pope's words might certainly be applicable to the protagonists of 'Target One' and 'Let the Ants Try'. Certainly it is pure hubris that brings about the doom of the narrator in 'The Ghost-Maker': he has already interfered with the system of things by propagating so many ghosts (upsetting the natural order was one of Pope's *bêtes noires*); and it is when he idly puts his ring to the tyrannosaurus rex without looking, while addressing 'some mocking phrase' to Brandon that he is himself ghosted. In a sense he is fittingly made a ghost, for he has just refused Brandon's offer of the return of his job, indeed he has renounced any of his former concern for scientific truth, so that he no longer belongs to the collective that previously gave him his identity. The narrator in the anomalous story 'Happy Birthday, Dear Jesus', by contrast, succeeds by separating himself from the collective, by abandoning his pre-vious identification with a materialist culture, leaving his job and country, marrying into a family of people opposed to the system.

Yet it would be absurd to suggest that conservatism and submission of the self constitute the sole ethic of Pohl's stories. Pope's dogmas were directed at making men submit to a broadly happy state of affairs, with an ultimately benign creator in control of an ordered and on the whole delightful universe. It is different when it comes to atomic deserts, exclusion from happiness, manipulation by others, or rejection. We sympathise with, rather than find absurd, many of the rebellions in the stories. Submission may be 'better' but it is not always nobler. Isn't Burckhardt's struggle towards awareness of the manipulations being carried out on the model Tylerton a finer thing than stupid ignorance – even if Burckhardt himself turns out to be other than a man? Isn't McGory's sense of the degradation of humanity in 'What To Do

. . .' at least as valid as the assertion of the Cheery-Gum-chewing Dr Yust that the disasters are real only to him (pp. 151–3)? Isn't Rafferty's painful hatred of Girty, however inaccurate and blindly personal, a better thing than the kind of happy acceptance of Big Brother than ends Orwell's *Nineteen Eighty-Four?*

Rebellion does not go away in Pohl's stories save in death, or, in the case of Burckhardt, when 'the maintenance crews take over' (p .141). Gideon Upshur still clamours at the lid of the cess pit, Rafferty presumably continues to express his rage at Girty from behind the bars of a prison, McGory cannot escape his isolated rejection of Cheery-Gum. Therefore several of the stories are essentially dialectical. They call for rebellion, indeed sometimes almost prescribe it, only to show it to be quite futile and dangerous. In part of course it is simply the case that without the rebellions there would be no story. But this is not quite the merely circular argument it might seem. It is often rebellion that brings the new worlds into being. Had it not been for Burckhardt, Tylerton would have remained Tylerton on 15 June to all its inhabitants: it is Burckhardt's abnormal consciousness that makes him aware of the fact that it never becomes 16 June and eventually find out what Tylerton 'really' is. It is the rebellions of the scientist protagonists of 'Let the Ants Try' and 'Target One' that bring about a world dominated by intelligent giant ants, and an overpopulated planet on the verge of discovering atomic fission by a different route. It is the revenge-seeking drive of Ehrlich in 'The Ghost-Maker' that makes a little company of released spirits, the human members of which are vividly characterised. In a sense the scientist is like God: he makes (though perhaps unwittingly) a new creation; the scientist in 'Let the Ants Try' is named Salva Gordy. The impulse of rebellion seems here directly linked to the impulse to create. The ants in 'Let the Ants Try', unlike Dr Gordy, do not create a time machine: they copy it. Gordy has brought them into being: they do nothing but cancel his being. Equally one can rebel at the new creation, as do Gordy or the narrator of 'Target One' or McGory at the invention of Cheery-Gum, or the narrator of 'Pythias' (ostensibly) at the powers of psychokinesis.

The very existence of all these different stories depends upon a 'rebellion' against the status quo of our reality: in each of them we start from a context which is an alteration of our world as it is now – a world in which travel through 'hyperspace' is possible, or atomic wars have been fought, or magic spells work, or matter can be directly manipulated by mind, or time travel is possible. And the world of each narrative is, as it were, in 'rebellion' against that of any other, in the sense that each is an 'Alternating Current'. In 'Let the Ants Try' human beings can travel through time, while in 'Target One' this is 'impossible by definition; matter cannot leave its locus in the chronon' (p. 100), though a special destructive particle known as a K-meson can be made to span time. In 'The Ghost-Maker' magic replaces plodding science as the wonder-worker; in 'Target One' scientific 'explanation' is given in terms of the operation of K-mesons, reactors, and Einstein's laws; in 'What To Do Until the Analyst Comes' the irreverent lay narrator's explanation of the process of manufacturing Cheery-Gum as told to him is by way of 'a substance in a common plant which, by cauliflamming the whingdrop and di-tricolating the residual glom, or words something like that, you could convert into another substance which appeared to have much in common with what is sometimes called hop, snow or joy-dust. In other words, dope' (p. 145). Thus we have Pohl the creator 'rebelling' against the external world in writing at all; each story 'rebelling' against others; and within each individuals rebelling against the conditions, or else rebelling against the results of their own rebellion. Pohl likes the idea of Chinese boxes, of events within events, worlds within worlds, rebel/creators within rebel/creators. Pope, by contrast, insisted on our entertaining the notion of only one external world, the supposedly empirical one about us: for him the artist was not a creator but a follower of nature. The very variety of Pohl's worlds suggests the contingency of ours: it is subject to alteration with the minimum of notice, whether by the creator or his creatures. Thus the fact of change, even if it is only of the mutant type, plays against implicit criticism of change.

So far as the protagonists of the stories are concerned, another motif of the collection is alienation. Most of the central figures are alone. Gordy in 'Let the Ants Try' has his companion De Terry only for the first part, till they arrive in the city of the ants, where De Terry is killed. Ehrlich in 'The Ghost-Maker' is a man on his own and against society, as is Rafferty in 'Rafferty's Reasons'. Burckhardt in 'The Tunnel Under the World' becomes isolated from his world by his own developing knowledge. The protagonist of 'Pythias' makes himself a condemned murderer to keep the secret of psychokinesis from mankind. McGory in 'What To Do

Until the Analyst Comes' starts as the brilliant member of an advertising team and ends as a man burdened with lonely gloom, cut off from the relief and integration with humanity that would be given by the Cheery-Gum he himself sponsored, if only he could eat it. The space ship in 'The Mapmakers' is lost, and Groden severed from the normal world by his blindness and alone able to see his way through hyperspace. The scientists in 'Let the Ants Try' and 'Target One' refuse to accept society as they find it: one irony of this is that the alternative societies they bring into being refuse to accept them. In stories in others of Pohl's collections, such as *Tomorrow Times Seven*, *Turn Left at Thursday* or *Day Million*, by contrast, there may be several protagonists, or the protagonist is in relative harmony with society. We are with a group of Earthmen defending themselves against Martians in 'The Middle of Nowhere' (1955);[16] the apparent tribesman in 'It's a Young World' (1941)[17] ends by stepping into leadership of a planetary council; 'The Day of the Boomer Dukes' (1956)[18] is told from a plurality of points of view; fellow-humans help the hero to escape from destroying Martians in 'Mars by Moonlight' (1958);[19] in 'The Man Who Ate the World' (1956) the gross protagonist ends by reintegration with himself and society; in 'The Day the Icicle Works Closed' (1959) a lawyer exposes an international fraud that has isolated the home planet from the rest of the galaxy; in 'The Seven Deadly Virtues' (1958)[20] a man outcast from society on Mars recovers his identity in the end. There are exceptions of course, such as 'The Hated (1961)[21] or 'The Fiend' (1964),[22] but it is remarkable how consistently *Alternating Currents* is different from others of Pohl's collections.

Together with the theme of alienation goes one relating to identity. Isolated, and without a social niche, a place that gives some validation to what one is, the characters in the stories lose their selfhood. The scientist Ehrlich in 'The Ghost-Maker' sinks to vengeful magician and thence to ghost. An outsider, opposed to the family, Gideon Upshur in 'Grandy Devil' is shredded in a waste-disposal unit. The similarity of the names among several of the characters – Gordy, Groden, McGory, Girty, Grandy Orville – suggests further a dissolution of self. 'The Tunnel Under the World' explores the dissolution not only of a self but of a world. His world becomes steadily stranger to Burckhardt as the story proceeds. His wife has dreamed the same terrifying dream as he has, an outrageous voice screams commercials from a van parked in the street without the police intervening; Barth, who is never absent from the office, is so on this day; the cellar of Burckhardt's house is no longer plain concrete but a thin sheath of concrete over a floor, walls and ceiling made of copper; the interior of the boat he had built now appears unfinished; and repeatedly Burckhardt is encountered by the desperate features of an aquaintance named Swanson in the streets. And then there are the neat touches that really distinguish Pohl: it is not that Burckhardt's world is simply becoming less normal, it is also the fact that it is losing its abnormalities, that is disturbing:

> It isn't the things that are right and perfect in your life that make it familiar. It is the things that are just a little bit wrong – the sticking latch, the light switch at the head of the stairs that needs an extra push because the spring is old and weak, the rug that unfailingly skids underfoot.
>
> It wasn't just that thing were wrong with the pattern of Burckhardt's life; it was that the *wrong* things were wrong. (p. 117)

And so the story continues until Burckhardt finds that the world he thought was his is no longer his at all, but a completely alien one with only the simulation of some normality remaining. His world drops away from him; and finally his own identity drops away from himself. He finds that he is not a man, that as a man he died in the explosion he thought he dreamt. Now he is reduced to a midget; and the humanity he thought he possessed turns out to be an electronic reproduction located in a robot. By the kind of circularity that often reinforces Pohl's coolly ironic tone in these stories, Burckhardt's own job in 'real life' was associated with the very factory that thus engineered the transference of human memories, minds, emotions and habits to vacuum-tube cells: he himself ends as one of his own factory's products.

Perhaps the fullest and most suggestive account of alienation is the least fantastic story of the collection, where we are much closer to a tormented psyche – 'Rafferty's Reasons'. Rafferty has lost his former identity as an artist during the machine age, when he became unemployed: now, under the Mudgins Way, everyone is given full employment and machines are abolished. This has meant two things: first, people must do the work formerly done by machines, which means largely repetitive labour; and secondly, artists such as Rafferty will be degraded to manual workers, while morons will succeed. At least, this is what one gathers from odd hints in the story, which refuses to come clean with its own context, almost like Rafferty unable to speak or act openly, or to piece out his 'reasons'. Thus Rafferty, who once was worth something, is treated as trash by his boss Girty, who is far from being a better man. It is this refusal by Girty and the world he represents to give Rafferty his own valuation and identity that is the spring of his rage – though by the time of the story his rage has become so large and formless that it has almost lost touch with any identifiable cause (the motive has lost *its* identity) and Rafferty can only burn with fury at Girty's physical being.[23] Rafferty has lost all notion of what 'the studio' or 'Art' were, though he senses vaguely that they were better than the New Way (p. 124). The enforced sameness of the world of Mudgins and the New Way is fused with the sameness of the anger that Rafferty always feels, 'He sat down and ate what was before him, not caring what it was or how it tasted, for everything tasted alike to Rafferty' (p. 85). When his fury takes him, the normally clear and neat numbers which 'the artist that lived in Rafferty' enjoys making (p. 84) become 'hot red and smouldering black, and they swirled and bloated before his stinging eyes' (p. 87). Rafferty's words and feelings have no identity, remaining unuttered, as with his acts which remain undone. The girls at his table in the cafeteria do not notice him. His whole object in the story is to whip himself up to such a point that he will make some overt definition of himself to the world. His constant mental harping on how he will carve and slice Girty is an image for cutting his way out of himself, and for shaping himself by actually carving someone else's flesh. He fails to accomplish these dramatic acts, but in his failure he reveals a truer self, that of helpless protest.

Clearly outcasts everywhere will be inclined to identify with Rafferty: but we have to remember that he is a creature in a work of science fiction, and that his failures may not be simply psychological but created by the new machines which have been set to turn humanity into unthinkingly obedient operatives before the machines are finally dispensed with. When Girty, announcing to the workers on the Project that an important visitor is coming, tells them all to ' "try to act like human beings this morning" ' (p. 86), the words carry no little unintended irony. Constantly the story presents us with definition, only to pull it away. As Rafferty searches for Girty, looking in the free-market restaurants, he presses 'his forehead against the glass like an urchin on Christmas Day, only with the blackness coming out of no urchin's eyes' (p. 88). That phrase 'blackness coming out of no urchin's eyes' suggests that it comes out of a nothingness, before we read it aright; and the effect of the whole has been to give us a clear scene of a street urchin and Christmas time before whisking both away. When Rafferty, who has only two dollars, takes a taxi to follow Girty, 'The driver . . . never knew that murder was right behind him. But it was only a short ride – fortunately for Rafferty's two dollars' (p. 89): at that 'fortunately' we think the reference will be to the taxi-driver who has escaped Rafferty's murderous intent, but in fact it is directed at the two dollars; the sentence starts in Rafferty's melodramatic idiom and then shifts to the dry tone of the author.

Throughout the story Rafferty is constantly being portrayed as saying terrible things to people, whether to Girty, a stranger, the taxi-driver or a masseur, before this is taken back and we realize that they have taken place only in his imagination, not in reality at all. Rafferty's hatred is both present and not, burdened with intent and starved of act. Lying on the massage slab in the steam baths to which he eventually follows Girty, Rafferty rages at 'the darkened, shapeless core of the light' (p. 94): it is as though he is raging at an image of his own hate. That hatred has lost definition as, in a different way, has Rafferty's past, of which he retains only a hazy notion: he dimly recollects having been at the baths before, but loses certainty in a thicket of vague pronouns and shuffled tenses, 'Once upon a time, it seemed to Rafferty, a long, long time ago someone who *then* had been that which was Rafferty *now* had been in a place like this. That was during what they called the "Old Way", although it seemed to Rafferty, they hadn't called it that then' (p. 90).

The steam-baths where the story ends are symbolic. They are hot, like Rafferty's rage. They are impersonal, like society – functional, anonymous square rooms, functional attendants. Those in them have to go naked, which suggests revelation of the true self. Yet at the same time the steam obscures everything, reducing people to dim shapes, enabling Rafferty to conceal himself from Girty, even (for a while) when he lies down on the slab beside him for massage. This double aspect, of revelation and concealment, mirrors Rafferty's eventual revelation of his feelings to Girty and the world, and at the same time his delusion that he has revealed them far more violently than in fact he has, 'After he committed suicide, he sat there and watched his victims running about. It was several seconds before he noticed that he wasn't dead' (p. 95). When Girty suddenly recognizes Rafferty in the massage room, it is then that Rafferty reveals his true self by getting slowly off his slab, voicing his incoherent hate and assaulting Girty: as Girty penetrates through the steam to Rafferty's physical identity in the baths, so he discovers something of Rafferty's inner being.

It has taken that to bring Rafferty to act: he has been lying passively on his slab waiting for 'some sort of signal' (p. 92), and one may suppose that had Girty not recognized him he might never have acted at all – in short that Girty, in a way, has brought Rafferty 'into being'. Rafferty depends on the very world he hates to stimulate him: perhaps it is more a part of him than he knows. Nor can he make his act fully his own: it is always like something else, like somebody else. He uses multiple analogies, seeing his eventual movements as being 'fast as lightning or the star rays that shoot across the void', even mixing his metaphors, as when he describes himself as 'an avalanche waiting on cue in the wings of a spectacular drama' (p. 91). When he attacks Girty and those about him, 'It was the moment of the knife', and

> He was a Spartacus, and a Lizzie Borden, swordsman and butcher. He stabbed every one of them to the heart and ripped them up and down, and for the first time in longer than he could know, Rafferty was Rafferty, *Mister* Rafferty, a man who had once been a human being and, God save the mark, an artist, and not a mere flesh ersatz for a bookkeeping machine. Kill and slice and tear! They overturned furniture, squealing and thundering, like a trapped horse kicking at the flaming, booming walls of its stall. But he killed them all, many times, this Rafferty who was Spartacus and Lizzie Borden –
> And, at last, a warrior of the Samurai as well. (pp. 94–5)

The circularity of the first paragraph suggests the isolation from reality, from which the only escape is the suicidal gesture of the final sentence, a gesture which is quite imaginary. Just as Rafferty denies his true self in these analogies, so his own words lose identity. He uses cliché throughout – 'the moment of the knife',

'God save the mark'; his words are repetitive – 'Dirty, dirty, dirty', 'I have a knife to cut you with and stab you with'; and they are exhausted, short-breathed, lacking the emphasis even of an exclamation mark: ' "I'll kill you, Girty" '; ' "Fat, soft thing. You're dirty, cow" '; ' "Your mother loved hogs" ' (pp. 90–4). Rafferty does in his way succeed in identifying himself, but the identification is limited. How far he realized he had deluded himself about the knife we do not know, as he is carried out, weeping. As for the world, he has left little mark on it: he had hoped literally to make a mark with the knife, and Girty's death, but all he has done is give Girty's body some temporary bruises. As far as Girty's mind is concerned, to it Rafferty is mere riff-rafferty, the kind of degenerate who will snap under pressure. True, Girty is left vaguely wondering at Rafferty's reason for attacking him, but that is all. All we know is that a few others not unlike Rafferty may exist, such as Girty's friend, who dislikes the harshness of the Mudgins Way, but voices his criticism only to himself. In the last section of the story the conversation of Girty and his friend largely walls off Rafferty's act from comprehension.

In this and the other stories in *Alternating Currents* Pohl is not bent on making a point or in putting over a message, which makes them all the more effective. The story of Ehrlich in 'The Ghost-Maker' may be shown to illustrate 'pride punished' or the Faustian theme of the perils of going beyond permitted limits of knowledge and power, but Pohl never says so, never reduces the story to these lessons, and the result is that it conveys these meanings and many more. Similarly in 'Let the Ants Try' and 'Target One' the moral thread may be the danger of playing God, but this is no more than hinted in the name *Salva* Gordy, which leaves the story free to work at other levels. In 'Rafferty's Reasons' we deal with a very mixed person in Rafferty, who is not reducible to any formula. Always Pohl prefers the oblique, or the dryly detached: 'Sometimes he screams, sometimes he wheedles, threatens, begs, cajoles . . . but his voice goes on and on through one June 15th after another' (pp. 142–3);

> It was entirely my own fault and carelessness; but I wish I had not been so free to conjure up the ghosts of lions and lizards; I have wished it more and more since N'Ginga came running to me, face almost pale, to show me what lizard-teeth had done to the wraith of the Boy. (p. 34)

(That 'almost pale' is a marvellously precise touch in the midst of horror: it suggests under-statement, until we recall that ghosts are already pale.)

In other collections of his stories Pohl sometimes does look over his shoulder at an audience, or hector his readers directly, and the result is far less potent narrative. 'Day Million' is an example. In this story Pohl's object is to show us how provincial and contingent some of our values are. He describes the peculiar marital relationship of a couple in the far future, where the man is a one hundred and eighty-seven-year-old cyborg composed mainly of metal parts, and the woman is genetically male, seven feet tall and with a body part-seal, smelling of peanut butter; and during this absurd portrait he turns to lash us for our blinkered perspective, 'Balls, you say, it looks crazy to me. And you – with your aftershave lotion and your little red car, pushing papers across a desk all day and chasing tail all night – tell me, just how the hell you think you would look to Tiglath-Pileser, say, or Attila the Hun?'[24] If one were to put the next story from the same collection, 'The Deadly Mission of P. Snodgrass', beside 'Target One', the point is still more evident. The Snodgrass story has its scientist protagonist return to the time of Christ with the generous object of providing the benefits of twentieth-century medicine to the suffering humanity of the time. The result is a dramatic decline in the mortality rate, and the population of the world swiftly doubles and redoubles. Pressure of population forces an early industrial revolution and scientific advance to sustain the population; but even so, by the sixth century A.D. all the available land mass of the earth is covered with humans. Eventually a time machine is constructed to send back a man to kill Snodgrass, whereupon 'To the great (if only potential) joy of some quintillions of never-to-be-born persons, Darkness blessedly fell.'[25] The 'story' is simply direct extrapolation of what would happen after a single dramatic event; and with its projections of how humanity would eventually outweigh the universe, it, like 'Day Million' goes to extreme lengths. As a warning against overpopulation it is much less effective, because much more naively direct, than the more oblique 'Target One', which fully dramatises a situation of overpopulation and its effect on human beings, and shows us something of what it would feel like. 'The Deadly Mission of P. Snodgrass' also limits its effect by ending with a happy reversal of the disaster, where 'Target One' does not; one thinks too of the failure of Gordy to reverse his manipulations of the past in 'Let the Ants Try'.

One of Pohl's *fortes* in *Alternating Currents* is the neatness with which every detail fits. The narrative of 'The Tunnel Under the World' is written from an initial position of ignorance, where we think we know where we are but slowly discover, with the narrator, anomalous factors, such as the unchanging date and weather, the explosion remembered from the 'dream', the strange commercials for unfamiliar brands, the unusual cigarettes, the absence of Barth from Burckhardt's office and so on, all causing increasing puzzlement: and then, when this has reached a pitch, every single piece fits into one explanation, one unsuspected world which seems more real because it answers everything in the story. This is, if we like, where Pohl's stories have a further kinship with Pope: every part that seemed to stand out in the end proves to be part of a larger whole ('Parts answ'ring parts shall slide into a Whole'; 'All Chance, Direction, which thou canst not see; / All Discord, Harmony not understood'[26]). In this Pohl is quite different, for example, from an author and a story whose publication he himself ensured – Cordwainer Smith's 'Scanners Live in Vain' (1950). In Smith's story the process of 'cranching', of coming out from being a scanner or bio-telepath into normal humanity is as contingent as the name: a golden-sheathed wire is wrapped about the scanner, plugged into a control in his chest, and a wire field sphere at its end thrown into the air, where it is caught and held by the force-field round the scanner before glowing and producing the change. There is nothing necessary or even symbolic about this apparatus so far as the story is concerned, apart perhaps from its relative absurdity. With Pohl the apparently random becomes patterned: in 'The Mapmakers' – and the title itself says it – the seeming chaos of hyperspace becomes ordered in the mind of Groden.

It is this 'fitting' that makes the new worlds of Pohl coolly attractive. One of the finest examples of this is 'Let the Ants Try', where, in contrast to 'The Tunnel Under the World', we start with an apparently all-knowing narrator, one indeed who proposes to refashion the chaos of the world into his own pattern. But the very pattern he creates contains a logic and a further pattern that he did not foresee. Intelligent ants will not coexist with humans; and events will neatly circumscribe every attempt to reverse the process by which they came into being. Things get out of hand:

here the narrative is symbolic, for it suggests a runaway
chain-reaction, and it is precisely away from the results of such
chain-reaction, in the form of devastating atomic war, that the
scientist Gordy is trying to manipulate history. (In this and such
sceptical stories as 'The Ghost-Maker', 'Target One' and 'What
To Do Until the Analyst Comes' Pohl is again like Pope – 'Man,
who here seems principal alone, / Perhaps acts second to some
sphere unknown, / . . . / 'Tis but a part we see, and not a
whole.'[27]) The circularity of the narrative, whereby Gordy comes
to live through his own unrecognized scream, is again symbolic:
he is caught in a temporal pincer-movement, just as the ants have
outflanked him to catch him in their physical pincers. Somehow
the story is so tightly woven, so precisely balanced, that we do not
question why the ants could not have used Gordy's time machine
themselves rather than build a new one, or how they knew for
what he had disappeared into the past, and to what precise time in
the past. If anything makes Pohl's stories 'scientific', it is that they
work like equations.

Neatness, wit, clarity: it is Pohl's instinct for accuracy that
makes him so able to write well about a man such as Rafferty who
lives an 'inaccurate' life, a man who struggles and fails to define
himself. It is because the scientists in 'Let the Ants Try' and
'Target One' do not work out the possible consequences of their
actions that they meet disaster. Ehrlich in 'The Ghost-Maker'
meets his fate partly because he has ceased to care for accuracy,
whether the accuracy of a scientist, or that of simply looking where
one is going: he himself becomes ghosted because he has refused
definition. In many of the stories the characters end by coming to
a clearer, if often unpleasant, awareness – Gordy, Burckhardt
finding the true nature of Tylerton, the protagonists of 'Target
One' realizing the real nature of the world they have made,
Ehrlich coming to see that ghost-carnivores can devour ghosts,
McGory doomed to be the sole clear and undrugged consciousness who at the end of 'What To Do Until the Analyst Comes' sees
the full effect on the world of Cheery-Gum.

Pohl always gives the fantastic events of his stories 'definition'
by tying them to the everyday and identifiable. While the captain
of the space-ship in 'The Mapmakers' considers the mysteries of
Riemannian space he simultaneously observes that a spaceman is
out of uniform and that 'The enlisted women's quarters needed
floor-polishing' (p. 63). Part of Rafferty's mind is preoccupied

with the price of his Swedish Rub massage as he prepares to slay Girty. No better way could have been found to convey the narrowness of Gordy's escape from the ants than the severed insect leg still thrashing about on the floor of the time machine. And Pohl has a marvellously sharp ear for tones of voice and attitude – Gordy in 'Let the Ants Try' addressing the ants like a collection of ignorant natives, the pompous formalities of the narrator in 'Target One' before he is bundled away by the dingy representatives of the new society he has brought about, the smart flippancy of Ehrlich in 'The Ghost-Maker', the wry self-exposure of McGory in 'What To Do Until the Analyst Comes'. Detail, precision, scepticism, wit, astringent irony and above all an insider's view of *this* world – whether the interior of a steam bath, a museum or an advertising company: all these go into Pohl's tone. In some ways, as we have suggested, he is like Pope; in others, particularly in his juxtaposition of the familiar and the strange, or his carrying a situation to its logical limit, or in the interplay between serious and comic in his stories, his method recalls that of the metaphysical poets: but ultimately these likenesses serve only to point more precisely to his own individuality.

4 Brian Aldiss, *Hothouse* (1962)

To his friend Frederik Pohl Brian Aldiss owes the first publication in the US of his science fiction.[1] His work has much of the astringency of Pohl's, and like him he is an expert in the finely-tuned short story of which he has similarly published about as many collections as novels – though with Aldiss both types have been produced throughout his career. But his imagination is on the whole much freer than Pohl's – where Pohl will carefully document the physical changes necessary to turn a man into a cyborg capable of survival in the bleak environment of Mars, Aldiss will create aliens who live happily in their own excrement, or a fantastic vision of the end-time world of Earth or of travel into the remote past. Aldiss, like Clifford Simak, who was also brought up in a rural environment, loves the portrayal of landscapes,[2] where the environment of Pohl's work and of much science fiction tends to be urban or a construct. (In *Non-Stop* (1958) Aldiss turns a star-ship into a jungle.) Much of Aldiss's work, like Pohl's, is satiric: but the objects of his satire are less particular, more philosophic – not the power of advertising, the dangers of scientific meddling, the perils of consumerism, the menace of racial prejudice, but rather the divided psyche of modern man from which these spring. Most of his novels have been relatively short and have involved the activities of technological man on this planet: his recent 'Helliconia' novels – *Helliconia Spring* (1982) and *Helliconia Summer* (1983) are lengthy parts of an unfolding epic of life on a remote planet in which man as we understand him has little place. But in their relative primitivism and sense of nature's strength these Helliconia novels mark a return to the idiom of Aldiss's strange and powerful *Hothouse*.

Aldiss has tended to view his Hugo award-winning *Hothouse* as a changeling in his work, 'a novel from which I always feel distanced'.[3] What is certain is that the jungle landscape of the

57

book is drawn from one with which he was continuously in contact during one of the most telling experiences of his life, his time of service in Burma during the war and in Sumatra after it.[4] Most of the contexts of his other books – apart perhaps from the Thames-side of *Greybeard* (1964) or the Norfolk acres of 'The Saliva Tree' (1965) – are more or less wholly imaginary: but this book, and perhaps something in its story too, come from very close to the author; it was written at a time of great stress, when his first marriage was breaking up and he was, like Gren in the book, having to learn to survive on his own. It is arguably the most imaginative and suggestive of his works: imaginative in the sheer variety of fantastic flora and fauna that are described; suggestive in the way that we are drawn to trace patterns of meaning and development in the narrative which the solidity of the images resists.

The narrative, if we can call it such, in this science fiction classic, is of a group of devolved miniature humans trying to survive in a world far in the future, when the sun is much hotter and about to go 'nova', the earth has stopped spinning, and the land area of the planet facing the sun is covered by a single banyan tree, hundreds of feet in height, that has spread and conquered all other vegetable forms.[5] In this plant world the few humans have to contend with a whole range of exotic predators, most of them near-vegetable in nature. The humans are portrayed as being only just human: they have cunning enough to outwit many of their adversaries, but they are largely devoid of purpose, and never speculate on or question their experiences, however bleak. For them, whatever happens, ' "It is the way" ': they are determinists. Without the sense of themselves as capable of individual acts of will and self-definition, they are slumping towards the vegetable state. Certainly their identity is unstable: at one stage a group of them travels to the moon, where each member mutates to a winged creature called a 'flyman'. Later we meet a collection of fisher-folk, all of whom are joined to a tree by tails: they feed themselves and the tree with the fish, and the tree in turn protects them; they recall Kingsley's Doasyoulikes, who devolved through sloth from men to apes. And we are to meet the 'sharp-furs', a people half-dog, half-human, and the howlers, the products of the conjunction of man and sheep.

The earth is on the point of dying, though paradoxically the increase of the sun's heat has produced an enormous burst of fecundity in the form of the banyan and its inhabitants:[6] Aldiss has inverted Wells's vision of a dead world beneath a dying sun. In this world all the life-forms are immune to cosmic radiation. Space travel has become possible for life, in the shapes of the traversers, giant spider-like plants a mile or so in length, which over millenia have created out of their dead bodies an atmosphere capable of sustaining them on the moon. Between the moon and the earth they make regular journeys, almost like immense airships, except that for them biology and the need to reproduce dictate their movements. It is by means of the traversers, together with the help of sealable capsules gathered from another plant, that humans are able to make the journey from the earth to the moon also.

The story begins with Clat, one of the small group of humans living in the banyan, falling from a branch on to wide leaf: while the others gather to rescue her, 'green teeth sprouted through the leaf all about her.' Before she can escape, the teeth catch her by the waist:

> Under the leaf, a trappersnapper had moved into position, sensing the presence of prey through the single layer of foliage. The trappersnapper was a horny, caselike affair, just a pair of square jaws, hinged and with many long teeth. From one corner of it grew a stalk, very muscular and thicker than a human, and resembling a neck. Now it bent, carrying Clat away down to its true mouth, which lived with the rest of the plant far below on the unseen forest Ground, in darkness and decay.
>
> Whistling, Lily-yo directed her dumbler back up to the home branch. Nothing now could be done for Clat. It was the way.[7]

Everything is functional, the jaws, the teeth, the stalk, even the response of the humans. As the second paragraph of the book tells us, this environment 'was no longer a place for mind. It was a place for growth, for vegetables' (p. 7). There is, however, some vestigial gesture at a funeral rite. This rite involves taking the 'soul' of the dead person – the soul being a piece of wood shaped to the rough form of the departed and previously kept in his or her dwelling – up to 'the Tips', the highest point of the banyan tree. Death is called 'falling to the green': yet it is matched by an ascent to the heights. None of the humans, however, is aware of this built-in antithesis, with its suggestion that the way down is the way up – a paradox to be more explicitly stated near the end of the book (p. 203).

Once at the Tips, a capsule is with difficulty found for the soul and attached to the web of an approaching traverser: as the traverser runs down the web its hairs brush up the capsule, which is then conveyed by the traverser on its next journey to the moon. These obsequies over, the two women who have performed the task return down to the group. But they – that is the females Lily-yo and Flor – now begin to feel that they are too old for the group and that it is time for them, too, along with several others, to 'Go Up' to the Tips and the traversers. This they do, leaving a group of three young males and six females under the leadership of the girl Toy to find their way down from the Tips and make a new life for themselves in the jungle world. What governs most of these actions is unthinking instinct. There is no reason to go to the Tips, no foresight of what may lie beyond: only this blind, largely biological urge. The leaving of the children is not far from the behaviour of animals towards their young: and the human young in this case are correspondingly less childish than their years might suggest to us, and more able to look after themselves. Having journeyed to the moon, at the cost of two of the six, the humans find that they have mutated to the form of the more intelligent race of flymen they formerly hated, who there greet them, help them over their self-disgust at their new bodies and train them for an invasion of Earth.

At this point the narrative returns us to the remaining members of the group left on Earth. One of the males, Gren, proves self-willed and rash, and quickly comes into conflict with the leader Toy. On their way through the Tips they encounter a white, hose-like object moving down past them into the depths. It is the enormous proboscis of a suckerbird, which lies on the Tips and pays out its giant tongue to feed off the highly nutritious soil on the far distant ground. The children trap it by pinning its tongue to a tree trunk with a rope: they then set about the creature to kill it for food. The attack is foolishly carried out, since with their relatively small weapons the humans cannot damage the vast creature for a long time, by which point it has broken itself free and flown off with them still clinging to it. As the bird becomes increasingly wounded, it loses height, and finally crashes on a rocky promontory at a coast. Thereafter the group of humans becomes split up: the banished male Gren becomes the centre of narrative interest, and apart from his companion the female Poyly, the others are forgotten.

During his wanderings in an extremely hostile environment, Gren encounters a morel, a dark brown conglomerate of cells which attaches itself to his head and sends down feelers into his brain. The morel is a living brain, and it confers upon Gren a perception and purpose that he had not before possessed. But it is the morel's purpose, not Gren's: Gren becomes increasingly subject to its dictates, and at the same time unable to remove it. The morel is curious about everything; its eventual plan is to destroy all the inimical life on the planet and make for itself a paradise. It reveals to Gren, after probing his deep unconscious, that it was once inside the head of man when he was great: that is, that 'human' intelligence was always the result of symbiosis between morel and man, a symbiosis that began as with Gren, with morels fixing themselves to the outsides of primitive men's heads until evolution brought them in. But with the increase of solar radiation the morels inside human skulls died, and men returned to the primitive state; only now have the morels developed a strain resistant to radiation, a strain which may start the whole cycle once more. But the morel tires of Gren and his stubbornness, and seeks to pour itself from his head to that of his child Laren: and at that point it is tricked and its hopes smashed, by the interposition of a gourd, into which it falls, between it and the baby. Thereafter Gren is said to be intellectually more advanced than he was before he met the morel: 'the morel . . . had found Gren's mind like a little stagnant pool and left it like a living sea' (p. 180). Gren's awareness of his world is now further increased by an articulate dolphin-creature called Sodal Ye. He then encounters the people of his old group, who have returned to earth as fly-people. They, warned by the Sodal that the earth is not far from its end, resolve to set out on a traverser for new worlds in deep space, and implant the morel in the traverser to govern its direction. But Gren will not go with them, preferring to return to his old home environment of the jungle of the banyan tree, sure too now that he will be more able to survive against predators.

What then is the book about? One of its central themes might appear to be the development of Gren from an unthinking to a more thinking state: at first animal, he is altered by the morel and the Sodal. Yet that thinking will be largely useless as thought, for it will only enable him the more surely to stay alive, not to create anything new. The 'development' as such is only 'there' at the end, after the morel has left Gren. And Gren and thought will go again in the end. In this direction the book is often quite bleak in outlook. If we think that thought is a good thing, we can see that it often only serves to foster megalomania and tyranny. This applies not just to the doings of the morel and its lust to cover the planet with fungus (p. 75), but to the Sodal Ye, borne about and served by the hopeless human slaves he degrades, and even to Gren's attitude to the ignorant 'tummy-belly' folk, kicking them about with contempt and ignoring their wants. If on the other hand we would dispense with thought, we seem left either with the hedonism of the tummy-bellies, attached by umbilical cords to their tummy-trees, or the mindless viciousness of the many predators. It is true that at the end Gren, free of the morel, is said to be more intelligent than before, and thus could represent a mixture of the opposites, of mind and body, thought and thoughtlessness. But even if the book might make us feel that this is so, the facts of human evolution as described by the morel make it false: for human intelligence was possible in the past only as long as the morel brain remained in symbiosis with the human one. And there is also the fact to consider that Gren is capable of considerable powers of deduction before he meets the morel – as when he alone of his group works out a cunning method of escaping from the devouring bellyelm (pp. 63–4). Finally we have to consider that from this point of view, even if Gren chooses the jungle at the end where he did not before, he is still returning to his place of origin, into the engulfing banyan, in a circularity which must suggest mental enclosure, especially when compared to the linear evolutionary movement pursued by the morel and the others as they leave earth for a new planet on a traverser. Thus, if it cannot be denied that some sort of mental development on the part of Gren is proposed, it cannot be asserted either that this theme is clearly and unambiguously present.

Suppose we consider another possible theme: Gren's maturation, his development to a true sense of self. Much can be made of this: he is left as a child at the beginning and has to learn how to survive on his own. Here we can view his return to his jungle home at the end in more heroic terms: the others, Lily-yo, Haris, even the morel, all leave the world to find another, because they are told this world will end. They project their personal insecurity on to the cosmic stage: they refuse to see that, as Gren points out, the end of the earth will not come in their lifetimes or in that of their children's children. They have no home, because they are not at home in themselves. To their warning to Gren, ' "You don't know what you are doing," ' he replies, ' "That may be true; but at least I know what you are doing" ' (p. 206). His name is Gren, suggesting his kinship with the green world. Lily-yo and the others began by leaving the earth for the moon on a traverser, and they leave earth thus again at the end for deep space: they are wanderers. We last see Gren dismounting from the traverser, climbing down 'into a bower of leaves' (p. 206). For most of the narrative Gren has wandered, from jungle to sea, from sea to the dark lands beyond the termination of earth's sunward side, and now back again. He has found himself, and in doing so, self no longer matters to him: he is free of the megalomania of the morel and the fears of the other humans. For much of the story, too, he has been carried or used as a carrier, indicating his lack of self-sufficiency. First the suckerbird bore him to the coast; then the morel dropped on his head and began to dominate; then he is swept by boat to an island in the sea, and by boat and then iceberg to another island; then he journeys on a walking seed plant beyond the terminator; and finally makes his way back to the jungle by traverser. At the end, descending from the traverser, he says, ' "I'm tired of carrying or being carried" ' (p. 205). He is not the only creature carried in the novel: the morel and Sodal Ye both depend on others to carry them and make them able to act; they are in their way emblems of the helplessness of mere intelligence.

The earlier half of the book also has a number of images of enclosure, suggesting the womb, from which Gren must escape. It is true that he has in a sense 'escaped' it early on, when the adults abandon the children, who are then forced on their own resources: but the 'womb' that he is escaping for most of the narrative is one that his elders themselves have not escaped – it is the womb of dependence, of the resignation of will to instinct, of the blind determinism of 'It is the way.' There are the urns in which Lily-yo and the others transport themselves to the moon; and the body of the traverser in which they return. While on the coast in the 'Nomansland' between the giant banyan and the inhospitable sea, Gren is caught in a tree-cage let down by an oak, and a little later, after he has been rescued, the whole group find themselves trapped for food inside the hollow trunk-stomach of a bellyelm tree. (The originals of both these trees and others of Nomansland were driven there by the all-conquering banyan, which halted short of the shore, leaving them to adapt to survive.) It is Gren who works out how the others may escape from the bellyelm. Later he and two female companions, Poyly and Yattmur, are drawn by the Black Mouth. The Black Mouth (an idea perhaps taken from E. H. Visiak's *Medusa* (1929)), is a volcanic cone in a wasteland, out of which from time to time comes a Circe-like song so fascinating that it draws all creatures from miles around towards it to hurl themselves into the cone; inside they are devoured by a creature the only evidence of which is a huge white hand of waving fingers that beckons from the cone during the song, and is slowly withdrawn at its completion. Gren and the others first escape from being engulfed by the Black Mouth by another form of engulfing – a camouflaged stomach-plant called a greenguts, out of which they cut their way just in time, only once more to be called by the Black Mouth. But just as they arrive near the edge of the cone the song suddenly stops, and they are free.

That some kind of development is implied is suggested by the way enclosures now no longer take them, and by the fact that there are not so many in the later part of the book. On an island another kind of womb rejects Gren. He and the tummy-bellies have found a cave in a strange rock pitted with many of what look like regularly-spaced eyes; and inside it they are given a vision of a vegetable paradise. But just as Gren thinks to have this paradise, it is withdrawn from him, and he wakens rejected and alone on the cave floor. The tummy-bellies have been taken because they, unlike Gren and the morel, are mindless. The last enclosure from which Gren is removed is that of the morel, which has surrounded his head and leaves him, as it intends, for Laren, only to drop into an enclosure itself (the gourd). With the disappearance of the morel, which in its tyrannic control over his will could be seen as a symbol of his own early determinism and dependence, Gren is a wholly free agent, aware of the nature of choice and able to make it.

Yet still one must be careful with such patterns. Ostensibly, Gren's behaviour alters not one bit from beginning to end of the story. His decisions are not evidently increasingly mature as the story progresses, because for most of the time he is in the grip of the morel, unable to do anything but its bidding. It is only on the last page that he chooses against the others to stay on earth. Nor has he been devoid of such independence of choice before. Indeed it is precisely his stubborn rashness, his refusal to conform, that makes the adults of the group suspicious of him from the beginning. When they go to the Tips he does not take the safe route of climbing the Tree, but instead whistles up a dumbler, an obliging winged seed-plant, which conveys him upward without effort but at great risk of his being devoured by flying predators. It is he who is rash enough to hack off the suckerbird's tongue so that it flies away with them all; he too who refuses to go with the others when they escape from the castle on the promontory to the shore. He always chooses on behalf of himself alone. Although he works out the means by which all of the group including himself can escape from the prison of the bellyelm, he does all in his power to stop other members of the group from going back to rescue one of their number who remained stuck in the bellyelm with a deadly plant threatening; and for this he is expelled from the group. At the end, when he chooses to stay on earth, the adult male Haris tells him, ' "You were always as difficult to deal with. You don't know what you are doing" ' (p. 206), which shows that for one person at least his choices at the end are no more enlightened than they were at the beginning. We cannot be sure at the level of his character and behaviour alone that Gren has changed. The only indications are really at the level of the changing symbols in the narrative.

But then it can be argued that these are the real vocabulary of this writer in this novel. He is primarily responsive here to the creation of images and fantastic individuals. There is not very much concern with developing psychology, or indeed with anything directly connective in the narrative. In fact there is not much 'narrative' as such, for there is no particular goal. The adults at the beginning know only that they must 'Go Up', but not why. They go to the moon and then are sent back with no more than a platoon of flymen, supposedly to conquer the earth. This motive has been forgotten by the end of the book, for when they are met their first object is to escape from the world. Gren's motives for most of the narrative are negative: he wishes to go with the suckerbird because he does not want to be left alone in the jungle, he seeks to escape from Nomansland, from the morel and finally from the dark lands beyond the terminator. Most of his journey is random. Even the morel, when it has charge of him, has only a vague idea of overrunning the world with itself. Hence the diverse creatures in the book tend to exist as imaginative islands:

we start with the world of the predatory vegetables in the giant banyan or in the Nomansland between the banyan and the threshing seaweeds of the sea; then we encounter the mysterious force of the singing and devouring Black Mouth from which Gren and Poyly are just saved; later Gren unearths a yellow object with numbers of switches which, when played with by Gren and the girl Yattmur, cause the thing to fly aloft and start shrieking long-forgotten political slogans; and beyond the terminator we find strange dog-like men called 'sharp-furs' and the talking fish Sodal Ye being borne about by a man bent permanently double.

The first thing that strikes us about these and other images in the book is their originality. How did the author manage to think of the burnurn plant in the Tips, a plant which develops transparent seed-pods that can be used to focus the sun and burn an enemy? Or of the terrible battle continually waged between the highly-adapted trees of Nomansland, and the seaweeds, where one side flails the water with bramble-like extensions or even hurls explosive bombs, while the other lashes with barbed fronds or burns with bladders of acid? Doubtless something is owed to John Wyndham's triffids, but Aldiss has gone far beyond this. Much of the book is devoted to the detailed portrayal of the freak flora and fauna encountered; trappersnappers, wiltmilts, burnurns, traversers, suckerbirds, termights, killerwillows, sand octopi, greenguts, crawlpaws, stalkers, tummy-bellies, all receive detailed accounts of their appearance and evolutionary histories so that in some ways the book becomes a sort of fantastic work of biology. The sheer 'this-ness' of the creatures strikes us quite independently of any significance.

Yet, however strange these creatures, everything about them is functional and conditioned by their environment. Their very freakishness and multiplicity have to be there, because the world in which they are set is one in which under the influence of the sun life has rioted into a plenitude of the bizarre. Suppose, for example, we consider one of the strangest and most elaborately thought-out creatures of the book – the stalker, the extraordinary plant that Gren and Yattmur find when marooned on an island and are forced to contemplate by the morel. Arrived on the island, which is pervaded by a delicious air of sloth, they take in among other features 'seed pods towering in the air at the top of tall stalks' (p. 130); later Gren observes how these grow in groups with a shared root system (pp. 133–4). They also notice strange objects shaped like hands, which swim ashore from the sea and burrow into the ground; these they call 'crawlpaws'. But later Gren finds out what happens to make these 'stalkers'. The flowers, which grow at ground level, each have behind them 'a disproportionately large seed pod, a sexfid drum, from each face of which protruded gummy and fringed bosses resembling sea anemones' (p. 139). When an insect lands on the blossom and pollinates it, the plant responds with violence: 'With an odd shrilling noise, flower and seed drum rocked up skywards on a spring that unravelled itself from the drum'. Thereafter, warmed by the sun, the spring 'straightened and dried into a tall stalk. The six-sided drum nodded in sunlight, far above their heads'. The morel forces Gren to remain watching, as three more stalkers from the same clump are flung skywards. When the fourth has risen, a breeze catches it and bumps it against its neighbour: at which, 'the anemone-like protruberances stuck against each other, so that the two cases remained locked, swaying quietly on their long legs' (p. 141). At this the morel tells Gren that ' "These blooms are not separate plants. Six of them with their communal root structure go to make up one plant. They have grown from the six-pronged tubers we have seen, the crawlpaws." ' Eventually all six flowers are pollinated and the six pods fuse together to make one body on six long legs.

At this point the legs detach themselves from the root system beneath, and the whole plant actually begins to walk. It walks directly towards the sea, into which it wades, heading for the mainland coast. The morel is now able excitedly to announce, ' "There lies our escape route, Gren! These stalkers grow here, where there is room for their full development, then go back to the mainland to seed themselves. And if these migratory vegetables can get ashore, they can take us with them!" ' (p. 142). Another flowering stalker plant is found, and by stimulating the pistils the travellers are thrown aloft with the seed pod until they sit on the body of a stalker. Then they move off through the sea to the coast. But they find that the stalkers do not stop there: they march on beyond the terminator, to the dark lands, finally to stop in a twilight zone high up on a mountain that still catches some of the light from the sun. There the stalker waits, until slowly its legs give way and it sinks down to the muddy ground, on impact with which the six seed drums burst, scattering seeds all around. This is the stalker-plant's solution to the problem of overcrowding in the sunlit lands: it has ventured into the less habitable lands to ensure the continued propagation of its kind. From the seeds will grow the crawlpaws, which will return via many obstacles 'to the realms of true warmth and light, there to root and flower and continue the endless vegetable mode of being' (p. 155).

We can think of analogues for this stalker – it is like a spider or one of H. G. Wells's Martians, and there is much of Olaf Stapledon's plant-men in the idea of a plant uprooting itself and becoming mobile: but clearly the whole account, and in particular the thoroughness of botanical explanation, is highly original. One would like to emphasise the point in relation to the scientific explanation: the account is not simply fantastic, the peculiarities of the stalker's life are not there only for themselves, but each one has a biological reason so that its very oddity is part of a scheme. And it is in part this combination of freakishness with sense that gives almost metaphoric life to the picture. There is need for space, the island alone permits the growth of the plants as the hostile shore would not, but the shore must be reached to continue the life cycle; hence the need for legs, since once arrived at the shore the plant must travel much further to find one particular location suitable for its future development – propagation by airborne seeds would here have been useless, since the chance of any seed striking a favourable location would be slim. And of course the form of the stalker is functional in another, unintended way: it precisely serves the purpose of a group of people stuck on an island. Thus in all ways the peculiarities of the stalker are integrated with its environmental needs and with those of the narrative in which it is set.

Furthermore there are certain submerged patterns in the narrative into which the stalker can be seen to fit. In the first place, apart from the humans, few of the creatures seen in the narrative till now have been mobile – if we except the giant vegetable traversers, which do not belong to earth at all but fly through space. The banyan tree is simply *there*, rooted over the land surface of the planet. The seaweeds, the trees of Nomansland, the Black Mouth, all are confined to one area or place. The predators, the wiltmilts, fuzzypuzzles, rayplanes, suckerbirds, leapycreepers, oystermaws, tigerflies, are some of them mobile, but they prey in one locality. The change from the static to the mobile in what is met occurs when Gren, Poyly and Yattmur encounter the tummy-bellies and cut them loose from their tummy-tree, to become the unwilling companions of their travels. It is interesting that just before this episode, Poyly, physically and spiritually exhausted after the Black Mouth asks, ' "What happens to the world here? Does it go mad here, or fall apart? Does it end here?" ' and the morel says, ' "Where it ends may be a good place for us to start it going again" ' (p. 97) – in other words some kind of conclusion is felt here, and it will be followed by new movement. For the rest of the narrative the creatures met are in some way mobile and directional – the stalker, the heckler Beauty, the 'sharp-furs', Sodal Ye and his assistants, the fly-people.

A second pattern is the switch away from the feeding and predatory habits of creatures to their life-history and reproductive cycles. Up to the episode with the tummy-bellies, everything has been hostile, everything a devourer – the menaces in the dense foliage of the banyan, the seaweeds, the trees of Nomansland such as the engulfing bellyelm or the tentacular killerwillow, the Black Mouth. Typical is the following:

> By now, the din of the sea battle was abating. Several trees had been dragged down into the water. At the same time, much seaweed had been fished out of the sea. This was now being eargerly tossed among the victor trees, anxious as they were for nourishment in that barren soil.
>
> As the group crept forward, a soft-pelted thing rushed past on four legs and was gone before they had their wits about them.
>
> 'We could have eaten that,' Shree said grumpily. 'Toy promised us the suckerbird to eat and we never got it.'
>
> The thing had scarcely disappeared before there was a scuffle in the direction it had taken, a squeal, a hasty gobbling sound, and then silence.
>
> 'Something else ate it,' Toy whispered. 'Spread out and we'll stalk it. Knives ready!'
>
> They fanned out and slid through the long grass, happy to engage in positive action. This part of the business of living they understood. (pp. 57–8)

There is a kind of plenitude of gastronomy: everything is about to eat or be eaten; the 'soft-pelted thing' is characterized only so far as a potential menu for the next predator. The humans, too, at this stage in the narrative are concerned mainly with fighting against a hostile environment and with eating. Later in the story however, their interests shift. After seizing the boat of the tummy-bellies and while drifting downriver, Gren and Yattmur make love, and later still a son Laren is born to them. Where in the first part of the story humans were constantly leaving one another in hostility or indifference, whether the adults leaving the children at the beginning, or the remnant of the group rejecting Gren, the later part shows them coming together. Into this new concern with racial continuance the portrait of the stalker fits. And all this can be seen as part of a larger shift from literally 'the law of the jungle' to wider, more diverse and more reflective modes of existence: it is in this section of the narrative that the Sodal Ye is encountered and the potency of the morel develops, together with its schemes for self-propagation over the world.

Yet the assignment of significance is elsewhere not so clear-cut – as can be seen when we relate the appearance of the stalker to another motif – that of growing ambiguity in the characters, and of increasing instability of identity. What is portrayed in the stalker is a process of metamorphosis, a shift from plant to semi-animal, a process of becoming. Every creature in *Hothouse* is the product of metamorphosis. The bellyelm, with its deceptively rotten-looking hollow trunk, in which it traps passing creatures, or the oak-tree with the wooden cage it drops on its prey, or the killerwillow with its subterranean mode of travel are all developments of original elms, oaks and willows brought about by the needs imposed on them by their environments. But we do not see that metamorphosis in the narrative: it is over and done with and is given to us only by the omniscient author; so that the shapes the trees have in the narrative itself are fixed. Later on, however, things change as we watch. The human characters change the tummy-bellies by separating them from their trees and forcing them to live more fully but pathetically on their own. Gren's identity becomes uncertain as he is progressively taken over by the morel, until Yattmur asks herself, 'could it be that he was still human?' (p. 156). The rod-covered cave turns to eyes and back again (pp. 121, 123); even the land can be active, 'This whole tumbled area was one of darkness, lit occasionally by ruddy beacons where mountains thrust themselves up in stony imitation of living things to reach the light' (p. 157). When first met, the creature Sodal Ye appears thus to Yattmur:

She could not understand him properly, for his head, an

enormous fish-like affair with a broad lower lip which turned
down so far that it nearly concealed his lack of chin, was out of
all proportion with the rest of his body. His legs, though bowed,
were human in appearance, his arms were wrapped unmoving
behind his ears, while from his chest a hairy, head-like growth
seemed to emerge. Now and again she caught a glimpse of a
large tail hanging behind him. (p. 172)

This humanoid fish eventually turns out to be in fact two
creatures, the one a fish, the other a man bent double to carry the
fish about – emblem enough of the degradation of humanity in this
world. The companions too of the sodal, the tattooed women who
appear and disappear to the beholder as they travel into the future
and back, are also pictures of unstable identity. Despite their
peculiarities, these humans are essentially dull-witted and un-
questioning in their slavery to the sodal: thus both their humanity
and their exoticism are countered, rendering them an uncertain
mixture. The sharp-furs are capricious, appearing first hostile,
then merely irritable with their barks and squabbles, then finally
savage as they turn on the tummy-bellies they have allowed to live
with them and kill and behead them. Yet here again there is
another point of view; indeed it might be said that just as identity is
ambiguous in this book, so is any assigned meaning. We have
already seen how the appearance of change can be related to the
new motif of reproduction and racial continuance. In the mobility
of its changes the stalker can also be viewed as a product of that
medium in which it grows and which forms part of the environment of Gren and Yattmur in the second half of the book – the
fluid sea. The sodal is later to claim that the sea is the origin of
thought (p.184). The other medium of the second part of the book
is semi-darkness, in contrast to the brilliance of the sunlit lands of
the first half: here again darkness is a medium of release from
fixity, the fluid medium of the unconscious. Thus so far as Gren is
concerned, we can read this motif of metamorphosis in two
directions. Looked at one way, it suggests removal of stasis for the
fluidity of spiritual development: looked at another, this instability of identity suggests the symptom of devolution towards
universal final entropy that the morel later describes (p. 204). We
may play with the patterns, as for instance by suggesting that the
way down is the way up, that by going into the darkness beyond
the terminator Gren goes towards the light, but this really will not

hold. We can observe that while most of the beings of the earlier half of the book have to do with physical struggle and 'body', there is much more 'mind' and contemplation in the latter half, whether in the morel, the vegetable transporter or the sodal. Yet as we have seen these minds are often warped, or filled by power lust. And body continues to exist, now rendered supine and futile in total dissociation from mind – the tummy-bellies, the sodal-bearer, the vacant women. Thus whether the emphasis on mind towards the latter part of the book is an advance remains in doubt.

Still, there are more certainties to be derived from another motif – that of widening vision. This is what marks out the morel:

> The life forms of the great hothouse world lived out their days in ferocity or flight, pursuit or peace, before falling to the green and forming compost for the next generation. For them there was no past and no future; they were like figures woven into a tapestry, without depth. The morel, tapping human minds, was different. It had perspective. (p .74)

The description of the stalker's growth is spread over time: we are aware of how Gren has to sit still and watch the process unfold. The women with the sodal can travel through time; though this does not give them much insight into life. The morel continually gives Gren perspective, making him think and contemplate before he acts, making him plan the future as he never did before; though always under its control. The strange cave-transporter by contrast renounces time for an eternal present: it is 'some flux apart from time' where 'Life had replaced time' – and it rejects Gren (pp. 122, 123). Both the morel and the sodal extend the humans' awareness of their past history and that of the planet enormously. At the end Gren is able to use the temporal perspective the morel has given him to answer warnings against returning to the jungle:

> 'You know this Earth will suffer a fire death, you fool man!'
> 'So you said, O wise morel. You also said that that would not come for many generations. Laren and his son and his son's son will live in the green, rather than be cooked into the gut of a vegetable making an unknown journey.' (p. 205)

Which is right, though, going or staying, is still not fully clear.

There is also a growth in spatial perspective throughout the book. At the beginning of the story things are close to, and usually about to come into direct physical contact. The banyan's density prevents any far-sightedness; and the frenzied activity of Nomansland gives little time for it – though even by then the humans have leisure to contemplate the war of the trees and the seaweeds. Later, objects become more distant, and are seen on their own rather than defined through their conflict with one another. The Black Mouth calls from far off, we see the islands long before reaching them, we watch traversers high up in the open sky, we wade parallel to the coast on the stalker, we gradually approach the distant terminator, we see Sodal Ye and the sharp-furs from afar at first, we look down over the world at the end. There are fewer creatures in the latter part of the book, and these are much more spaced out than in the bursting plenitude of the first part (see for instance the account of Nomansland coming to life when two fighting ray-planes fall into one of the trees, pp. 61–2).

These perspectives are complemented by another, whereby more than two characters are in operation at once. While Gren and the others are in the jungle or on the shore early on, each antagonist they meet appears in turn. They meet the trappersnapper, then the tigerfly, then the oystermaw, then the burnurn, then the wiltmilt, then the seaweeds, then one after the other the assortment of mutated trees and finally the Black Mouth. But later on what they do has a background. They are accompanied by the tummy-bellies whose reactions of fear or pleasure to their various adventures counterpoint those of the humans themselves. The lazy reactions of Gren himself are contrasted to those of the morel. The figures met become multiple – the sharp-furs, the sodal and his attendants, the many stalkers, in contrast to the normally single creatures met earlier, *a* tigerfly, a sand octopus, a bellyelm, *the* Black Mouth. And each figure is often a double creature (the 'howlers' or sheep-humans, the sharp-furs or ape-men, the morel-man Gren), or one creature used by another (the attendants and the sodal) or one being that has a life-cycle with another (the crawlpaws and the stalkers). Encounters orchestrate several different individuals. When the humans speak with the sodal, they also address the assistants. When Yattmur flees from Gren to the sharp-furs, her conversation is shared between them and the tummy-bellies. When Gren takes farewell at the end, he takes farewell of the sodal, the morel, the other humans and their opinions all together. Gren and Yattmur have not only each other, but a child. There is much more conversation, much more thought, much more awareness, in particular, of the wider world about one. In the first half of the novel only the reader is told how the various botanical freaks have emerged over time (for example, pp. 59–60): in the latter half Gren himself is told by the morel or the sodal about the transporter, the stalker, the devolved humans, the changes wrought by the sun.

At the same time language has developed perspective and range. In the first part of the book we find that the names of the various predators are usually in baby-language: there are trappersnappers, wiltmilts, leapycreepers, burnurns, dripper-lips, thinpins, rayplanes, suckerbirds, fuzzypuzzles, crocksocks, pluggyrugs, berrywhisks. All these names reflect the relative mental infancy of the humans – and we might add the bellyelms, killerwillows, snaptrap trees and whistlethistles they later encounter and which they could not have named themselves. They are often exact descriptions of what the creatures do or how they appear: the names are strictly functional; but to that extent of course they lack the detachment of names such as 'lion' or 'horse' which in themselves do not delineate. Functional names such as 'stalker', 'crawlpaw', 'leatherfeather', or 'sharp-fur' do occur later in the narrative, but these names are usually given by the stupid tummy-bellies or by the less intelligent human, Yattmur. The sodal gives the sharp-furs their 'proper' name, 'Bamboon' (p. 186); and 'Sodal' and 'morel' are non-functional names: in them we have reached a measure of adult detachment from phenomena. We may notice also that syntax has developed over the book, from short sentences registering immediate stimuli to more complex forms involving deductive processes. And Gren, who complained earlier in the book that he lacked words to express his ideas (p. 50) now has a much larger vocabulary.

This broadening of perspective, such as it is, is symbolized in the flying slogan-machine or heckler, named Beauty by Yattmur. In itself its recovery is an image of the acquisition of a new temporal dimension, for it is the only relic from man's technological past in the book. Beauty flies after Gren and the others as they travel on the stalker to the shore:

> As they looked towards it [the shore] hopefully, a pair of large
> black birds rose from the forest. Spreading their wings, they

sailed upwards, hovered, and then began to beat their way
heavily through the air towards the stalker.

'Lie flat!' Gren called, drawing his knife.

'Boycott chimp goods!' Beauty cried. 'Don't allow Monkey
Labour in your factory. Support Imbroglio's Anti-Tripartite
scheme!'

The stalker was trampling through shallow water now.

Black wings flashed low overhead, thundering with a whiff of
decay across the stalker. Next moment, Beauty had been
snatched from its placid circling and was being carried
coastwards in mighty talons. As it was borne off, its cry came
back pathetically, 'Fight today to save tomorrow. Make the
world safe for democracy!' Then the birds had it down among
the branches. (pp. 147–8)

Beauty's message is comically irrelevant to this world; yet at the
same time in its battered way it points to the fact that many
alternative views of life are and have been possible. Of course
neither Gren nor Yattmur understands a word it is saying: but at
the level of symbolism its appearance in the narrative and chain of
images at this point may be said to be significant; it says
something about their perspective, if nothing to them. The duality
of the symbol here is caught by its presentation: a cold machine, it
is 'Beauty' to Yattmur; a mechanical device, it is treated still as
prey by the ignorant birds; personified as pathetic and also as
delicately female, 'she' is still an 'it'; masterpiece of the engineering mind though Beauty is, it is at the mercy of primitive nature.
And there is the marvellous duality of perspective in the passage,
with the humans and birds in their zone of awareness, the stalker
indifferently trampling on, the approaching birds, the squawks of
Beauty, all playing against one another.

All this widening of vision may seem progressive enough. But,
once again, broadened perspective does not necessarily lead to the
right conclusions. The philosophic morel who sees all life as
devolving and losing identity (p. 204) is too absolute. First, the
variety of the life in the book disputes projected uniformity, just as
the vigour of existence on the overheated earth contrasts with the
expiring condition of the sun. Secondly, the very movement
through the book is an evolutionary one through vegetables that
have become increasingly sophisticated and proto-mental, until
we arrive at an intellectual fish. Thirdly, insofar as Gren himself

develops, he overturns the idea of universal devolution: from being less of a man he becomes more of one. Then equally there is the question of Gren's educated choice at the end. It can be argued that he does not choose the jungle out of his developed being and perceptiveness so much as use his development to justify what is still an instinctual and irrational preference.

Nevertheless considered broadly the patterns of the creatures and events in the book do suggest a real expansion of outlook, and certainly some kind of maturation, even if this is not clearly present at the level of character. In this direction it is also significant that after a point in the narrative the beings and landscapes no longer express Gren. When Gren is freed of the morel he ceases in more ways than one to have any part in it. He is no longer being absorbed or carried by things, and he sees them at greater distances from him. It is they, the morel, the sodal and the other humans, who are examined by him and seen critically. In thus being free of phenomena, Gren has achieved a measure of self-definition.

Aldiss's *Hothouse* is indeed a book of stunning images. Whatever their original source in his Far East experience or reading, the dominant impression we have with them is of prodigious vitality and inventiveness. Here we have tried to fit some of them into patterns and to explain some of the ways they might be said to work; and we might add that the very way the parts come together to make larger patterns mirrors the way the isolated, localised vision of Gren is spread and deepened. But still a large part of the 'thisness' of the images remains. Still defiantly themselves are those incredible images of the seaweeds and the trees at war, of the tigerfly larvae in the traverser, of the fire-making burnurns, the tunnelling willows, the fingering Black Mouth, the intellectual fish squatting thick-lipped on its human porter, and many others. Perhaps Aldiss might say that these are no more wonderful than nature itself: but he made this nature. The tension between the meanings the images supply and the integrity that they retain makes *Hothouse*, in the words of the blurb from the *Daily Telegraph*, 'a real work of art'.

So the work remains, still enticing interpretation. We shall offer a few more slants on it in considering Frank Herbert's *Dune*.

AFTERWORD

It might be possible to put more definite meaning into *Hothouse* than considered by itself it supplies by looking at it in the context of others of Aldiss's earlier science fiction novels – *Non-Stop* (1958), *Bow Down to Nul* (1960), *The Dark Light Years* (1964), *Greybeard* (1964), *Earthworks* (1965) and *An Age* (1967). Throughout these novels Aldiss is often satiric concerning human development. *Non-Stop* portrays a decline to a savage state inside a gigantic enclosed space ship that the humans inside have come to believe is a world; *Bow Down to Nul* has humanity the slaves of an alien master race, the Nuls, and saved not by themselves but by chance; *The Dark Light Years* shows man, spreading across space, as a ruthless destroyer incapable because of his vanity of appreciating the different kinds of intelligence of other races encountered. In *Earthworks* overpopulation is turning the world to a desert of wretchedness: the appropriately-named protagonist Knowle Noland ends by setting in chain a nuclear war which will destroy most people and permit a fresh start. The post-holocaust world of *Greybeard* is one in which sterile humans, now old, are almost the only survivors. *An Age* is a twin of *The Dark Light Years* in the temporal direction: it shows the futility of visiting all time when one has not properly plumbed the self; its telling imagery is of the time-travellers who may not have any contact with the ages they visit; and it ends with a fitting piece of entropy, when the past is shown actually to be the far future. *Hothouse*, seen in this light, could be fitted into the idea that intellectual evolution at least is of dubious value, set as it is at a time when everything is near destruction by the sun, when almost all of human civilisation has disappeared and man has devolved, and when the intellectual progress enjoined on Gren by the morel is shown in part to be futile.

And there are other themes that could be used to throw light on *Hothouse*. Aldiss seems in many of these novels to be 'for' the primitive and integration with a natural habitat; against the city (especially in *Earthworks*, but also in the wild contexts of the novels); against control (the Nuls, the tyrannical Earth explorers of *The Dark Light Years*, the slave society of *Earthworks*); against severance from the world (the walling-off of the space-ship in *Non-Stop*, the protective suits of the characters in *Bow Down to Nul*, the alienation of humans from other forms of sentient life and from their own physicality in *The Dark Light Years*, even the anaemic representatives of a utopian future of 'homo uniformis' forced to confront their primitive ancestry on a far planet in the later *Enemies of the System* (1980)). Reading from these one could see the morel in *Hothouse* as the dangerous controller – and there is also a strong vein of anti-intellectualism in these other novels (mind in isolation makes ugly bodies in the later novels *Frankenstein Unbound* (1973) and *Moreau's Other Island* (1980)). Gren's decision to go back to his jungle home would then be the 'right' one; and the whole novel would become a sort of primitivist manifesto.

But so to interpret *Hothouse* is to oversimplify. This is one book where Aldiss does not allow us easy certainties, even if some patterns may be found.[8] The polarities are clear in *The Dark Light Years* – the happy and generous utods, integrated with their muddy environment and their physical selves, against the rapacious, egoistic humans, divorced from theirs; and we know only too clearly where our sympathies are to lie. But there is more ambiguity in *Hothouse*. Whether Gren's decision to return to the jungle at the end is right is not simply clear, nor whether he has 'learnt', nor whether his learning or not learning may be good or bad things. The morel's interstellar journey with Sodal Ye and the other humans may turn out to be futile, but is the only hope for the continuance of life from the solar system, insofar as such continuance is of value. Gren may have matured, and his awareness broadened, but his free choice of the jungle at the end, much as it may be an act of integration with his larger self, is also a refusal of evolution and further change: from this view, however 'choosing', he still ends at an animal level, in stasis. Its ambiguity, its full acknowledgement of the complexity of life, imaged in the extraordinary variety of the beings portrayed, is a large part of the strength of the novel: here indeed Aldiss achieves his aim of 'celebrating life in all its unkempt beauty'.[9]

5 Frank Herbert, *Dune* (1965)

Frank Herbert's *Dune* is frequently viewed as a science-fiction masterpiece.[1] It is in some ways a mixture of the mode of the *Koran*, the rise of a messiah, and the story of Lawrence of Arabia, who made himself one with the Arabs. It grew, Herbert has said, out of the image of a planet covered by desert sand, and from his wish to write an analysis of humanity's need for a messiah or superhero.[2] Its origins were thus both imaginative and intellectual, and in the bonding of the two lies much of its strength. It has been argued that *Dune* was also written as a reply to Asimov's *Foundation* trilogy, out of Herbert's dislike for impositions of science on history: thus Herbert replaces Seldon's mathematics with Paul Muad'Dib's wild unconscious, and order and civilization are put together with anarchy and primitive nature.[3] Certainly it can be said that *Dune* might not have been written had the example of Asimov's epic not been there.

The desert planet Arrakis or Dune has beneath its surface great deposits of the spice melange, which is mined for export to other planets of an empire. The natives of the planet (though in fact they were originally exiles from another) are the Fremen, an Arab-like people in appearance and customs, whose primary concern is the conservation of water and whose strengths lie in their patience, in their fanatical loyalty and in their powers of concealment. The last is particularly important, for unknown to the rulers of the planet and the empire at large, the Fremen are busy covering parts of the desert with self-sustaining plants that will eventually make an atmosphere suitable for vegetation. The Fremen are also, however, waiting for a messiah to lead them from the wilderness on a *jihad*, or holy war.

To Arrakis from the tropical world of Caladan comes the newly-appointed overlord Duke Leto, with his son Paul. Leto plans a more humane treatment of the disadvantaged people of the planet than was the case under his predecessor, the evil Baron Vladimir Harkonnen. But the machinations of Harkonnen, helped by disguised troops of the Emperor, bring about the death of Leto, the flight of Paul and his mother Jessica, and the re-establishment of Harkonnen rule. Paul and Jessica, the circumstances of whose escape have convinced the Baron that they are dead, travel across the dangerous desert and meet with the Fremen; after a number of trials the Fremen accept them. Paul himself has considerable mental powers, including the power of foresight, and indeed he gradually becomes to the Fremen more evidently the Kwisatz Haderach, the promised messiah. Under his guidance the Fremen carry out guerilla activities all over the planet which finally leave them in virtual control apart from the central city of Arakeen. Their control over the spice of the planet leads the Emperor to intervene personally, but he and the Harkonnens are overthrown in a surprise attack by the Fremen, and the Baron is killed. It turns out that much depends on the nature of the spice, which, apart from being a trance-inducing drug, is indispensable to the men of the Guild who steer the space-ships about the Imperium: with it, they can find direction from an inner mental knowledge of the spatial configurations about them; without it, they are blind, and there can be no more interstellar travel. Because the very existence of his empire depends on the ability to travel through it, the Emperor is subservient to the Guildsmen. Through exercise of his power Paul ensures the confinement of the Emperor to his former prison planet, and new dominance for the Fremen. By the end of the book the Fremen are poised on the edge of an interstellar war of conquest that Paul does not want but which he knows he cannot stop.

The world of the planet Dune, so far as landscape goes, is much simpler than that of the earth in Aldiss's *Hothouse*. There are no plants, save those that the Fremen grow artificially; there are few animals, save the usually concealed giant sandworms that guard the spice, and the desert mouse after which Paul is named, 'Muad'Dib'. The whole planet is covered with sand and rock. The land in Aldiss's book is covered by a single banyan tree over one hemisphere: but within that vegetable environment we are introduced to a host of creatures; and we are taken to the sea, where the plants and animals are again different, and beyond the terminator, where they live an entirely different mode of life. *Dune*, it would appear, deals with a barren planet; *Hothouse* with one distinct in its endless fertility and metamorphoses. There is little sense that being is plastic on Dune, small reference to a long history of evolution. Here we are dealing rather with man in a landscape than with man as one animal among others. Here too man has to be protected from his environment, in still-suits that retain every drop of the body's moisture; in *Hothouse* man goes naked, long since adapted to the destructive solar radiation that now blasts the earth, fighting his environment with only his wits. Dune seems a bleaker, simpler, much more arid world. Yet its aridity is in part only of the surface. Beneath the sand lie the rich deposits of the spice on which the whole fabric of the empire depends. The duality of aridity and richness here is almost metaphoric.

And the motif of concealment is central to *Dune* and its manner.[4] It is there in the Fremen, whose nature and plans remain till too late hidden from the Imperium. It is there in the concealed evidence of Paul Muad'Dib and his mother. It is there in the way in which much of the behaviour in the book is political or polite, one line of behaviour concealing another purpose, manners putting a gloss on hatreds, accusations, threats, love, loyalty, forgiveness. It is there in Paul's hidden powers and nature, which only gradually become revealed to himself as the book proceeds. And it is there in the concealed motives of the Emperor and in the unknown value of the spice to the Guildsmen: throughout the book until the end we do not know the natures of some of the central figures. There are concealments in *Hothouse*: the oystermaw that makes itself seem part of the bark of a tree, the killerwillow beneath the sand, the 'greenguts' or vegetable stomach that appears to be a little copse; but these are local, not involving the whole narrative, and they are local in time too, in that the concealment lasts simply until the next meal. In *Dune*, concealment is of the essence, and is bound up with waiting over long periods of time.

Indeed *Dune* is much more concerned with the future than *Hothouse*. *Hothouse* considers the present only, the immediate action of survival against hostile plants or beasts. Where it looks along time it looks to the past, in describing how the various biological freaks described in the book have evolved from their original, and in giving the past history of mankind. Its narrative does not directly look to the future: Gren is simply wandering without an aim, and we have no way of predicting or anticipating what event may happen for him next. At the end there is some account of the future development of the earth, but even this is left in doubt with the uncertainty over when it will happen and the dominant impression behind us of so implacable a force of life as to make its destruction seem theoretic. In *Dune* on the other hand the future is always before us: the future of the Fremen, of Paul Muad 'Dib the Messiah; and people are waiting till the time is right for them – the Baron to destroy Duke Leto, Paul till he gains his powers, the Fremen till they gain their messiah. At all times we are made aware that Paul has hidden power, and are looking forward to see what will come of him and it.

There is much greater passivity in *Hothouse*, where events are taken as they come. People are able to fight against the predators, true: but they do not try to alter their environment to their advantage – for example, by burning large areas of the banyan, as Gren plans to burn a way through the hostile trees of Nomansland using a piece of mica or glass; they simply adapt to existing conditions. Nor do they come together into any larger social units than about twenty individuals, which means that they are without the manpower and diversity of skills which would permit full social organization. Things are different in *Dune*, where the central activity is the harnessing of a planet for human ends, and the primary emphasis is on social relations, and, in the case of the Fremen, the construction of a larger social fabric from individual 'sietches' or tribes which in themselves are many times larger than the groups in *Hothouse*. In *Dune* the Fremen have long learned how to harness the gigantic devouring sandworms to their own purposes: they are able to ride them, and use them as a means of transport over the desert; the picture of a sandworm used till it is exhausted is a striking one of nature's subservience to man in this book. This is not to say that nature is not powerful and to be respected, in the form of the desert: but like the sandworms, it can be tamed and utilised. In *Dune* man struggles with the environment not merely to live but to get more from it. Of course to some extent this point emerges from the fact that the environment in Aldiss's book is much more specifically antagonistic to all other forms of life: everything is crowded together, thanks to the burst of life produced by the sun, and therefore everything is ravenously ready to eat everything else. The sandworms of *Dune* with their readiness to devour even a mobile spice-gathering factory, are the only equivalent, and their primary 'motivation' is protection of the spice.

Many of these differences spring from the fact that where *Hothouse* could be said to concern itself with body, the medium of *Dune* is mind. The whole of the novel, typically of Herbert's fiction, is bent on finding things out.[5] The same motive operates in Asimov's *Foundation* series, but in Herbert the concern is more with finding out what one is than with where something is – with what is one's true being rather than with becoming. Paul has to find out if he is a Kwisatz Haderach, and this he does only through the development of his mind throughout the book. He and his nature have been trained in the 'Bene Gesserit' school of teaching, which is directed to the control of one's own emotions, to perceiving the hidden motives of others, and to controlling others through voice intonation. The powers of a Kwisatz Haderach are mental powers – primarily the ability to see the course of events in the future. The Fremen are concerned to find out if Paul is their messiah. The Baron Harkonnen, early on, is bent of finding Paul's location; the Baron is also preoccupied with the Emperor's motives and objectives. A Mentat, or brilliant practical mind, helps Leto and the Baron with their plans. There are other motives governing the action; but these recur. In *Hothouse* the primary concern is physical, ensuring one's physical survival, or experiencing one's physical destruction. A particular vividness accompanies those passages describing the impact of one body on another: it is as though things cannot exist on their own, but only as they collide with others; there is, as we have said, a relationship in antagonism. But what might be physical in *Dune* has often become an extension of the mental. This, for instance, is a section of a conversation between the Baron and the imperial envoy Count Fenring, who has arrived on the Harkonnen home planet: Fenring has been demanding that the Baron destroy Thufir Hawat, his Mentat, who used to be Mentat to Duke Leto –

'But he's useful!'
'And he knows too many things no living man should know.'
'You said the Emperor doesn't fear exposure.'
'Don't play games with me, Baron!'
'When I see such an order above the Imperial seal I'll obey it,' the Baron said. 'But I'll not submit to your whim.'
'You think it whim?'

'What else can it be? The Emperor has obligations to me, too, Fenring. I rid him of the troublesome Duke.'

'With the help of a few Sardaukar' [élite imperial soldiers]

'Where else would the Emperor have found a House to provide the disguising uniforms to hide his hand in this matter?'

'He has asked himself the same question, Baron, but with a slightly different emphasis.'

The Baron studied Fenring, noting the stiffness of jaw muscles, the careful control. 'Ah-h-h, now,' the Baron said. 'I hope the Emperor doesn't believe he can move against *me* in total secrecy.'

'He hopes it won't become necessary.'[6]

When we come to the sword-fight between the Baron's son Feyd-Rautha and Paul Muad'Dib the weapons are only a concretion of what has been going on in much of the book, a series of intellectual duels. During Paul's fight with Feyd-Rautha the latter wounds him with a drugged sword which Paul is able to control using his mind to realign the metabolism of his own body. Then

Again Feyd-Rautha leaped, stabbing.

Paul, the smile frozen on his face, feinted with slowness as though inhibited by the drug and at the last instant dodged to meet the downflashing arm on the crysknife's point.

Feyd-Rautha ducked sideways and was out and away, his blade shifted to his left hand, and the measure of him that only a slight paleness of jaw betrayed the acid pain where Paul had cut him.

Let him know his own moment of doubt. Paul thought. *Let him suspect poison.*

'Treachery!' Feyd-Rautha shouted. 'He's poisoned me! I do feel poison in my arm!'

Paul dropped his cloak of silence, said: 'Only a little acid to counter the soporific on the Emperor's blade.'

Feyd-Rautha matched Paul's cold smile, lifted blade in left hand for a mock salute. His eyes glared rage behind the knife.

Paul shifted his crysknife to his left hand, matching his opponent. Again, they circled, probing.

Feyd-Rautha began closing the space between them, edging in, knife held high, anger showing itself in squint of eye and set of jaw. He feinted right and under, and they were pressed against each other, knife hands gripped, straining.

Paul, cautious of Feyd-Rautha's right hip where he suspected a poison flip-dart, forced the turn to the right. He almost failed to see the needle point flick out beneath the belt line. A shift and a giving in Feyd-Rautha's motion warned him. The tiny point missed Paul's flesh by the barest fraction.

On the left hip!

Treachery within treachery within treachery, Paul reminded himself. (p. 460)

The conversation between the Baron and Count Fenring is like sword-play, a continual probing. (Much of the book involves the search for weaknesses or strengths, from the veiled hostility of Paul's father's dinner-guests at his first arrival on Arrakis to the continual inquiry into Paul's nature, both by the Fremen and by himself.) First the Baron seems dominant and elusive, calling out the apparent outburst from Fenring of ' "Don't play games with me, Baron!" ', and refusing to submit; but then Fenring shifts the command away from himself (' "You think it whim?" ') to the Emperor, so that he fights now with a greater shield ('force-shields' are used in physical contexts), and can speak with much more penetrating indirectness. ' "He has asked himself the same question . . . but with a slightly different emphasis" '; ' "He hopes it won't become necessary." '

The fight between Paul and Feyd-Rautha is much more a contest of intellects than of physical powers, in which '*the cutting edge is the mind*' (pp. 353–4). Paul pretends to be slow, then shifts to sudden speed, catching his opponent off-balance; but his conviction that Feyd-Rautha has the poison dart on his right hip almost undoes him. The very existence of a poison dart and trickery emphasises that the contest with sword and knife is itself only part of what is going on. The same is true of Feyd-Rautha's earlier fight with the gladiator (pp. 315–20). The account is scattered with italicised thoughts of Feyd-Rautha as he tries to assess whether or not the gladiator has been programmed by the possible treachery of the Baron's Mentat to slay him: usually the gladiators Feyd fights are slightly drugged, but this one has been left undrugged to make the contest seem more spectacular. The fight turns finally not on physical ability but on a word. Feyd-Rautha, in fact, is in danger of being killed by his opponent and has to resort to 'a key word [that] had been drummed into the man's unconscious to immobilize his muscles at a critical instant' (p. 315); that word, appropriately enough, is ' "Scum!" ', and its utterance gives Feyd a moment to scratch the man with his poisoned sword. In his own fight with Feyd-Rautha, Paul has been given a word ('Uroshnor') which will similarly immobilize his opponent, but he refuses to use it: yet it can be said that here again, whatever Paul does, words win the struggle; for when most tempted to use the word he says out loud, ' "I will not say it!" ', and this itself catches Feyd 'in the merest fraction of hesitation' which 'was enough for Paul to find the weakness of balance in one of his opponent's leg muscles' (p. 461). Such 'outwittings' operate in every struggle in the book (see for example pp. 164–5, 268, 290).

The concern with mind, both conscious and unconscious, and its development is to be found throughout Herbert's work. In *Dune* it is given some local explanation in an oblique reference to the abolition of mechanical minds or computers under a movement known as the Butlerian Jihad (p. 17): thereafter the unaided human mind had become super-developed. There is a physical world in *Dune* – the desert, the worms, the spice, the human body – and this among other things marks the book off from Asimov's *Foundation* series: but it is a physical world largely harnessed to the purposes of intelligence; even the wild desert operates as a colossal spice farm, if the worms have to be avoided. (In the Lynch film of *Dune*, by contrast, there is great emphasis on the heavily or the disgustingly physical.) The very first episode of the book portrays the dominance of mind over body. The old Reverend Mother of the Bene Gesserit school has come to Paul's home on Caladan to try to find out whether he may be the Kwisatz Haderach, and her central test of him involves his putting his hand in a box which exactly simulates the pains caused by slow incineration of the hand: he surmounts the pain, keeps his hand voluntarily in the box longer than anyone else has done before. Nothing escapes the governance of mind. A Kwisatz Haderach is the potential product of generations of careful breeding and genetic control:[7] Paul is no random gift of nature, but nature bent to serve the purposes of man (though he has come earlier than the Bene Gesserit planned). When he meets the Fremen, they have been prepared, though they do not know it, by Bene Gesserit missionaries, to believe in the myth of a messiah who will lead them from the wilderness, and hence prepared to accept him eventually as their leader. Arrakis is itself a place for asceticism, for denial of the body. It is those who depend on the body and the physical alone who are finally weak – the Guildsmen, who have become addicted to the spice.

The book is full of formality and rules, organizing and containing the physical: the conduct of a fight or a meal is beset with tales and traditions; the life of the Fremen is shot through with rituals and codes which govern every action, from the distillation of water from a corpse to the initiation ceremony of riding a sandworm. And nearly everyone is in one way or another highly *trained*, whether as a fighter, such as the Duke Leto's officers Gurney Halleck or Duncan Idaho, or Feyd-Rautha Harkonnen; or as a Mentat or counsellor-cum-security guard, such as the Baron's Piter or the Count's Thufir Hawat; or as a Bene Gesserit such as Paul or his mother; or as a Fremen with their high social awareness and reverence for water; or even as a Sardaukar, one of the terrible Imperial/soldiers who have been hardened on the prison planet of Salusa Secundus. No one is undisciplined in the novel and few let their passions get the better of them: Paul decides when to grieve over his father's death (p. 192), Halleck fights down his rage against Rabban (p. 245). Those who fail do so by miscalculating – the Baron, for instance, through ignorance of the true value of the spice to the Guildsmen, and through underestimating the potential of the Fremen. The Baron survives a murder directed at his more passional side: a boy with whom he is enjoying himself in private has had a poison dart implanted in his thigh, but the Baron notices it. Similarly Feyd-Rautha wins and loses his fights through relative skill, not feelings: as Gurney Halleck, who trains Paul, tells him, ' "What has *mood* to do with it?" ' (p. 38). The attempt by Dr Yueh to use his master Count Leto to kill the Baron out of revenge for the Baron's slaying of Yueh's wife fails. It is miscalculation and ignorance of the truth that destroys Count Leto: he is betrayed by his servant Yueh and is in ignorance of the true motives of the Baron and the Emperor. Quite simply *Dune* can be said to be *about* mind: at its centre is the development of mental powers in Paul.

Mental development is mirrored in the narrative itself. We start with a narrow purview, and only as the book goes on are connections made. This imitates the expansion of mind in Paul. At first we see only the narrow sphere of Paul's life at home. Then, on Arrakis, he takes his place at table to represent his family to the people of that world. Then, exiled, he goes out to the people of

Arrakis, the Fremen, all the time finding out more about himself, his powers and his origins until all comes together with his meeting with the Emperor at the end. In the same way we only gradually become aware of the larger pattern. (The process recalls that in Asimov's *Foundation* series, but there is one distinctive difference: Asimov always gives us the impression, however illusory, that we know where we are; Herbert makes us feel uncertain throughout.) The piece left missing till the end is the Guildsmen and their crucial position in regard to the spice. We know that Leto has been given the fief of Arrakis in place of the Harkonnen family: we come to realize that this is so that Leto, who is favoured among a faction hostile to the Emperor, will be in a place where he can be destroyed, apparently by the Harkonnens alone, without too many questions being asked; we come to see what being a Kwisatz Haderach means, and only the Fremen have been prepared with appropriate mythology to accept Paul. Our minds are thus opened out like those of the central figures. Everyone is trying to find something out, to conquer more territory with mind. And the whole book is draped with a mind that knows its end long before we do: the mind of the Princess Irulan, authoress of the 'Manual of Muad'Dib', quotations from which prefix many of the chapters in the book. It is between the knowledge of her mind and ours that the whole book moves.[8] The first chapter has as epigraph:

> *A beginning is the time for taking the most delicate care that the balances are correct. This every sister of the Bene Gesserit knows. To begin your study of the life of Muad'Dib, then take care that you first place him in his time: born in the 57th year of the Padishah Emperor, Shaddam IV. And take the most special care that you locate Muad'Dib in his place: the planet Arrakis. Do not be deceived by the fact that he was born on Caladan and lived his first fifteen years there. Arrakis, the planet known as Dune, is for ever his place.* (p. 9)

What is 'Bene Gesserit', what 'Muad'Dib', why the stress on balances, why the importance attached to the child we are to meet on the first page as mere Paul? We are to move throughout the book to the mental awareness of this passage, even to awareness of the writer: and the narrative may be defined precisely as the gap between one level of insight and another; throughout we move between ignorance and knowledge, the knowledge of the epigraph playing against the ignorance in the material until the gap is closed. Actually we the readers have to work very hard as in all Herbert's fiction to make the links, which are often hidden in the narrative or understandable only with considerable effort: and in this way Herbert forces our minds into something like the greater awareness he portrays in his characters.

To a great extent the mass of thinking that goes on in the book is conditioned by the fact that people are in varying degrees isolated from one another. Leto, surrounded by potential enemies, is perpetually on his guard, as his son must be too. In *Hothouse* everything acts: one is struck, and then strikes back; there is little anticipation. In *Dune* one guards perpetually against being struck in the first place: hence the need for Mentat watchdogs, for anticipation and suspicion. There is a traitor in Leto's household: Thufir Hawat, Yueh, even the Lady Jessica, are suspected. The Baron has to guard against his own offspring. Paul has a private mental world that isolates him from his mother. The Fremen of Dune keep themselves to themselves, their fastidious isolation symbolised in their still-suits, which insulate them from the desert, conceal all but the eyes, and preserve the body's moisture from loss. The Guildsmen are never seen, and their interests are for long unfathomable. Each moves forward on a separate thought-path. Gurney Halleck, Paul's old soldier fighting instructor, has long suspected Jessica of engineering Leto's downfall: when he meets with Paul after being ambushed and learns that Jessica is with the Fremen too,

> *The she-witch alive!* Gurney thought. *The one I swore vengeance against, alive! And it's obvious Duke Paul doesn't know what manner of creature gave him birth. The evil one! Betrayed his own father to the Harkonnens!*
>
> Paul pressed past him, jumped up to the ledge. He glanced back, noted that the wounded and dead had been removed, and he thought bitterly that here was another chapter in the legend of Paul Muad'Dib. *I didn't even draw my knife, but it'll be said of this day that I slew twenty Saurdaukar by my own hand.*
>
> Gurney followed with Stilgar, stepping on ground that he did not even feel. The cavern with its yellow light of glow-globes was forced out of his thoughts by rage. *The she-witch alive while*

*those she betrayed are bones in lonesome graves. I must contrive it that Paul
learns the truth about her before I slay her.* (p. 403)

The illusion of conversation increases the sense of separate minds
here. The separateness of the characters is heightened by the
narrative mode. Each chapter is an isolated episode, cut off from
the next not only by a reflective or Olympian epigraph but also by
sudden switches to the actions of quite separate characters. We
shift back and forth between the Baron's doings and those of
Count Leto, and later between those of the Fremen and of the
Baron; and within the life with the Fremen we move between
Paul's life and that of his mother. In *Hothouse*, by contrast, the
chapters are often arbitrary-seeming, mere periods in a con-
tinuous action: we are with Gren and his limited perspective for
most of the time. But for all the isolation of the minds in *Dune* such
isolation is not desirable to them. The characters wish to make
connections, to find out who is a spy and who not, whether Paul is
Kwisatz Haderach, what are the real plans of the Emperor. As the
book proceeds the minds come together in the sense that they
come to understanding, even, in some cases, by actually merging.
And as they do, the world turns from being only a battleground of
isolated egos, to a place of shared and even communal interests.
Gurney finds out the truth about Jessica and is reconciled. Paul's
own mother was a Harkonnen, and the Baron is his grandfather,
even if he must die. Paul himself is the product of the best
blood-lines of the galaxy. The secret interest of the Guild in the
spice stands revealed, and hereafter they must cooperate with
others to obtain it. Paul, meanwhile, comes together with the
imperial house by marrying the Princess Irulan. Yet still there is
the mental isolation of Paul, locked in his own high destiny and in
the intermittent vision of the future afforded him by his unique
and estranging power.

No description in *Dune* is left to stand by itself like those in
Hothouse: always a mind enters to try to mould it. For instance, the
following description might seem at first largely unfiltered, 'for
itself':

Again there came the clatter of boxes being unloaded in the
entry. Jessica sighed.
    Against a carton to her right stood the painting of the Duke's
father. Wrapping twine hung from it like a frayed decoration. A

piece of twine was still clutched in Jessica's left hand. Beside the painting lay a black bull's head mounted on a polished board. The head was a dark island in a sea of wadded paper. Its plaque lay flat on the floor, and the bull's shiny muzzle pointed at the ceiling as though the beast were ready to bellow a challenge into this echoing room.

We can say that some of this portrays Jessica's feelings of desolation. The 'like a frayed decoration' seems to refer to something of her emotions, as does the forgotten piece of twine, the bull's head ('divorced' from the body), lying flat on the floor, the epitome of passion amid emptiness. But straightway we find that the scene means something quite different to Jessica; and if we thought that the description was there only to give a striking picture, we see its every detail being rendered meaningful:

Jessica wondered what compulsion had brought her to uncover those two things first – the head and the painting. She knew there was something symbolic in the action. Not since the day when the Duke's buyers had taken her from the school had she felt this frightened and unsure of herself.
The head and the picture.
They heightened her feelings of confusion. (p. 51)

Every action is seen as part of a meaningful design.[9] It is as though the world were choked full of interconnections, the least thing being of importance. As Paul later comes to see it, 'the most minute action – the wink of an eye, a careless word, a misplaced grain of sand – moved a gigantic lever across the known universe' (p. 282).[10]

The primacy of mind in *Dune* is seen in the very fact that Paul overcomes the Baron and the Emperor. For he has an ideal, some belief larger than himself to fight for: they are concerned only to keep hold of the power and the physical objects they possess. The Guildsmen depend on the spice, and the Emperor on the Guildsmen. Paul, however, has before him the vision of the new world the Fremen might make out of Arrakis: he fights for them as much as to regain his rights. Loyalty to a larger group is characteristic of those who are to overcome: the Baron and the Emperor, with their shifting alliances and manipulations, are simply out for themselves.[11] What is involved in Paul's nature and in his relation to the Fremen is heightened by the presence of his mother, who right from the start when she yields the young Paul to the terrible test of the *gom jabbar* of the old Reverend Mother, has been able to put aside her maternal feelings for the larger good. So she does continually when she wants to protect her son against the challenge of the Fremen Jamis, or the trial of riding the sandworm. The Fremen are capable of this negation of self for the greater good, as each makes over the water of his body for the use of the tribe, or sietch. When Paul slays Jamis, Harah, Jamis's wife, at once transfers her allegiance to Paul as she is expected to do by the tribe. And to the Fremen themselves Paul is himself in part an idea, the living realization of the messiah they have been promised in the mythology long instilled into them by Bene Gesserit missionaries. This idea creates fanatical zeal in them. Many of the epigraphs in the book insist on the moral and intellectual nature of Paul's experience and outlook: '*Greatness is a transitory experience. It is never consistent*' (p. 123); '*My father once told me that respect for the truth comes close to being the basis for all morality*' (p. 199); '*You cannot avoid the interplay of politics within an orthodox religion. This power struggle permeates the training, educating and disciplining of the orthodox community. Because of this pressure, the leaders of such a community inevitably must face that ultimate internal question: to succumb to complete opportunism as the price of maintaining their role, or risk sacrificing themselves for the sake of the orthodox ethic*' (p. 381); '*How often it is that the angry man rages denial of what his inner self is telling him*' (p. 403).

The intellectual world in which Paul moves is seen as eventually dynamic and mobile. As an ideal of course, it is necessarily so, since an ideal is in quest of realization. But it is not just the objective of the ideas that is at issue here, but the nature of the ideas themselves. As Paul sees it, an idea is dead as soon as it has met realization, for then it is stagnant.[12] (Here for many is the greatest difference between *Dune* and Asimov's *Foundation* trilogy.) As a Bene Gesserit proverb puts it, ' "*Any road followed to its end leads precisely nowhere. Climb the mountain just a little bit to test it's a mountain. From the top of the mountain, you cannot see the mountain*" ' (p. 70). Elsewhere, '*it is possible to see peril in the finding of ultimate perfection. It is clear that the ultimate pattern contains its own fixity. In such perfection, all things move towards death*' (p. 361). Paul recognizes that, on the paradise world of Caladan where he and his family lived before Arrakis, there was no striving for perfection when perfection was all around, '*And the price we paid was the price men have always paid for achieving a paradise in this life — we went soft, we lost our edge*' (pp. 243–4). The opponents of Paul and the Fremen are essentially stagnant. They wish to keep what they have, they have no wish to chart new areas of experience. They are symbolized at the beginning of the book in the aged Reverend Mother whose tests of the young Paul are overcome. The old are surpassed by the young. Through ninety generations Bene Gesserit Reverend Mothers have sought by genetic engineering to produce a Kwisatz Haderach who will be Emperor: when he comes in Paul, one generation early, they do not know it; and when they do, he refuses to do their bidding (p. 453). The Emperor wishes to keep his throne, the Guildsmen to keep their spice, the Baron Harkonnen his power. All are trying to preserve something static, and all therefore lose it. At the end they are symbolically reduced to immobility in the destruction of the recumbent battle-fleet, the noses of its rockets shot off by Fremen fire. Like one, like all: '*The Guild navigators [had] . . . chosen always the clear, safe course that leads ever downward into stagnation*' (p. 468; compare p. 209).

But Paul represents a new idea. Unlike his antagonists, he himself is new to all he meets: among the high society of Arrakeen, with the Fremen, and with the remnants of the Emperor's court at the end, he is the unknown of unexpected power; and in this he is quite unlike the Baron or Count Fenring or the Emperor, whose personalities, if not their ultimate motives, are known and familiar. But Paul is unknown even to himself, is continually encountering new powers in himself throughout the narrative, seeing how far and how wide his prescience will go, finding out his capacity to assimilate all humanity in himself. He *grows*. Compared to him, the Baron's son Feyd-Rautha is a perpetual savage adolescent; and the Baron himself is capable of only a narrow range of set responses. But Paul we feel changing throughout, from boy to youth to man, from uncertain grasp of the world to a greater inner strength. And he grows because he takes risks: he gains because he lives on the edge of loss.[13] Throughout the book he courts danger to live and develop: he takes the ornithopter into the sandstorm to escape the Harkonnen Sardaukar, he crosses the desert with his mother under the threat of sandworms, he accepts the knife-fight with Jamis and later with Feyd-Rautha, he dares to cause himself near-death by killing the Fremen sandworm, he passes the initiation test of riding on a worm. And he moves too throughout the novel in the literal sense of travelling about Arrakis, as a nomad with the Fremen, where the others are stuck in their cities. But his journey is also directional: in coming from Caladan to Arrakeen, and from Arrakeen to the Fremen, he removes his distance from the truth. It is with the Fremen that he finds himself as he could not otherwise have done: finds himself only where he has lost himself and much of his past identity as an Atreides of the royal line. In taking away the distance between himself and the Fremen, in stripping himself of the comforts of urban life for their wilderness economy, he has opened himself to the truth: his journey towards them is a journey into the interior, to that trance of mystic vision where he finally perceives his mental power (pp. 422–3). The whole planet with its barren aspect concealing hidden riches and strengths is itself an image of the unconscious mind into which Paul journeys; '*I have seen this place in a dream,*' he says (p. 302; see also p. 304). The motif is one of insight, of seeing to the concealed, from a lost haversack beneath the sand to submerged mental powers. He, thanks to the indoctrination of myth, is already a part of the minds of the Fremen: they, though he finds it out only when he meets them, provide the key to his own mind. It is among the Fremen, too, that Paul discovers the secret needs of the Guildsmen and the Emperor as the Baron could not: he has put himself where the spice is, and thus is directly in contact with the truth.

The continual movement has its price. Paul realizes that when he has helped the Fremen to gain Arrakis they will want to go on a *jihad* or holy war across the other planets of the empire, and that he will be unable, despite his wish, to stop them. Paul's object, even if it is defeated, must be the maintenance of a delicate balance between extremes. Balance is a word central to the first sentence of the book, '*A beginning is the time for taking the most delicate care that the balances are correct.*' In himself Paul is a combination of opposites. '*He was warrior and mystic, ogre and saint, the fox and the innocent, chivalrous, ruthless, less than a god, more than a man*' (p. 442), which may explain why as a person his character is often elusive. He sees that while life is divided into 'Givers' and 'Takers', he himself joins both, ' "I'm at the fulcrum . . . I cannot give without taking and I cannot take without . . ." ' (p. 423). When he drinks of the Fremen Water of Life he is '*both dead and alive*' (p. 415). He 'felt himself at the centre, at the pivot where the whole structure turned' (p. 344). Such balancing of the opposites ensures that

Paul will never slip into stasis: he will not settle for one side or the other. Reality is said here to be dialectical, each side of an extreme needing the other in order to be. '*To attempt an understanding of Muad'Dib without understanding his mortal enemies the Harkonnens, is to attempt seeing Truth without knowing Falsehood. It is the attempt to see the Light without knowing Darkness. It cannot be*' (p. 19).

Dune then is pervaded by mind: but why? It is here that we enter on the paradoxes by which Herbert's work moves. He, it must be said, is most happy when writing his books in such an intellectual mode. But there is mind and mind: there is the conscious mind, and there is the unconscious. And for all the stress on control and intellectual grip – on what Herbert called 'hyperconsciousness' – in the book, it is arguable that what it is there for is to beget out of its very certainties and supposed grasp on experience an indeterminacy over which it has no power.[14] No long-term scheme or attempt to alter the world works in the book. The plan of the Bene Gesserit to create a Kwisatz Haderach out of the union of Atreides and Harkonnens is thwarted when Duke Leto persuades Jessica to bear a son to him instead of the projected daughter. Leto's plan to kill the Baron goes awry. The Baron's scheme to make an élite force out of the Fremen is destroyed when they make war on him. The attempted use by Jessica of the Fremen to serve Atreides purposes puts herself and Paul at the mercy of forces they cannot control. The planned transformation of Dune through the spread of vegetation is in later works to be seen to destroy the worms and the spice with the desert. The 'plans' that work are those that go with the grain of reality, and do not try to manipulate it at a distance: and in particular those which are momently conceived, momently executed, such as the parries and thrusts during conversations or combat. Leto II sees 'how dangerous it was to be *right* in this universe' and that what is needed for survival is 'an understanding of the limitations in every moment'.[15]

Herbert drives us to an awareness that beneath the individual consciousnesses and desires of his characters lies a deeper and unconscious prompting over which they have no control. The book continually widens perspective. It does this through context in the journey of Paul from city to open desert (and eventually to spreading over all planets on the *jihad*). At first the force driving the characters seems merely that of factional struggle, whether with the Bene Gesserit trying to create an all-seeing Kwisatz

Haderach or with the Harkonnens or the Atreides. Later we find out how spice is the key to the behaviour of many of the factions, right up to the Guildsmen and the Emperor himelf. But what seemed to be a mere struggle over a treasure is also turning into something else, as we begin to see the hint of deeper motives behind. Similarly the motives of the Fremen extend outwards to further and further levels. At first they seem bent only on self-preservation and on gradual and concealed transformation of the planet; and then they acquire in Paul a leader under whom they can overthrow the Harkonnen tyranny. But their underlying drive through their messiah is seen to be *jihad*, a wild religious war across the universe, an expansive surge of conquest and colonisation. Yet there is a further purpose too. Behind the desire for *jihad*, behind the actions of all the characters, lies a deep historical prompting against stasis, a collective pressure of all men to liberate the damned-up forces of life, like a spice-blow. *Dune* portrays what Herbert has called a *nexus*, a focus for all these forces and a point at which they become not only concentrated but transformed. The ultimate force of mind behind the book is racial rather than individual. (Herbert was an adherent of Jungian psychology.[16])

> [Paul] found that he no longer could hate the Bene Gesserit or the Emperor or even the Harkonnens. They were all caught up in the need of their race to renew its scattered inheritance, to cross and mingle and infuse their bloodlines in a great new pooling of genes. And the race knew only one sure way for this – the ancient way, the tried and certain way that rolled over everything in its path: jihad. (p. 192; see also p. 457)

Having a Kwisatz Haderach, an all-seer in the book is symbolic of the all-seeing that is needed by the reader. For Paul such insight does not give but takes away power: it occurs on the unconscious plane and perceives unconscious drives it cannot halt and only hope to steer; he realizes, '*I am a prey to the imperfect vision, to the race consciousness and its terrible purpose*' (p. 361).

Thus arguably Herbert produces so dominant an impression of the conscious powers of the mind in the book to create the opposite effect of the strength of powers beyond its control or purview. In this view the 'intellectual' emphasis of the book is there to exhaust our love for it, to turn us against it as, unconsciously, the human race turns against stasis throughout the book. (In an analogous process Herbert has said that he made Paul a hero precisely to show us the emptiness of hero-worship in later books.[17]) In such a case we are dealing with no *volte-face* but with a steady process of erosion or undermining of that which seems to be being built up. (Erosion, we may add, is of the nature of the desert medium.) The reader will say, rightly, that most of the book concerns itself with Paul as hero and brilliant mind, and with his immediate personal objectives, and that there is scant reference to the *jihad*, to his powerlessness and to the unconscious urges (putatively) behind the narrative. But the book's medium is concealment, and Herbert operates through paradox: what looms most large has its opposite behind it. If we are surprised when we find Paul powerless or inhuman, we have not seen far enough. If we think a few references near the close of the narrative insufficient to alter our opinion of Paul we forget Paul's own awareness of the enormous potential of the tiniest movements (p. 282); and we forget too the symbolism of the Fremen, whom the Baron for long thought too pitiful and peripheral to take into consideration. And if we think to settle even with this awareness we are again mistaken: Paul *is* hero as much as he is not, and all is double-edged; so too here stasis is as necessary as flux, conscious as unconscious, for each is part of a living dialectic that cannot be caught in any formula.

All is planned; and yet everything is unplanned. In a later book Paul's son Leto is to create indeterminacy out of history precisely through thousands of years of rigid control.[18] Everything is a mixture: it is not surprising that Herbert called the spice of Dune *melange*. Seen thus the very fabric and mode of working of his book is an image of historical forces at work, the 'overwhelming impression' bringing forward its reversal, the control of mind liberating anarchy; '*One cannot have a single thing without its opposite.*'[19] As Herbert hoped, his work thus works as a metaphor at many levels:[20] but this last level would make it revolutionary as a literary form, in oversetting the assumptions and certainties that the reader has been allowed, even encouraged, to build up during the narrative; 'Every system and every interpretation becomes false in the light of a more complete system.'[21] In such a way the reader could be said to participate in the very life that the book portrays, the turning of a revolutionary cycle whereby he is forced to overthrow his own static modes of thought – and yet not even be allowed to rest easy in any anarchic revolutionary fervour, but be forced to live through Herbert's work at the level of the indeterminate. (And certainly Herbert in succeeding 'Dune' novels gives less and less away concerning historical process or even what is happening.) If we can see *Dune* in this way, we can see it as a work of considerable, if unusual, literary power and stature.

In the succeeding books *Dune Messiah* (1970), *Children of Dune* (1976), *God Emperor of Dune* (1981) and, most recently, *Heretics of Dune* (1984), the themes of *Dune* are considerably expanded and modified, if without its drama. Broadly what is described is a process by which Paul, having become increasingly passive, both to the external world of the *jihad* (whose operation we never see) and to his internal world of prescience and determinism, is superseded by his son Leto, who returns the planet and the Empire to mobility and life, if in order to do this he must exercise through his own near-immortality a three-and-a-half-thousand year tyranny over his subjects. These books are far more intellectual even than the first, so much so that the reader is often faced by life reduced to a subtle chess game of which he has lost track of the moves, or else to a rather naked-seeming analysis of themes and philosophies with physical actions coming as rather strange blurts only.

It must be said however that to be disappointed by this is in a sense inadequate, for the whole of the first four books at least have dramatised a progressive movement into mind. It is by living perfectly within himself, in a state of *prana bindu* or mystic oneness, at the mercy neither of an apparently inexorable future like Paul nor the slave of a tyrannic past like Paul's sister Alia (taken over by the identity of her dead ancestor the Baron Harkonnen),[22] that Leto II is able to restore indeterminacy to history; and able too, by virtue of the perceptions derived from such an awareness to establish such a rule as will destroy in man for ever the desire for a messiah or any simple and absolute key or direction with which to approach the universe: there will be no more *jihads*. At least that is the object: whether we can believe in its success is another matter (*Heretics of Dune* offers a somewhat ironic perspective). Life will return to something like a state of checks and balances: all will be dialectical, governed by opposites. Leto, worm and man, is in a sense the balance, the 'Golden Path': he is neither helpless like Paul nor simply self-seeking and autocratic like the Bene Gesserit:

he uses autocracy for his own purpose, and when it is accomplished he chooses to give his life away. What he has given away also is the desire for any lasting control over history: sandworms will return to Dune and something like the old Fremen society will be restored, but it is Bene Tleilaxu and Ixians, technological races that have learned to synthesise spice and to enable the Guild Steersmen to travel by mechanical means, who at the beginning of *God Emperor of Dune* unearth the history of Leto, which they regard as dangerous: the future contains the very oppositions for which Leto catered but could not foresee. In *Heretics of Dune*, like the ouroboros or endless worm, Dune returns to its original desert condition and the sandworms that were there at the beginning now reappear.

Yet if this pattern of historical development informs these novels, it is hard in the end not also to see Herbert's return of Dune to its original condition as a literary return also – a wish to recapture the first fine careless rapture of *Dune* the book itself (though *Heretics* is not finally of the same character at all). The later books are a fine – if sometimes overly complex – working-out of tendencies latent in Paul Muad'Dib down the generations, and the whole series is a consistent unit. Yet how often – even if it was Herbert's point – during *God Emperor of Dune* did one long for some tangible proof of the effect of what Leto was doing on the people or the planet! From *Dune Messiah* onwards there seemed a steady shrinking inwards to the controlling mind and its interactions with people immediately about it, until by *God Emperor* one was mostly concerned with Leto in his tower, and such plots as remained to others were all carefully arranged and manipulated by him, including his own assassination. The claustrophobia may be intentional, but it does not make the later books attractive. It is *Dune* for which – perhaps unfairly – Herbert will be remembered, rather than for the cycle of which it is a part: and his return to its idiom cannot only be seen as part of the internal necessities of his theme, but as a journey back to the desert and the wild giant worms and adventures where 'To know the meaning you had to go through the experience and even then the meaning changed before your eyes.'[23]

6 Robert Silverberg, *Nightwings* (1969)

Robert Silverberg is probably one of the most prolific writers of science fiction in the genre.[1] In his early days, which means the mid-1950s, he was able to turn out on demand for magazines as many as twenty stories a month: scarcely a day seems to have gone by without his being able to produce 7000–8000 words of copy (for him first was final draft). He himself allows that much of this early material was of little value. But from the mid-1960s he began to produce science fiction works of real originality, and this became even more marked with what he has portrayed as a great divide – the burning in 1968 of part of the mansion in New York that he and his family had made their dream home. After the burning, he found that the original creative torrent that had poured forth words had reduced to a trickle and he was forced to a plod (in his terms only). It was from this point that he began to control and order his style much more than previously, and his science fiction became subtler and more resonant, in such works as *The Masks of Time* (1968), *The Man in the Maze* (1969), *Downward to the Earth* (1970), *Tower of Glass* (1970), *A Time of Changes* (1971), *Son of Man* (1971), *The World Inside* (1971), *Dying Inside* (1972), *The Stochastic Man* (1975) and *Shadrach in the Furnace* (1976).[2] It was in the immediate aftermath of the fire that he wrote 'a curiously lyrical novella, "Nightwings", to which I added a pair of sequels some months later to constitute a novel'.[3] The novella won a Hugo award in 1969: and with its thoroughness of imagination, its originality of speculation and its sturdy realism it deserved it. But the novel fully lives up to and extends the promise of its original.

Silverberg's science fiction of this period is distinguished by its moral concern and its stress on human relationships; he tends to play down the specifically science fictional element,[4] and to deal rather with human situations than with the kinds of exciting adventure that formed the staple of his work up to the mid-1960s.[5]

In this he is nearer the concerns of the realistic novel than many other writers of the science fiction genre. The moral emphasis is seen for example in *Thorns* (1967), in the indictment of the tyrant Duncan Chalk for his delight in inflicting pain; in the expiation of his sin against the aliens of the planet Belzagor by the hero of *Downward to the Earth*; in the punishment of Krug the master-scientist's arrogance in *Tower of Glass*; or the descent of the imperial surgeon in *Shadrach in the Furnace* (1976) from his lofty isolation to an understanding of the need for him to help the disease-afflicted peoples of earth. Isolation from or by others is a recurrent motif – the exile to the far past of political detainees in *Hawksbill Station* (1968), the self-immolation on a far planet of the rejected hero of *The Man in the Maze*, the hunting-down of the man who has dared to stand against the cold impersonalities of his society in *A Time of Changes*, the lonely insight of Mattern in *The World Inside* into the aridities of life in the urbmons and the possibilities in the world beyond them, the slow departure of Duncan Selig's telepathic ability to be at one with others in *Dying Inside*.[6] Equally, though, Silverberg can look to a communication with others so absolute that the boundaries of the self and its demands will be completely melted: Gundersen and the nildoror in *Downward to the Earth*, Kinnall Darrival and his 'bondsister' Halum in *A Time of Changes*, Clay and the men of the future in *Son of Man*. Always the concern is with the human spirit, with the recording of pain or pleasure, with the sense of human isolation, with the need for humility and a coming together with others. There is a mystical streak in Silverberg, but it emerges more from a sense of human unity than through any transcendent force.[7] All these themes are explored in *Nightwings*: human pain and joy, moral development of the hero and of mankind, and isolation, here followed by growing intercommunication.

Nightwings describes our Earth in a period known as the Third Cycle tens of thousands of years beyond our time. The First Cycle covered the development of man from the beginning to the point where he first made contact with beings from the stars. The Second covered a prodigious development of human science and power, whereby man became the dominant being in the galaxy: so great was his power and his xenophobic contempt for 'outworld-ers' that he began to put aliens in zoos for the amusement of his kind, and such aliens eventually included intelligent races living comparatively near to Earth. But man was to ruin himself: he constructed at least one hundred vast towers across the globe, which contained machinery capable of altering the weather, and of adjusting Earth's magnetic poles in such a way as to unfreeze the polar oceans with a view to altering continental shapes for his own purposes. The experiment got out of hand, and resulted in the submergence of most of North and South America, vast loss of human life and world-wide social and technological collapse.

It was galactic aliens who helped to salvage what was left by constructing energy pylons which would once more stabilise Earth's axial spin, and by distributing relief: man now existed by the charity of others. There was no means by which humanity could repay the aliens for their assistance, and man's only hope lay in a 'quitclaim', an absolute release by the aliens. But while negotiations on this were under way, the inhabitants of a world known as H362 intervened, offering full compensation to man's helpers provided they were given sole rights to Earth, which they would take over when they were in a position to do so. The people of H362 had long ago, while still at a primitive level of development, vowed revenge on Earth for caging representatives of their race in its zoos. When they became absentee landlords of Earth they were still incapable of interstellar travel: but it was their intention to take over Earth when they developed that capacity, and then those who had put them in zoos would themselves become a gigantic zoo for the amusement of galactic tourists.

The time of this transaction marked the beginning of the Third Cycle, the period of the book. Earth people have organized themselves into a rigidly stratified society of guilds, each of which requires a particular function of its members. A guild of wandering Watchers has been formed to carry about and operate antiquated machines capable of detecting any approaching fleet from the stars, and a guild of Defenders makes up the army. The threat from H362 has gradually receded in time to the point of mythology, but still the Watchers perform their by now almost ritual function of probing the stars at fixed times every day. But there are other guilds – the Pilgrims, who journey to Jorslem (old Jerusalem) to receive redemption (not of any of our religions); the Rememberers, who try to piece together and make sense of the past, the Servitors, who perform most of the public service activities, the Dominators, who rule, and so on with Scribes, Indexers, Artificers, Musicians, Communicants, Somnambulists,

Manufactories, Vendors, Transporters, Merchants, Clowns, Sentinels, Masters and Fliers (a winged race of humans created by science in the Second Cycle). There are also Changelings, but they are human mutants outside guilds.

But the reader knows none of this at the outset of the story: he is simply set down outside Roum with a nameless wandering Watcher whose function is obscure, a winged girl Avluela who can only fly by night and without clothes, and with an enigmatic Changeling called Gormon. It is not until the Watcher, who is the narrator of the story, becomes a Rememberer much later on, that the history of man is revealed in his researches into the memory tanks. Till then we have a vague and mysterious threat from Outside and people performing tasks in a society we do not understand. We do not know why the girl should only be able to fly at night, or why she constitutes the title of the novel. All that reassures us is the sanity and common sense of the Old Watcher as he himself tries to comprehend the world and his own feelings: right from the outset, as he stands wondering before the city of Roum or cannot understand how Avluela's gauze-like wings can sustain even her fragile weight, he is our intermediary. We know, or come to know, that Roum is old Rome, that Jorslem, Perris, Agupt, Afreek, Sud-Amerik, Stralya and Talya are Jerusalem, Paris, Egypt, Africa, South America, Australia and Italy. Yet they are not reducible to these places, but have changed often beyond recognition, like Sud-Amerik which is now a chain of islands, or Stralya which is covered with frostflower fields;[8] or Eyrop which is now joined to Afreek by a land bridge across Lake Medit.

Quite deliberately, it would seem – for in others of his stories he is much more quick to provide backgrounds – the author dislocates us, removes us from certainty. And why? The world itself is at the time of the story a place without meaning, a place without coherence, a hiatus between one disaster and another to come. The Watcher has to move because that facilitates his perception of any alien threats, true: but his moving makes us unable to fix on anything for very long, as he moves to Roum for no particular reason, and, it seems equally reasonlessly, after the alien invasion, to Perris and to Jorslem. At Jorslem he is to fix, because by then man is no longer the helpless pawn of events, whether in dimly awaiting aliens or in experiencing their mastery of him: now the road to his eventual (bloodless) victory over them is clear. But till then the world is out of joint. People are often disguised – Gormon the Changeling, who turns out to be a concealed alien, the deposed Prince of Roum who must pass himself off as a Pilgrim, his mistress Olmayne who must do likewise. Events happen without explanation being given till later. The Watcher tells us that he must watch, but for long we do not know why; not until they have invaded do we learn why the invaders came and why they have been so long expected; only long after their first appearance do we learn the function of starstones for a Pilgrim; we have to wait till late in the story to find out the origin of the Fliers. This is quite different from the delay of knowledge we find in Asimov or Herbert, for there there is a constant direction towards its discovery, but here things are left hanging inert, almost as though it is hardly worth telling us the details.

Sometimes, even, we are refused narrative certainty, as when, having reached the land bridge by which the Watcher and his companion are to cross to Afreek, the story continues with a long account of a car lift they were given by a wealthy Merchant long before they reached the bridge: this back-tracking account which goes on as though it contained the linear version of their journey lasts for five pages (pp. 137–42), before it shuffles back without notice to a description of the approach to the land bridge which we have already covered. And during the entire book we have little clear vision of objects in the external world:

> The morning's light was bright and harsh, as though this were some young world newly created. The road was all but empty; people do not travel much in these latter days unless, like me, they are wanderers by habit and profession. Occasionally we stepped aside to let a chariot of some member of the guild of Masters go by, drawn by a dozen expressionless neuters harnessed in series. Four such vehicles went by in the first two hours of the day, each shuttered and sealed to hide the Master's proud features from the gaze of such common folk as we. Several roller-wagons laden with produce passed us, and a number of floaters soared overhead. Generally we had the road to ourselves, however. (p. 16)

There is not much in the way of an emotional response to the material described: things are described, and that is all. The first sentence is not elegiac: it merely recounts a fact. Without a vital relation to the scene it becomes rather inert and blurred. We do not know what neuters, roller-wagons or floaters are, and the perfunctory mention of them does not give us the energy to attempt visualisation. What was a chariot – which to most readers is a small open vehicle – in the second sentence, becomes a closed carriage in the third. We do not really see the road: the apparently significant detail of four Magisterial chariots going past in the first two hours is not meaningful at all. The fact that the road is largely deserted is repeated in the last sentence as though not said before. That we do not see things vitally must be partly attributed to the detached and lost spiritual state of the Watcher here; and it is also the expression of a world without meaning or relation, imaged in the next paragraph:

> The environs of Roum showed vestiges of antiquity: isolated columns, the fragments of an aqueduct transporting nothing from nowhere to nowhere, the portals of a vanished temple. That was the oldest Roum we saw, but there were accretions of the later Roums of subsequent cycles: the huts of peasants, the domes of power drains, the hulls of dwelling-towers. Infrequently we met with the burned-out shell of some ancient airship. Gormon examined everything, taking samples from time to time. Avluela looked, wide-eyed, saying nothing.

This is a wreckage of the past, a jumbled mass of discrete objects and ages thrown together in a heap. Antiquity is reduced to vestiges, an aqueduct to fragments, a temple to mere portals, dwelling towers to hulls, airships to burnt-out shells. Gormon's examining of all he sees may suggest some purpose, but his lack of discrimination undercuts this: Avuela's 'nothing' to his 'everything' seems to underline the fact.

But though the book does traverse from non-meaning to meaning, it cannot be said that the description of Jorslem is any more *precise* than that of Roum:

> The city of Jorslem sits some good distance inland from Lake Medit on a cool plateau guarded by a ring of low, barren, rock-strewn mountains. All my life, it seemed, had been but a preparation for my first glimpse of this golden city, whose image I knew so well. Hence when I saw it spires and parapets rising in the east, I felt not so much awe as a sense of homecoming.

A winding road took us down through the encircling hills to the city, whose wall was made of squared blocks of a fine stone, dark pink-gold in colour. The houses and shrines, too, were of this stone. Groves of trees bordered the road, nor were they star-trees, but native products of Earth, as was fitting to this, the oldest of man's cities, older than Roum, older than Perris, its roots deep in the First Cycle. (p. 167)

Again there is the curiously inert geographical description. We scarcely see the rock-strewn mountains or the plateau; when Tomis the Watcher mentions the dark pink-gold colour of the wall and then of the houses and shrines, it is difficult to have a clear notion of the colour; and the plurals throughout – 'mountains', 'spires', 'parapets', 'hills', 'blocks', 'houses', 'shrines', 'groves', 'trees' – refuse focus. The groves of trees are described in terms more of what they are not (star-trees) than of what they are (the general 'trees of earth'). Yet there is much more in the way of an emotional response to this place: Tomis tells us that all his life has been a preparation for glimpsing it, that he felt 'not so much awe as a sense of homecoming'; and in his final sentence in particular the rhythmic cadences and the simple, almost elemental character of the language put over a sense of a profound experience of the city. Throughout, the syntax is longer and more flowing than in the passage on Roum; and purposeful too, in that we are kept moving towards Jorslem rather than gazing on it from a static viewpoint. The difference with Jorslem is that this is a place Tomis has seen already, so that the image itself is in a sense unimportant at a physical level, while being much more so at a spiritual one. Jorslem is the end more of a metaphysical than a physical journey.[9]

And if we think back to the account itself of the physical journey, we may recall how little real description there was of the rigours of the way and the weariness. The pilgrims are across the land bridge in a sentence; one sentence tells us that Olmayne preferred to travel by night to avoid the heat (p. 148); another that they kept to the coast, avoiding the hot sandy interior of Afreek (p. 147); another that as Pilgrims they never were hungry or in need of shelter (p. 147). The rest of the account is really a series of digressions: their experience with the starstones, the visit to the sick people in an Aguptan village, the hospitality of the alien Earthclaim Nineteen at his villa and the post-prandial philosophical discourse there, the divergence to the old surgery of the Second Cycle and the attack by mutants. It is as if the effect of the outer world on the psyche is of little account. It is others who are ill or slain, not the central figure. The external world is subject to mind, in some ways an extension of it. One chapter tells us, 'We travelled mainly by night and clung to our hostelries by day'; the next begins, 'Several days eastwards of that place', as though we had been put in any place (pp. 148, 150). Although they have reached Agupt after travelling apparently for weeks in Afreek, the narrator thinks that from the lakeside villa of Earthclaim Nineteen 'I could detect Land Bridge jutting forward to my left, and even Eyrop at the far side of the lake' (p. 155). Such telescoping of distances makes the outside world seem ghostly, a chimera to be manipulated as the mind pleases.

The paradox of the book is the realism with which Silverberg has presented this faded world. Perhaps realism and level-headedness are uniquely consonant with a world where there is little drama or purpose left. There is the description of the Watcher's machine, which he drags about with him in a little cart, a strange mixture of the semi-medieval and the technologically advanced. And the machine itself, though capable of throwing the mind of its user among the stars, is decrepit and weatherworn. We do not see it precisely, but the *idea* comes over strongly through the juxtaposition of these opposites. 'I went to the cart, opened my cases, prepared the instruments. Some of the dial covers were yellowed and faded; the indicator needles had lost their luminous coating; sea stains defaced the instrument housings, a relic of the time that pirates had assailed me in Earth Ocean. The worn and cracked levers and nodes responded easily to my touch as I entered the preliminaries' (p. 10). It is particularly vivid that the worn levers should work so responsively, as perhaps new levers would not have done. The same blend of the ancient and modern is seen in the guild-structure of society, ruled by a despotic Prince, and yet protected by quite sophisticated armaments against extra-terrestrial attack. And it is also seen in the way that the Third Cycle people live amid the wreckage of the First and Second Cycles, are indeed still ignorantly dependent on some of the Second Cycle machines.

Realism also stems from the lack of sensationalism and narrative thrills in the book. There is some suspense as the aliens' attack is looked for, even if for most of the time its approach is no longer believed. But after that attack, when the Watcher loses his function, the narrative loses all direction, as the ex-Watcher simply quits Roum. The Flier Avluela has gone, and his other companion Gormon has revealed himself to be an alien in disguise. Events seem simply to happen at random: the Watcher meets the blinded Prince of Roum, helps him on his way to Perris, becomes a Rememberer at Perris, and then when he thinks he has betrayed the human race to the aliens to save the life of the corrupt Prince, he sets out as a pilgrim for Jorslem. And the deeds in the narrative are not often violent or romantic either: they have the prosaic character of real life. Even catastrophe is not clear-cut: the collapse of Terran civilization at the end of the Second Cycle was not total; the takeover of Earth by the anonymous H362 will not be the shattering transition supposed. When the aliens arrive the human defences are ineffectual but there is not much killing and the invaders do not act as tyrants. Though the jealous husband of Olmayne the Rememberer kills her lover the Prince of Roum, and she in turn kills him, the deaths and their manner are reported. When death happens it is often blundered upon without anticipation. While the Pilgrims are travelling through Agupt they are asked to turn aside to a village whose people are suffering from a star-borne disease which makes their flesh turn crystalline: but they can do nothing. A Surgeon who accompanies them persuades them to visit a building by the way where miracles of surgical manipulation were accomplished during the Second Cycle: they are accompanied by a strange alien tourist shaped like a cylinder covered with eyes. During their visit a group of Changelings (mutants) enters the surgical building and a missile they throw severs the alien's body and kills it. There is no drama in the event; and the Changelings are stopped by one of their number friendly to the travellers. It turns out that the Changelings regard the surgery as a shrine, although with a casual and shocking irony unknown to them, their wretched deformities are the rejected detritus of surgical experiments on man carried out long ago in that very building. Such meetings of opposites make much of the life of the book.

But there is also the steady, undemonstrative way in which the story is presented, the sense of an imagination firmly and precisely in control. There is none of the freewheeling of the imagination that we find, say, in Silverberg's *Son of Man* (1971). When the Watcher perceives the approach of the aliens, he is reluctant to quit his mystical and empathetic contact with his machine to let others know: 'Lingeringly, lovingly, I drank in the sensory data for what seemed like hours. I fondled my equipment; I drained from it the total affirmation of faith that my readings gave me. Dimly I warned myself that I was wasting vital time, that it was my duty to leave this lewd caressing of destiny to summon the Defenders' (p. 48). That fine phrase 'this lewd caressing of destiny' is the kind of precise aperçu that an imagination working in full control can throw out.

And everything in the book, however random the world in which it appears, is thoroughly imagined at this intellectual level. Each guild has its duties, each its codes of conduct. The apprenticeship required of a would-be Rememberer is carefully described (pp. 88–9). The proper responses to Pilgrims or Watchers are precisely delimited. A certain category of Mendicant is admitted within the precincts of the palace of Roum, where others have to remain outside. Pilgrims must go masked in gilded metal face-screens. The highest levels of Rememberer are those engaged on synthesis and interpretation of the myriad facts from the past unearthed by other workers in the guild. No member of one guild knows of the work of another: when Gormon the supposed Changeling shows the Watcher some coins he has picked up near Roum and bids the Watcher look at " 'the faces of the Caesars!" ' he is told that he has done wrong in picking up relics and that only Rememberers should do so; and is asked whether with his knowledge of the Caesars he is not in fact a Changeling at all but a Rememberer (p. 11). When Gormon interrupts the Watcher's communion with his machine, the latter controls his anger because 'one does not show anger at a guildless person no matter what the provocation' (p. 10). Here we see the isolation theme so common in Silverberg's novels of this period.

No-one has a name: one is simply a Watcher or a Pilgrim or a Servitor; only those outside regular guilds have names, such as Gormon or Avluela. Even the aliens are without names, being known as Earthclaim Nineteen, Manrule Seven or Victorious Thirteen. Part of the life of the book comes from the interplay between the individual self and the guild-self, as we see it particularly in the Watcher, with his mingled sense of futility and devotion to his task: and he himself comments on it in the Rememberers,

Individual Rememberers whom I had known had struck me generally as pompous, disdainful, haughty, or merely aloof; I did not find them charming. Yet is the whole greater than the sum of its parts [notice how the Watcher is characterised through his rhetoric], and I saw such men as Basil and Elegro, so vacant, so absent from ordinary human concerns, so disinterested, as part of a colossal effort to win back from eternity our brilliant yesterdays. (p. 89)

The strength of the book comes not only from the imagination of a world, but from the pattern of change that is described as taking place within it. At the core of the novel, amid the seemingly random actions, is a scheme of spiritual development on the level both of the individual and the species. The invasion of the 'outworlders' of H362 is specifically a punishment for mankind for putting their kind in zoos in the Second Cycle while they were still at a primitive level of development. But the invaders themselves, although not tyrannical, although they are gently, if impersonally spoken and politely behaved, are guilty of pride and must themselves lose control over Earth: this is foreseen at the end through a new oneness of humanity, which will be achieved through harnessing the powers given by the Watcher machines, the Pilgrim starstones and the process of redemption.[10]

And at the centre of it is the Watcher and the moment in which in his own eyes he betrays mankind to the outworlders. Wandering from fallen Roum he has encountered the disguised and blinded Prince of Roum escaping the wrack. Despite the latter's unpleasantness and his known vice, the Watcher helps him on his way to Perris. In Perris, the Watcher, now an ex-Watcher, joins the guild of Rememberers under the guidance of the female Rememberer Olmayne. Olmayne becomes acquainted with the Prince of Roum, and despite her own sacrosanct marriage to another Rememberer becomes his mistress. This fact becomes known to her husband Elegro, but he is unable to overcome the Prince himself. He sees his opportunity in informing the aliens of the Prince of Roum's whereabouts, since they are anxious to track him down. But, afraid to face them himself, he persuades Tomis (the new name of the narrator now that he is a Rememberer) to go, threatening to reveal that he helped the Prince escape from Roum if he does not. Tomis agrees, but for his own reasons. Thanks to recent intensive researches he has carried out, he has found film evidence, long concealed by man, of the actual incarceration of past inhabitants of H362 in Earth zoological compounds. He knows that the aliens of H362 will want this information badly: they invaded Earth on the basis of an age-old threat founded on their knowledge that some of their people had been reduced to exhibits on Earth, but there was still no concrete evidence. And such evidence would give final moral justification to the outworld-ers for their invasion of Earth, an invasion they otherwise must apparently feel morally shaky (p. 113). Tomis gives the aliens this information in return for their giving the Prince of Roum safe conduct both from themselves and from Elegro on a continued journey on a Pilgrim to Jorslem. He concludes, 'Thus did I betray my Earthborn heritage and perform a service for our conquerors, out of loyalty to a blinded wife-stealing Prince' (p. 116).

In the event, however, Elegro slays the Prince and the action is made futile at this level. But at another level it was morally right and necessary, even though Tomis is expelled as a traitor by the Rememberers and is for long burdened with a sense of enormous guilt. From one point of view it was an act of total fellowship, a commitment to the human race as a whole on the part of Tomis: had the Prince of Roum been his friend the motive would have been narrower and more local or personal, but because he does not even like the man but does it out of a simple refusal to betray any single man and in recognition of their companionship on the road, it is most simply a humanitarian act. And yet, paradoxical-ly, to accomplish it he must in his own eyes simultaneously betray the human race. The story, however, is to suggest a larger vision. What Tomis has done is plumb the depths of the depravities done by man. He has shown the aliens the worst; but he has also stripped away the last of man's illusions. It may not be evident to many others, but with that done, with a kind of moral bottom having been reached for mankind in this way, it becomes possible for man to become better: he is no longer shifting and uncertain, but stands revealed for what he was in truth. And knowing the self is the beginning of wisdom. It is a case of Hardy's 'If way to the Better there be, it exacts a full look at the worst.' And exposure of one's sins to others is the humiliation and the shame that can wipe away all false pride.[11] From his individual predicament Tomis cannot see this and must suffer (for example, pp. 135–6): but when by the end of the story he is able to share in the corporate spiritual life of other humans, and to fly with Avluela, the

narrowness of his perspective becomes plain to him (p. 192). At
the same time he is given a vision in which the Procurator of the
aliens, Manrule Seven, says, ' "We have been sent to this world as
the devices of your purgation. We are instruments of the Will" '
(p. 178; compare p. 157). Seen thus, all actions, those of Tomis in
particular, are part of a pattern of redemption or purgation rather
than of punishment, in which apparent evil is in reality good: the
Surgeon tells Earthclaim Nineteen this (pp. 157–8).

But that is not the whole truth. Earthclaim Nineteen continued
from the Procurator, ' "On the other hand, permit me to disagree.
The intersection of Earth's destinities and ours is purely
accidental" ' (p. 178). The random is as much a part of reality
here as the purposive. And evil is real: it has to be cut with surgical
spiritual knives from Tomis during his process of redemption
(pp. 178–9). Here again is realism, the refusal of facile patterns.
This is perhaps the moral equivalent of the apparently random
character of the book, the way we happen from place to place and
person to person without any immediately evident cause. Nevertheless the random and the purposeful are not of finally equal
status: looked at closely, the apparently meaningless reveals in its
very lack of connection a deeper spiritual interrelationship.

Tomis himself develops through the narrative from the purposeless to the purposeful. He begins without direction, his feeling
of the emptiness of his occupation as Watcher a symbol of an inner
void: he has lost faith;

> 'For twice your lifetime, Changeling, I've listened to the stars
> and done my Watching. Something done that often loses
> meaning. Say your own name ten thousand times and it will be
> an empty sound. I have Watched, and Watched well, and in the
> dark hours of the night I sometimes think I Watch for nothing,
> that I have wasted my life. There is a pleasure in Watching, but
> perhaps there is no real purpose.' (p. 36).

The Watching for the aliens is suggestive of the watching for the
return of Christ at the Last Judgment that He required of His
disciples, in a passage from St. Mark 13, 33–7 which Silverberg
himself quotes at the end of *Son of Man*: 'Take ye heed, watch and
pray: for ye know not when the time is. . . . Watch ye therefore: for
ye know not when the master of the house cometh, at even, or at
midnight, or at the cockcrowing, or in the morning: Lest coming

suddenly he find you sleeping. And what I say unto you, I say unto all, Watch.' Thus, in whatever spiritual dryness, the Watcher continues his functions until his machine at last detects the arrival of the aliens.

At this point he loses his guild, for Watching is now irrelevant: at a spiritual level, from being static he is now mobile, and can choose his guild, from Pilgrim to Rememberer to Redeemer. The journey itself, from Roum to Jorslem, is a journey from secular to sacred; previously he had refused the invitation of a Pilgrim to make it. It is by no means direct, lying by way of a valley of humiliation in which the Watcher feels that he has betrayed his kind. And, as in the pilgrimage of *Downward to the Earth*, it involves no fastidious turning away from the corrupt world, but rather a deeper immersion in it: a journey with an amoral Prince and later a lecherous woman, the wickedness of each heightened by their disguises as Pilgrims. And, like a kind of Christ, Tomis the ex-Watcher helps these people despite some personal repugnance: he gives all in the vain attempt to save the life of the Prince, putting a kind of divine love for one man above obligations to humanity in general. It is he who later feels for the sick people of the village in Agupt as the woman Olmayne does not.

Yet even then he is still a fatalist, his constant calm the image of resignation. He can tell Olmayne when she is terrified of being infected, ' "You wanted atonement. . . . It must be earned" ', but he sees what has happened as the direct action of 'the Will', a divine moral force, ' "This village has earned the displeasure of the Will" '; to which Olmayne replies, ' "How neatly you serve up the mysticism, Tomis. . . . I misjudged you. I thought you were a sensible man. This fatalism of yours is ugly" ' (p. 153). Tomis replies that his 'fatalism' arises from having seen his world conquered and the Prince of Roum overthrown, but we sense that his neat vision of pain in simply moral terms of sin and punishment is not fully adequate as an account of our mortal condition: he himself admits to being 'smug in my piety' here. This point is debated in the later subtle discussion between the alien Earthclaim Nineteen and the Surgeon accompanying Tomis and Olmayne (pp. 156–8), where Earthclaim argues away the simply destinal view of events by saying that ' "if the Will is omnipotent, it must have decreed the sin of your ancestors that made the punishment necessary. . . . Where is the element of choice that makes suffering meaningful?" ' (p. 157). To this the

Surgeon replies that humans have the wills to choose, but the choices they make and the consequences they experience of those choices can be viewed as part of a pattern of cosmic action as well, *ex post facto*. And Tomis himself has made free choices throughout the book from the point where he ceased to be a Watcher: from an automaton he became a free agent. And fatalist or not, he has faith as he never had before: the world has become a meaningful pattern of events to him, and he believes and trusts in the divine will, to which he gives himself freely, as he tells Olmayne when she hangs back for fear of the crystallisation sickness.[12]

The man whose life was a meaningless rite based on fear has become a man whose life is devoted to helping others. In the vaults of the Rememberers he learned guilt for the sufferings caused by the human race. In the loss of his old guild self as Watcher he begins the long journey to understand that although guilds may define a man's abilities, they do not cancel the essential shared humanity of all men in all guilds. He learns this partly through the mundane jealousies of the Rememberer Elegro, or the lechery of his wife Olmayne; he learns it through the use of Changeling or Pilgrim disguises by Gormon the alien, the Prince of Roum and Olmayne; he learns it finally through the guildless Changelings themselves, such as Bernalt, and he sees 'the human soul beneath the strange Changeling surface' (p. 188). And as he does so, he himself acquires an individual name, Tomis, and others do too. At the end the man who seemed severed from people, closed in on himself with his machine, a mere wanderer over a world whose fellows quit him, becomes a man surrounded by people, a man who at least becomes part of a city, a man whose final apotheosis is to lose his obstinate ego in sharing thoughts, feelings and lives with others:

> And I became the Surgeon and the Flier and the Renewer and the Changeling and the Servitor and the rest. And they became me. And so long as my hands gripped the starstones we were of one soul and one mind. This was not the merging of communion, in which a Pilgrim sinks anonymously into the Will, but rather a union of self and self, maintaining independence within a larger dependence. It was the keen perception one gets from Watching coupled with the submergence in a larger entity that one gets from communion, and I knew this was something new on Earth, not merely the founding of a new guild but the

initiation of a new cycle of human existence, the birth of the
Fourth Cycle upon this defeated planet. (pp. 188–9)

This movement out of the isolation of the self to embrace others is
a recurrent concern in Silverberg's novels.

At the beginning of the book, watching the Flier Avluela, the
Watcher 'felt, as always, gross and earthbound, a thing of
loathsome flesh' (p. 8); 'Up she rose, glorying in her freedom from
gravity, making me feel all the more leaden-footed' (p. 9). She is
almost like the soul, fluttering aloft. But the total dichotomy of
height and depth, of aspiration and dull limitation is there.[13] The
division between earth and sky is heightened when the Prince of
Roum makes Avluela serve his coarse pleasures: thereafter she
disappears from the story till the end. Not that she is idealised: she
is a seventeen-year old girl with a skinny, underdeveloped body;
and the physical, even gross makeup of her gossamer wings,
joined by a 'sturdy ligament' to her back, is precisely recounted.
But her departure does symbolise a spiritual void; and she returns
only at the end when the regenerate Tomis meets her in Jorslem.
And when she returns she has changed: before, she could not fly
by day, because 'the terrible pressure of the solar wind would hurl
her to the ground' (p. 9); but at the end she can fly in broad
sunlight. The soul has as it were become tempered through the
novel; and it has 'returned' to the former Watcher, to the body.
Simultaneously the 'body' has become lighter. Now Tomis, and
his fellows, because of their sympathetic capacity to enter the
being of others in community, can experience Avluela's flight with
her, as though aloft themselves (pp. 191–2).

The book has come full circle: we begin with Avluela making
her devotions before flight, and so end. But conditions have
changed too. The darkness in which alone she could fly before has
now become light. Avluela herself has changed from a pouting
teenager to a creature of spiritual delight. The old Earth has
sloughed itself off in the working out, partly through the agency of
Tomis, of man's past sins: the Fourth Cycle is about to dawn, and
the invaders will be absorbed, not overcome, by the new human
understanding. At the individual level, Tomis has put off his old
body and regained that of his youth: he has lost the emptiness of
spiritually barren age for the plenitude and hope of early
manhood, and with it he has become more lyrical and passionate
than before: 'I was engulfed in joy that came in mighty waves, like

the surging tides of Earth Ocean' (p. 181); 'I gave myself to the violence of joy' (p. 183); ' "I feel it", I whispered. "The cool wind against bare flesh – the wind in my hair – we drift on the currents, we coast, we soar, Avluela, we soar!" ' (p. 192).

Now Tomis can relate to someone else as never before; he can have sexual feelings for Avluela, he can enter others' lives. Before, he was merely an old man doomed to watch the relations of others from outside – Gormon or the Prince of Roum with Avluela, the Prince with Olmayne, even Olmayne's wayside couplings with Servitors on the journey to Jorslem. But now also there is no more narrow self, and no more guilds of the restrictive type. Sharing Avluela's mind and experience, Tomis is able to leave the narrow purview of earthbound vision that has previously broken things into categories, 'From this height one could not tell that our world had ever been conquered. One saw only the beauty of the colours of the land and the sea, not the checkpoints of the invaders. Those checkpoints would not long endure' (p. 192). It is a turning of cycle into apocalypse, a science-fiction version of the renewal of Earth portrayed in Virgil's Fourth Eclogue of the Golden Age, or of Blake's New Jerusalem. (In fact the whole story with its imagery of old men and young is reminiscent of Blake's *Songs*.) And it is convincing and moving because the whole story has led up to it. The Third Cycle was fundamentally defensive, an anonymous interregnum between the acts done in the Second Cycle and their consequence. With the Fourth Cycle which we see here born out of the rubble of the Third, a new purpose has been given to mankind, an ideal to strive for.

But if the Second Cycle had purpose, it is not that kind of purpose to which the book would have mankind return. Here again it is not cyclic but evolutionary. The new purpose is spiritual, not physical, based on love and not the desire to dominate out of pride. As the collaborator in man's pride, technology is often condemned, as in much of Silverberg's fiction of this period.[14] It was science that gave man the capacity to dominate other intelligent races in the galaxy. It was science and the megalomania associated with it that led him to attempt to control the world's weather and so ruin the world. Science however is not wholly bad: it enabled mankind to accomplish forgotten miracles of surgery, ambiguous relics of which are found in the graceful Fliers and the abortive Changelings, many of them 'a twisted, hunched mockery of the human form' (p. 164). It also enabled the skills of the Rememberers, who can with their machines recover the exact nature of the past, but this is still a science of an age oriented to the past, not the future, a past that Tomis for the time mistakenly overvalues because he sees no future (p. 89). It is science, too, that is behind the baths of redemption with their electrodes and their knives, by which Tomis is made young again and the evil flows out 'with flick after flick after flick of the little blades, cutting out guilt and sorrow, jealousy and rage, greed, lust, and impatience' (pp. 178–9).

But on the whole the book shows a movement away from technology. It is partly seen in what the technology itself does. Before, it built star-ships, made galactic zoos, changed the physical body, tried to change the weather. But now it is harnessed to more metaphysical ends. The machine of the Watcher is intended to survey space for approaching invaders, but it also has the function of putting the Watcher's spirit free amid the space of the galaxy, 'I cast my mind to the heavens and searched for hostile entities. What ecstasy! What incredible splendour! I who had never left this small planet roved the black spaces of the void, glided from star to burning star, saw the planets spinning like tops' (p. 14; compare pp. 26, 47–8). The starstones of the Pilgrims enable a merging of the self with others, a total loss of self in the cosmic Will, imaged in one striking passage in the total absence of sentence-subjects:

> And shared with all of them [the Pilgrims] the instant of submergence into the Will. And saw in the darkness a deep purple glow on the horizon – which grew in intensity until it became an all-encompassing red brilliance. And went into it, though unworthy, unclean, flesh-trapped, accepting fully the communion offered and wishing no other state of being than this divorce from self.
> And was purified. (p. 146)

The Watcher machine extends the self through all immensity; the starstone loses it in other selves: each is a metaphysical result. And the synthesis of those two, self-exaltation and self-denial, is accomplished by a modified form of the Watcher machine: here there is 'not the merging of communion, in which a Pilgrim sinks anonymously into the Will, but rather a union of self and self, maintaining independence within a larger dependence' (p. 188).

This machine has starstone grips, and is a fusion of the Watcher and Pilgrim devices. The machines themselves seem only part-machines: that of the Watcher, so worn and yet so responsive to his nature; the starstones of the Pilgrims whose scientific basis is only hypothesised (p. 145), and whose gemlike aspect, 'cool polished spheres . . . icy as frostflowers' (p. 130), seems closer in character to the near-mystic states of mind it produces. And at the end we are told that the final machine will no longer be needed (p. 187): man's mind alone will be able to produce the communion that previously could only be helped into being by artificial means. It is clear that the book looks forward to a future where mind and metaphysics, rather than science and physics, will be the medium of being.

Nevertheless the book shows a fascination with manipulations of the flesh. Right from the start we are with the large but frail wings of the Flier Avluela, attached by stout ligaments to pads on her back, and with her thin body and spindly thighs, adapted for flying. Her wings 'rose about her like a cloak whipped up by the breeze' (p. 8); she struggles to get aloft, 'She doubled her body and shot it out, head going one way, rump the other' (p. 9). Then there is Gormon's description of how the old Caesars would save or slay a gladiator by a finger movement (pp. 39–40). There are 'interrogation skulls' filled with nutrient fluids in the palace of Roum. The Prince of Roum has his eyes torn out by the long nails of Gormon, and these are replaced by mechanical grey ones. The same Prince carries a flesh pouch containing valuables, hidden within his thigh. The Rememberer Olmayne is the embodiment of sexual allure: yet at the baths of redemption her body is to shrivel to that of a child's. The Changelings in the desert are described in detail 'one with ropy tendrils descending from his chin, one with a face that was a featureless void, another whose ears were giant cups . . . another a creature with small platforms jutting from his skin in a thousand places' (p. 164; see also p. 23).

The effects of the crystallisation disease are lingered on: it produces a metamorphosis, initially painful, later ecstatic, and ultimately fatal, of all but the innermost organs of a human being to a replica of itself in precious gems. The crystallisation process is symbolic, in that it produces a beauty which goes nowhere, which is destructive. This metamorphosis is in contrast with the purposive changes in the human form that are brought about in the baths of redemption at the end. Till then the flesh seems often

tortured and awry. The narrator contemplates 'the golden hue of
. . . [Gormon], the thick waxen skin, the red-pupilled eyes, the
jagged mouth. Gormon had been weaned on teratogenetic drugs;
he was a monster' (p. 11). The different races of aliens are
described, xenophobically enough, as though their forms were
anomalous, as though the 'human form divine' were alone the
image, however often distorted, of the Will. Those from H362
have long arms reaching below their knees, but there are outworld
tourists of every shape (p. 78). A starborn tourist puts 'his
cratered red face' close to that of Tomis and 'vented hallucina-
tions in my nostrils' (p. 106). The outworlder tourist which
accompanies the Pilgrims to the desert surgery is 'a flattened
spike-shaped creature somewhat taller than a man and mounted
on a jointed tripod of angular legs; its place of origin was in the
Golden Spiral; its skin was rough and bright red in hue, and
vertical rows of glassy oval eyes descended on three sides from the
top of its tapered head' (pp. 160–1); it never blinks or speaks, and
seems more like a machine than a creature; it is the one killed in
the surgery by the Changelings.

  Silverberg is interested in others of his works in the idea of
metamorphosis and alterations of flesh. Perhaps *Son of Man* is the
most striking example:[15] but there the idea is one of mobility,
sex-changing for its own sake; here the changes are part of a
pattern. We have already commented on how the spiritual and the
physical are divided in this story – while at a general level it must
be said that the physical abnormalities of humans and aliens alike
are a material representation of the spiritual crippledom of man
himself, the discord of evil that he himself has created, on a more
local plane it is clear that the physical aspect of people need not
reflect their inner nature. This lesson is nowhere more strongly
borne out than in the case of the Changelings, who, simply
because of their mutant form, and not from any inherent
depravity, are rendered guildless. For much of the narrative the
separation of appearance and reality that prevails is carried by the
theme of disguise. Gormon the Changeling is really Victorious
Thirteen the alien, a disguised spy. The Prince of Roum has to
travel dressed as a Pilgrim; and so does Olmayne. At every step of
his way to Roum, and from Roum to Perris and Perris to Jorslem,
wittingly or unwittingly, Tomis is accompanied by a hypocrite.
Till the baths of redemption there is no correlation between
physical appearance and reality. Till then Tomis the old man has

found his age 'a sort of battered kettle at the heel': his feelings for Avluela are blighted to the avuncular; he is a young and true soul in an old and corroded body. Redemption gives him a young body to match his inner nature; to Olmayne, impartial, it gives the form of a regressing infant to match hers. The flesh, so twisted by the perversions of science, so distorted by the released evil of humankind, assumes once more its proper form. The moral precondition of human regeneration, ' "redemption for our ancient sins" ' (p. 142), has been in part accomplished by Tomis. All humanity is risen with this healing, this sloughing-off of old, dividing sin. The first peoples to be redeemed are the Changelings and those ravaged by the crystallisation disease. Now their true selves can be restored, ' "We will go into Agupt, into the desert where miserable Changelings huddle in an ancient building that they worship, and we will take them into us and make them clean again. We will go on, to the west, to a pitiful village smitten by the crystallisation disease, and we will reach the souls of the villagers and free them from taint, and the crystallisation will cease and their bodies will be healed" ' (p. 189).

It would be a mistake to see *Nightwings* as a function of Silverberg's philosophy. As he said of himself, 'I manage to hold all poses at once . . . probably the truth is that I have no consistent positions at all.'[16] If *Nightwings* is an optimistic novel finally, *Dying Inside* (1972) is not; if *Downward to the Earth* (1970) or *Shadrach in the Furnace* (1976) suggest progress and spiritual renewal, the perceptions of the hero of *The World Inside* (1971) vanish down the urbmon 'chute' with his corpse. There have been attempts to tie a darkening of Silverberg's views to his experience of loss, emphasised by himself, in the burning of his house, but he had already written numbers of bleak stories such as 'To See the Invisible Man' (1962), *Thorns* (1967), *Hawksbill Station* (1968) and *The Man in the Maze* (1969). It is mistaken here to look for a clear evolutionary path.[17] Silverberg finds pleasure and happiness as real and as continually present as pain. What counts is not the linking of the book to the author, but the degree of felt reality that the book on its own conveys. And on this consideration, *Nightwings*, with its hard-earned optimism, and its lyricism sustained on a bedrock of reality, comes over with indubitable power.

7 Philip José Farmer, *To Your Scattered Bodies Go* (1971)

Of all the writers considered in this book, Philip José Farmer is one of the most imaginatively ambitious. His urge, from his first well-known book, *The Lovers* (1952), is always to push his mind beyond the limits, to describe a world of the Last Days, to throw together in one context historical figures and personages from fiction, to create endless series of sheerly different worlds or images striking in their sheer inventiveness, even to write alien pornography beyond man's wildest imaginings. Always, at root, the urge is simply the basic one of a delight in making, though one can relate Farmer's prodigious creative appetite to the quest for an absolute.[1] But Farmer's absolute is always itself a maker, a creator – like the makers of his Riverworld or of his World of Tiers: there is a circularity, the artist in pursuit of a transcendent version of himself, rather than anything more metaphysical. Silverberg too, as we have seen, seeks a kind of transcendence, even if he finds it within creation rather than in a God: but Silverberg is more spiritual in his concern than Farmer. Even in Farmer's *Night of Light* (1966), which describes a brilliantly imagined process of self-discovery through suffering, the strange landscape and events of the planet Dante's Joy are at the centre.

The Riverworld series – *To Your Scattered Bodies Go* (1971), *The Fabulous Riverboat* (1971), *The Dark Design* (1977), *The Magic Labyrinth* (1980) and most recently *Gods of Riverworld* (1983)[2] – is typical of Farmer in its extremity of imagination, its transgression of cosmic finalities, its rapacity for experience and vast variety of character. But there is a difference: the landscape, once created, stays almost unvaryingly the same. In other works Farmer keeps throwing up fresh images and landscapes as from a fountain – the multiple perspectives of *Strange Relations* (1960), the constantly-

121

changing backgrounds of the amazing 'World of Tiers' series, the
endless inventiveness of *Dark is the Sun* (1979). Riverworld has one
context through four ever longer novels, the river and its
cliff-hemmed banks.[3] Its rigidity of aspect is in part an indictment
of the tyranny exercised over man by the makers of this world. But
its constancy also enables it to develop a symbolic force in the
mind that Farmer's more mobile images and worlds do not
produce.

Nevertheless Riverworld is increasingly taken for granted as the
series proceeds, and loses some of its original force while Farmer
debouches into the creation of incidental characters and plots.
Farmer continually refuses the reader the knowledge of the truth
behind Riverworld so that he may spin out the story: and to this
extent the series is not to be considered as a unity so much as the
longest distance between two points (like the river itself, which
winds for millions of miles over the planet before emptying into
the very polar sea from which it takes its source). The most
powerful and truly imaginative novel of the series is the first, *To
Your Scattered Bodies Go*, for which Farmer received a Hugo award
in 1972.

The story of *To Your Scattered Bodies Go* begins with a man being
slain and then reawakening to find himself once more strong, yet
somehow suspended in a void. In all directions, and at equal
distances from one another, he sees other bodies in rows stretching
away into the far distance. All are naked, and some even are
lacking their flesh; all are rotating about their 'longitudinal axes'.
Near the head and feet of each stretch long red rods from as far
'down' as the eyes can see to as far 'up'. The whole image has
something of the suggestion of a scaffolding, a lattice in which
human bodies form the cross members.

The perceiving consciousness of this scene struggles to reach
the rod a foot from his finger tips, only to encounter resistance.
Eventually he touches it, and as soon as he does so, starts falling.
He is able to grasp the rod and halt himself. But touching this rod
has removed the force sustaining all the bodies vertically above
and below him also, and they fall past him, at exactly regular
intervals. He himself now begins to climb down his vertical rod.
But as he does so, a strange canoe-shaped craft appears above
him, with two human-like figures aboard. They stop the fall of
bodies and re-establish the cocoon-like force about the man on the
rod, which tears his hands loose. As he drifts upward past the

canoe, vowing to kill the men on board, one of them sights at him along a pencil sized metal object: after which, 'Oblivion came again.'[4]

There follows a chapter containing a dream, in which God comes to one Richard Francis Burton and tells him that he is long overdue in his debt ' "for the flesh" ', and that if he does not pay God will be forced to foreclose. When asked on what He will foreclose, God dissolves into the darkness, and at this point Burton sees that God resembles himself.

In the next chapter the same Burton wakes up in broad sunlight to find himself lying naked in a meadow near a river. Beside him, all over the grass, are lying other naked bodies. Eventually all begin numbly to get to their feet. When consciousness returns fully, they begin screaming with terror. Burton runs away from them in his own fright. All of course think they are on Earth in the Last Days, about to face final judgment. Nothing happens; and Burton, more a sceptic, comes quickly to himself and begins the process of discovery of this new world. The river is the central feature. It is bordered on either side for a distance of two miles or so by a grassy plain, which then slopes into more hilly country. After a few more miles this hilly region ends at a vast mountain wall of rock which leaps almost sheer from the ground for an amazing twenty thousand feet. Subsequent exploration reveals that with some variations, such as river narrows, lakes and an occasionally lower mountain wall, this remains the topography as far as can be travelled.

As for the human environment, this proves to be made up of all the men who ever lived on Earth, apart from the physically or mentally deformed, and children under five. These 'resurectees' are spread along the banks of the river, which proves to be over ten million miles long. The scattering seems fairly random, so that prehistoric men or medieval warriors may be mingled with people from the nineteenth and twentieth centuries. Not all are humans: one of the figures resurrected near Burton, and who befriends him, tells him he is an inhabitant of the star Tau Ceti who came to Earth with others in the twenty-first century. His name is Monat; and it transpires that it was he, when his fellows were slaughtered by men, who caused a 'scanner' satellite to be activated to destroy many of Earth's inhabitants. Monat, therefore, precipitated a kind of Armageddon. (At least this is what we learn of him in *this* book: a wholly different account of Monat and his actions emerges in the fourth book of the series, *The Magic Labyrinth*.[5]) But who or what caused the resurrection is obscure. Burton, from curiosity and from rage at the violation of his privacy in death, resolves to try to find out by travelling the river.

Each human awakes in this new world to find a large cylindrical canister strapped to his wrist, one which only he and his body chemistry can open. At regular intervals along the river bank are huge stone mushroom-shaped objects which have concentric rings of depressions on their upper surfaces. On each of these, and in one depression, a canister identical to that which every human carries has been placed. Suddenly the stones erupt in a single huge explosion which sends sheets of blue flame twenty feet up from the surface of each stone, killing a man who has got too near to one of them. After a time it occurs to Burton to investigate the cylinder left in one of the stones; and when he does so he finds it full of food. And thus, by placing their canisters, or 'grails' as they come to be called, in the depressions in the 'grailstones', the inhabitants of this new world come to be fed via discharges that occur from the stones at sunrise and sunset every day.

It is eventually discovered that death no longer exists in the sense of its finality. Like the river, life is endless and identical at all times; like the river too, whose mouth is to prove where its source is, life begins where it ends. Anyone who is killed – and people still can be killed or hurt themselves – is resurrected at some other point on the banks of the huge river. There seems no limit to the number of times one can die and live again, though such a limit is eventually shown to exist. Death thus becomes a unique mode of travel, if a totally uncertain one, in that one can be deposited anywhere in one's next life. And people who were close together in the rod-filled void at the beginning (for that turns out to be the original reconstruction place for humanity) tend to be resurrected in the same place as one another. Thus Richard Burton, African and Arabian explorer, who is to be the protagonist of this novel, is on numbers of his eight hundred-odd deaths reawakened in the company of Hermann Göring. All resurrectees come to life in healthy bodies aged twenty-five, or under if they died on Earth earlier than that age. Ageing, however, seems to be at work in one area, since it is said that there will soon be no children, and adults are sterile (p. 95).

Where they all are is not plain. Monat points out to Burton that there is another sun near the one which most evidently traverses their sky: and fainter celestial bodies too can be seen. At night the landscape is lit by so great a blaze from multitudes of stars and gas clouds as to have almost the visibility of day, which would suggest somewhere near a galactic core. Already we are making a non-supernatural hypothesis: this place is on one star among others: how could it be so local and still be heaven or any approach to it? Nevertheless the possibility of eschatology is entertained throughout the novel. What the geographical makeup of the world is is not clear either. Since the mountains that rim the river cannot be scaled, there is no way of having a wide view of the landscape. Only after a number of individuals have travelled via death, and then by deduction rather than sight, is it realized that the length of the river and the size of the planet suppose a river which zigzags its way over both hemispheres, with the river winding in such a way that one gorge is 'stacked' against another. Even then it is wrongly deduced that the source of the river is at one pole of the planet and its mouth at the other.

The novel describes how Burton (who turns out to have been the waker in the void at the start) gathers a heterogeneous band about him and eventually constructs a sailing boat out of bamboo to sail the river and find its source and their creators. After much voyaging his ship is finally attacked and sunk by hostiles in one section of the river, and thereafter his mode of travelling is through death. At one point one of his band, Spruce, is unmasked as one of the makers of this world, and under threat of torture says that Riverworld was created as a means of developing the souls of the inhabitants. Later, however, Burton is visited by a stranger who tells him that he is one of those who has engineered this planet as an experiment to see how resurrected humans behave in different 'mixes'; this stranger says that he has turned against this experiment as being arrogant and cruel, and that he wishes to enlist Burton's help in overthrowing those who have organized it. He tries to put Burton through death into a position near the beginning of the river from which he can easily reach the central tower of these scientists, or 'Ethicals', as Burton comes to call them: but unfortunately Burton is murdered by the inhabitants of the place where he is resurrected before he can make a move, and when he awakes again, he is once more far down the river. Meanwhile the Ethicals (who indeed exist), aware of his object, try to track him down; so that from being the hunter he becomes the hunted. Eventually one of the deaths by which Burton seeks to escape them lands him in their council-chamber, where they try to explain to him the futility of his designs on them before returning him to the river bank with his memory of the meeting supposedly erased. But in fact that memory remains, and he awakes resolved to continue his quest with another voyage upriver.

Unlike the other books considered here, this one sets out to create a totally new ontology from the ground up. Other worlds are in varying degrees built on our own: but in this book the foundations of our own world have disappeared as surely as solidity from Burton as he floats in the void at the start. Indeed that void is suggestive: it is as though all past creation has been nullified and a new one is to be begotten *ex nihilo*. The void, in its way, measures the disjunction between our world and the new one. In this new world there is only one unchanging freak landscape, death is not final, food is provided by flames on stone mushrooms, one's next companion may be an ancient Hittite or the Joneses from next door. It is fair to say that the act of imagination required to create the book is more or less its *raison d'être*. The author's inspiration seems to have emerged from the Christian idea of all souls being reclothed in flesh in the Last Days:[6] it was then for him to imagine a world in which this might happen. What would occur within that world, indeed what was the reason for its being as it was, were secondary considerations. The plot of the Riverworld series – particularly the convoluted battles between the resuscitated Mark Twain and King John which rumble through three more long novels – is really of less interest, or has less fire behind it: it is Farmer exploiting his world rather than making it come to life. And the rush of garbled explanation of 'the truth' which comes at the end of the fourth volume, not to mention the series of *volte-face* which then run through the fifth, shows how much better things are when not fully accounted for.

It is in part the dialectic between the formlessness of mystery and the limits of certainty that gives life to the first book. The nameless character starts by sinking out of a highly precise moment, of which we know nothing in advance – a man in a room crying ' "My God, I am a dead man!" ' while his wife holds him in her arms 'as if she could keep death away from him', the door opening, a giant black camel outside, with the hot desert wind tinkling the bells of its harness, the huge dark face of a turbanned eunuch appearing at the door with a scimitar in his hand and then

'Blackness. Nothingness. He did not even know that his heart had given out forever. Nothingness' (p. 5). Where we are, who this is, and how it is that we are concerned with him after his death we do not know, and the narrative intimacy with the scene only increases our sense of disorientation. This is symbolized in the image of the abyss that follows. The character reawakens to an immediate sense of vigorous life, all pain gone and his heart beating strongly; yet he is in a void of neither up nor down, 'hanging in nothingness'. There are no limits to that nothingness. There is only a rod by him which 'came from above, from infinity, and went on down to infinity' (p. 5). Still, the rod gives him some bearings: it becomes literally something to hold on to as he struggles towards it. Unknown to him, there is also an identical rod at his feet, and it is this that he meets as he somersaults over in attempting to reach the one near his hands. Then he notices the bodies all around him, stretching away into the distance, and suddenly his previously numbed senses go clear:

> Something snapped inside him. He could almost hear it, as if a window had suddenly been raised.
> The world took a shape which he could grasp, though he could not comprehend it. Above him, on both sides, below him, as far as he could see, bodies floated. They were arranged in vertical and horizontal rows. The up-and-down ranks were separated by red rods, slender as broomsticks, one of which was twelve inches from the feet of the sleepers and the other twelve inches from their heads. Each body was spaced about six feet from the body above and below and on each side.

Now he is beginning to get some mental bearings. So too when at last he touches the rod by him and begins to fall, he finds out which way is 'down'. But at the end of this scene, mystery reasserts itself with the arrival of the canoe-like boat and the character's enforced return to his previous position.

The image is striking, but its peculiarities can be seen as serving to convey dislocation more effectively. Were it a complete void or a darkness this would be less. It is because the character can see, because there are no limits to the space he is in, and because he and the other bodies are revolving slowly so that what direction is up, down or to one side is at once asked and made impossible of answer, that the disorientation comes over more powerfully. In this the image serves as epigraph to the whole book, in which the disorientation of revived humanity in a strange new world and the attempt to find bearings, whether the configuration of the planet, the origins of the river, or the Ethicals and their motives, form the central subject and motive.

Throughout the story that attempt is both invited and frustrated. The sceptical Burton always seeks a scientific explanation rather than a supernatural one for the layout of the planet and the nature of those behind it. Yet the explanation is to elude him, and even the explanations given by the 'Ethical' are not entirely trustworthy, cast in doubt as they are by the later Council of Ethicals. Throughout the book the reader is left uncertain as to whether events have a natural or a supernatural explanation. Moreover, while wanting to know the explanation, the reader also does not wish to know, for to do so would be to lose the pleasure of mystery and free speculation: when the secret is apparently run to earth at the end of the fourth volume one feels tied down and restricted (though the Ethical Loga does say that there is a further and untraceable destiny for the human *wathan*, or spirit, beyond Ethical control[7]).

The landscape of the novel plays its part in this too. We think perhaps of heaven or the afterworld as a vague misty place where one is free to do as one wishes (given that one's wishes are all pure). But the landscape Farmer has given us is one very clear-cut and hard-edged. C. S. Lewis similarly portrays heaven as an extremely solid place in his *The Great Divorce* (1946): but even he has his ghosts and spirits wandering at will over an endless area. In Riverworld there is no such freedom, except to travel the river. The river itself is bounded by unscalable walls. The afterworld here has been set within very precise markers. (The author, we may note, is fascinated by precise measurements: he even has Burton count the bodies falling past him in the void till he reaches three thousand and one.) The stress is on locality – a mile across here, two miles there, ten miles down. Hardly anything is seen from far off, and despite aeroplanes in the later books, there is no distant aerial perspective given. Each adventure is *sui generis*, just as each settlement along the river is divided from the next by narrows or bends. We are often confined to the psyche and perceptions of one character – particularly, in this first book, those of Burton. Yet that very confinement awakens more strongly a sense of some larger dimension of which the fragment is a part.

Burton's mind will not rest within any local limits, but continually ranges outward. And for the reader too the limitation of purview enhances the imaginative energy of the book.

The main urges in the story are curiosity and the desire to master one's environment. The object of the characters in setting out to find the Ethicals is to gain control over their own lives – and, indeed, deaths. It is being controlled by others to which the protagonists object. Burton has a particular dislike at having been recreated without his consent, 'He did not feel gratitude because They had given him a second life. He was outraged that They should do this without his leave' (p. 177).[8] It is he who determines to travel to the makers of the planet and force them to account for themselves. He masters his environment as no one else in the first book. He alone begins to gain control over his condition in the void. He is quick to find his bearings within Riverworld and to find out its resources, quick to organize a group about him for exploration of the planet and eventually the construction of the bamboo boat with which to travel the river and locate the Ethicals. He is master not only of his life but of death, using it as a means of travel; and it is he who makes contact with the Ethicals, eventually being brought before their full council. In all this he is the example for humanity in general.

The planet itself is an example of man's – or at least mind's – control over matter. Its topography – the river, the endless gorge, the deep-rooted grass, the almost unfellable irontrees – all of those have been created by the makers of the planet as the new world for reborn humanity. Even the fish in the river are functional; as are the worms, sole fauna of the land and annelidan refuse service (p. 94). The planet is set at a fixed ninety degrees to the ecliptic, which means that the warm weather remains constant. More overt evidence of organization is seen in the grails and grailstones. The food provided by the grailstones is, incidentally, no nectar or ambrosia; it is usually twentieth-century food, such as antipasta, bacon and eggs, steak, soup, liqueurs, and, as supplements, cigarettes, cigars and even mind-trip drugs. Everything is purposive. Shut in by the gorge, humanity is to be barred from larger inquiry into the planet and its origins. For any thinking being, the fact that there is a designer behind the planet is quite sufficiently obvious: it is a perfect candidate for Paley's natural theology, the argument from scheme to Schemer. Nothing is random. On Earth there is such a thing as nature, and wilderness, where phenomena such as growth or death by disease or storms or wild beasts happen freely: here there is only nature methodised.

We are to find at the end of the fourth book that humanity itself even on Earth owed its sentience and self-awareness to the long-ago implantation deep in the Earth of special *wathan* generators which created psychic energies that attached themselves to men: this implantation was carried out on many planets capable of intelligent life by the same beings who have created Riverworld. So far as his self-knowledge goes, man has always been the creature of someone else. The Riverworld saga comes to an end with men overcoming the humanoid beings who have created them and the planet, and learning to be masters of their own destiny: in the end it is a case of Men Without Gods. By a piece of nonsense-logic derived from Lewis Carroll, a member of the human race, they gain control of a renegade computer that is on the verge of ending Riverworld; and in that sense they are no longer ghosts in the machine, questionable identities generated by scientific process, but fully existent individuals whose souls or *wathans* are now truly their own – or so they can believe.[9]

The emphasis of the book on control over the environment is heightened by comparison with a novel with which the author may well have been familiar – C. S. Lewis's *Perelandra* (1943). This describes a Venusian paradise with its own Adam and Eve, whom one Ransom, sent from Earth by angels, must seek to defend from the assaults of Satan in the body of a scientist Weston who has travelled there by his own space ship. The planet in Lewis's book is largely oceanic, and the Lady and her Lord, who are the sole human inhabitants on the planetary surface, live on huge mats of vegetation that float on the giant waves. In *Perelandra* innocence consists in voluntarily and gladly accepting whatever Maleldil (God), maker of the planet, sends, just as the islands shape themselves to the varying sea. The prohibition on Venus/ Perelandra is not to accept, to step out of the ocean of voluntary passivity on to a place called the Fixed Land, and to sleep there. But such assertion of the self against higher control is at the heart of the ethic in Farmer's book. Again, in Perelandra, there is no sense of control behind the environment: it is nature rather than a construct like the human-making rods that begin Farmer's story. And it is more free than controlled nature. The very violence and immensity of the ocean in which Ransom finds himself seem there to tell us that nature on Perelandra is no puppet, even if she gladly serves the purposes of Maleldil and on a planet of innocence will do no harm. But Lewis's object in his book is precisely to show and celebrate 'creatureliness' – the way in which man expresses and fulfils the creativity and purpose of a maker. The aim in Farmer's novel is for man himself to become the maker. This aim may be felt ironically unachieved by the end of the first volume, but not by the fourth. Yet even the first has throughout given pride of place to those who, faced by their strange environment, have grasped and manipulated it. For Lewis such an impulse is little other than megalomania: it remains to be seen with what kind of an ethic Farmer has credited his protagonists' behaviour.

The makers of the planet are called 'Ethicals' after one of them, Spruce, has claimed that the purpose of the planet is to prepare human souls for a higher life; and the name sticks, despite the assertion of the unknown 'X' who tells Burton that the whole planetary arrangement is nothing more than a gigantic experiment. If we consider morality in terms of caring for others and carrying out selfless acts, there is not much of this to be found among the protagonists of the book. For example:

> They got to the grailstone about a half-hour before noon. Things had changed. Their quiet little hollow contained about sixty people, many of whom were working on pieces of chert. One man was holding a bloody eye into which a piece of stone had flown. Several more were bleeding from the face or holding smashed fingers.
>
> Burton was upset but he could do nothing about it. The only hope for regaining the quiet retreat was that the lack of water would drive the intruders away. (p. 75)

The 'Burton was upset' momentarily seems to refer to the people harming themselves with the stones, and we are made all the more aware of Burton's concern with self when we see the true source of his upset. His attitude throughout is one of undermining what he sees as the false standards of other people – the sexual puritanism of Alice Hargreaves, the devoutness of those who accept a divine source for their rebirth, the idealism of those who believe that man is capable of being anything but a 'killer ape' (p. 85), even the loyalty of one friend to another when the pre-human Kazz refuses to come on the adventure with Burton in the bamboo ship the *Hadji* out of affection for Monat.

On the whole Burton is not answered. The possibility of moral behaviour in the accepted sense is scarcely entertained. An Israeli, Lev Ruach, tells Burton that he will not journey on the *Hadji* because the unmasked Ethical, Spruce, told them that ' "we should be striving for a spiritual perfection, not fighting Those Who gave us a chance to do so" ' (p. 146). Burton rejects the idea, ' "I didn't ask to be put here any more than I asked to be born on Earth. I don't intend to kowtow to another's dictates! I mean to find The River's end. And if I don't, I will at least have had fun and learned much on the way!" ' (p. 147). Here Burton puts his selfhood against any higher authority, whether tyrannical, benign or moral: it is a case of Parolles' 'Simply the thing I am shall make me live.' Yet what 'I am' is really the central issue: in seeking to overcome the Ethicals, Burton is seeking to have a self he can truly call his own; the quest of the book is a quest for identity. When Burton makes this statement he is in control of a little state the group have set up on the river bank, and in effect he is carrying out precisely the decision of Tennyson's Ulysses in leaving his kingdom to the governance of his son Telemachus while he sets forth on fresh adventures 'beyond the sunset': that is, looked at from one way, he is evading his responsibilities, and from another he is making a heroic and romantic decision. The book seems to come down mainly on the latter side, with Ruach abandoning his moral stance and admitting that he is really staying because he wants to settle down and cultivate his own little garden (p. 147). Elsewhere, by bringing into contrast people with peculiar moral principles, the suggestion is made that many moralities are born of personal need, whim or custom rather than from any fundamental imperative: 'Ruach described the despair and disgust of a Croat Moslem and an Austrian Jew because their grails contained pork. A Hindu screamed obscenities because his grail offered him meat. A fourth man, crying out that they were in the hands of devils, had hurled his cigarettes into the river' (p. 62).

Nevertheless by the end of the first book we do not know for sure that Burton's views are right because we do not know truly whether the principles on which Riverworld is founded are those of devotion or exploitation or neither. It is one of the main strengths of *To Your Scattered Bodies Go* that it leaves us and the characters in doubt, still unaware of which of the Ethicals has given the true explanation of events or of whether the Church of the Second Chance, whose believers hold Riverworld to be a place of spiritual testing, may be correct. Looked at from the standpoint of the whole series, however, we are to see that all moralities are wrong because they operate *a priori*, in applying the standards and beliefs of one world to those of another of whose principles they know nothing: their moralities are mere gestures, a grid imposed on the void. The pragmatic, more scientific Burton, trying to discover the true nature of things by personal experiment (it is he who first works out the use of the grail stones), works *a posteriori*, by submitting himself to learn from the new phenomena. His journey is to discover the ontology of the planet, without which no morality can have final substance. He travels to find out the new; the others sit still on the river bank holding on to the old. He commits himself to the fluidity of the moving water, or even of his many deaths; they keep to the static land.

This makes him tantamount to a moral hero;[10] and this turns out to be true in another way too. Spruce's assertion of the value of developing the spirit may have had some force in the first book, but it proves to be a fiction designed to keep people from attempting to reach his fellow Ethicals and their purpose. Had all people simply sat where they were, they would not only have remained docile fodder for an experiment, but ultimately victims of an experiment that goes wrong. Burton and his friends both save the human race and give them their true 'selves'. Only if we maintain that it is a better thing to die than merely to live for the sake of living, only then can we take a moral stance against the behaviour in the book. Otherwise we must accept that what is moral or good is determined by the nature of the world one inhabits. (Here science fiction is radically different from fantasy, in which the moral laws considered to be operative in this world are often taken into the invented one.[11]) In Riverworld the ethic becomes one of self-control, rationality and forward movement. Burton will let no-one have control over him, but he insists on keeping a grip on himself: he is always first to govern his passions; and his constant meetings in the latter part of the first book with Hermann Göring who is lacerated with guilt, are designed not only to heighten his relative probity, but also his steadiness. If the lengthy accounts, in volumes two to four of the saga, of the fruitless battles between Samuel Clemens in his various ships and Erik Bloodax and King John in theirs, resulting in the destruction of all ships save Burton's, have any purpose, it is to show how when one forgets the larger vision and goal, one is doomed to futility and stasis.

It is when we come to self that we come to one of the dominant interests of the book, as of the series. Faced by the possibility of becoming saintly enough for his *wathan*, or spirit, to 'go beyond' into the Over*wathan* of ecstatic oneness with God, the character Cyrano de Bergerac in *The Dark Design* refuses vehemently:

> 'No! It does not make sense! Speaking logically, why should the *wathan*, or the soul, be created in the first place? What sense is there to this creation when most *wathans* will be wasted, as if they were so many flies hatched only to be eaten or swatted? And those *wathans* who do survive, in a manner of speaking. What about those who achieve near perfection, sainthood, if you will, only to be cheated in the end? For surely to lose your self-consciousness, your individuality, your humanity, is to be cheated?
>
> 'No, I want to stand as myself, Savinien de Cyrano de Bergerac, if I am to be immortal. I do not want this spurious immortality, this beingness as an unknowing, brainless cell of God's body! Nameless and brainless!'[12]

And this ethic does seem to be behind much of the book. The whole idea of recreating men out of the nonentity of death which is the basis of the saga is obviously central to it.[13] In a sense nothing has a purpose: it is enough that it is or is done for its own sake. When one considers the motives of the Ethicals in setting up Riverworld as an experiment they seem rather tenuous. What will they prove by thus mixing humanity? What purpose will it serve? (One of them even asserts that they did it to escape boredom (p. 185).) Since most of the mixed societies they set up seem to be continuously at war with one another, the experiment does not appear to have been a very fruitful one.[14] We have to push away the 'experiment' motive as a smokescreen for the real urge, which seems simply to realize being in all its variety – as in much of Farmer's fiction generally. So too even with Burton's motivation: he is a traveller, and that makes him traveller; what he is is what he does. As we have seen, one of his prime motives is objection to the invasion of the privacy of his self by others: his aim is to become independent of them, first by eluding them and then by reaching them to wrest the secret of his true nature from them. In the book, death, which is normally the end of the self, is now only the gateway to return to the same self in another place; it can be said that there is truly no escape from one's identity. Self-realization is all. The age of twenty-five is the basic one for re-creation: it is an age at which the self is at its fullest, as the book sees it.[15] At first, whether in the anonymity of the void of rebirth where endless bodies hang suspended, or in the initial nakedness and hairlessness of all people who wake in Riverworld, all can seem very alike, apart from pre-humans and the few humanoid star travellers. Yet from this very superficial similarity at once springs the announcement of striking differences of character: it is as though their clothes and hair had been removed to heighten their real differences and true identities.

It is clear that part of the author's incidental pleasure in writing the Riverworld saga was in recreating the identities of figures lost to time. The author re-making Sir Richard Burton is like another kind of Ethical bringing humanity to new life.[16] He said that he wished to write more Riverworld books which would explore new characters. Certainly the leisurely books that follow the first are devoted in large part to a variety of characters, from Mark Twain to King John and Lothar von Richthofen to Cyrano de Bergerac. The character-sketches throughout are often a sort of *D.N.B.* entry, with bits of 'inside knowledge' thrown in:

> She had been born Alice Pleasance Liddell on April 25, 1852. (Burton was thirty then.) She was the direct descendant of King Edward III and his son, John of Gaunt. Her father was dean of Christ Church College of Oxford and co-author of a famous Greek-English lexicon. (Liddell and Scott! Burton thought.) She had had a happy childhood, an excellent education, and had met many famous people of her times: Gladstone, Matthew Arnold, the Prince of Wales, who was placed under her father's care while he was at Oxford . . .
>
> . . .
>
> She talked of Dinah, the tabby kitten she had loved when she was a child, the great trees of her husband's aboretum, how her father, when working on his lexicon, would always sneeze at twelve o'clock in the afternoon, no one knew why . . . at the age of eighty, she was given an honorary Doctor of Letters by the

American university, Columbia, because of the vital part she played in the genesis of Mr Dodgson's famous book . . .

'That was a golden afternoon indeed,' she said, 'despite the official meteorological report. On July 4, 1862, I was ten . . . my sisters and I were wearing black shoes, white openwork socks, white cotton dresses, and hats with large brims.' (*To Your Scattered Bodies Go*, p. 52)

There is a similarly full account of Burton (of whom one of the characters he meets had on Earth wanted to write a biography), with detailed questions about missing biographical facts and discussions of his poetry and his anti-semitic prose work (pp. 40, 92, 122). The book is full of debates: it is no adventure story simple but tries to canvas a range of different responses to the new world and of people to each other. There are those who believe the world is purgatory, those who believe it is hell, and those like Burton who believe it has a physical explanation. One man who thinks he is in a world made by devils, and feels unfairly treated because he devoted his life to piety and good works, is unmasked as one Robert Smithson, a tyrannical Victorian cotton- and steel-mill owner, by one of his former downtrodden female employees; and a long description of factory life ensues. Burton and Alice Hargreaves have frequent arguments about sexual prudery. Peter Frigate, Burton's former would-be biographer, debates with Burton how far man is subject to the territorial imperative (pp. 84–6), and frequently discusses Burton's previous life on Earth. John Collop, seventeenth-century English founder of the Church of the Second Chance, who believes that Riverworld is divinely-based and that the river is the Jordan, has several disputes with Burton.

All the time there are references to the natures and behaviours of the different races encountered, such as the Bronze Age Central Europeans who go in for whiskers (p. 167), or the effect on women from different times and places of the pre-human casually urinating in public like a dog (p. 77). Part of the impulse of the book is the mixing together at one level of people who on Earth were divided by time, race or class, such as Hermann Göring and a Jew, Kazz the pre-human and Monat the star dweller who become friends from opposite ends of time, Collop the Christian and Burton the sceptic, the factory girl and the owner, the high-born Alice Hargreaves and the low-class Wilfreda. The author devotes much of the first volume to refusing certainties and entertaining the sheer variety of possibilities, so that a multiplicity of viewpoints may be enjoyed – though he tends to come down on Burton's side. Considerable space is given in the book to investigations of the nature of the planet, such as its rocks, the behaviour of the fish in the river, the bamboo for hut- and boat-making. The author is quite content to suspend his narrative for description. After one discussion Burton says they all ought to be getting on with present issues and investigation of the cities of the river plains: at which Alice Hargreaves suddenly appears in clothes she has made out of grass, and a debate on nudity versus clothing develops (pp. 65–6).

Curiously, though, despite this insistence on identity, there is often a strange lack of it in the story. As we have seen, most of the people are portrayed as engaged in some kind of warfare. This is described as the only way of avoiding tedium (p. 169), as though there were no other possible pursuits, such as building, painting, writing or making music. Actually there is remarkable emphasis on physical rather than intellectual activities in the book. Nor does the author go very deep into his characters: he may 'cover' them with facts about them, but he does not penetrate them. Burton has some reality, it is true; but midway through the story Alice Hargreaves drops the prudery that increasingly has become her sole characteristic. The Jews have no other characterisation but that of detesting those who have persecuted their race. Hermann Göring, who is initially seen as something of a vicious monster, can later be regarded with something like comradeship by Burton, and the narrative endorses his leadership qualities. Göring is actually a case in point, as the author has tried with him to present the picture of a guilty man whose spirit is tormented with revulsion at the evils done by him on Earth. Yet even this aspect of him is presented rather at a distance, as 'something strange going on in Göring' rather than as a response we can understand to an evil we can recognize. Moreover he does not evince any sign of guilt when Burton first meets him in the little empire he has set up with the Roman Tullius Hostilius. Monat of Tau Ceti, initially presented as physically peculiar, loses even this identity as he is merged into the group about Burton. In the next book too, Samuel Clemens, or Mark Twain, ceases to be an author and becomes a warfaring captain. Nor is there a *strong* attempt to individuate the societies along the river: they may have different habits, but about their different characters, or that which distinguishes a pre-Mayan Colombian from an Ancient Etruscan, little is said. The different races that are mixed together are sometimes detailed simply as ingredients in a recipe – at one point we have 30 per cent pre-Columbian Samoans, 60 per cent 'Sumerians of the Old or Classical period', the 'ubiquitous 10 per cent of people from anywhere-everyplace, twentieth centurians being the most numerous' (p. 189).

Now all this is fair enough in science fiction, which is not generally concerned with the portrayal of character, but in a book where interest in individual identity is clearly present it is a curious anomaly. Its source may lie in the book's rejection of inwardness and of the spirit. We are not allowed to view the world from the eyes of the religious John Collop: only from the dispassionate ones of Burton. Burton does not have very much time for emotion: he has no particular or consistent feelings, whether of amazement, wonder or terror, about having been recreated in Riverworld. The otherness of the place never really strikes him. Nor does the otherness of others. The result is that progressively people come to speak the same idiom, the same slang. The levelling processes advances through the books, till we have a lisping sub-man or Titanthrops who swears 'Jethuth H. Chritht', or an Ethical leader who says he has just 'gotten' a message from a computer.[17]

For all that the first book devotes itself to research and argument, it has in it a tendency opposed to mental life, certainly to the spirit. Reflections are local and relatively unsustained. The first image of the book is one of returning to the flesh: Burton's immediate interest on awakening is not in the fact that he still has a self, but that he has a rejuvenated body: in that first scene he is not even named. The original Riverworld novel was called 'Owe for the Flesh'. The title of the first published novel of the series is *To Your Scattered Bodies Go*: there is no mention of the souls that do so; during the book the existence of souls is conjectured (pp. 130–1), but we are not introduced to *wathans* till late in the series. *Wathans* themselves are conceived of only as blueprints for recreation, not as functions of spiritual life. When God comes to Burton in his dream he tells him, ' "You owe for the flesh" '; and then, as though remembering, ' "Not to mention the spirit. You owe for the flesh and the spirit, which are one and the same thing" ' (p. 11). In later re-runs of this scene, it is only the flesh (pp. 49, 148). Flesh, normally viewed as mutable and subject to decay, is here almost eternally youthful: however often one dies, one will return to the same body, even if all else changes. The spirit may age, but the flesh does not, so that by the end Burton can speak of having a one hundred and one year-old spirit in a twenty-five year-old body – the reverse of the feeling known to terrestrial geriatrics. In our world spirit stamps its mark on flesh, more or less, so that there is some art to tell the mind's construction from the face: not here. (Farmer wrote a novel called *Flesh* (1960).) And just as flesh remains more or less constant, so does the physical landscape and environment of Riverworld.

This concentration on the physical has further implications. The Big Grail, or Dark Tower, at the north pole of the world, legends of which have filtered through Riverworld from the supposed sight of it by one man before he fell to his death, could well have formed part of a spiritual quest, just as the Holy Grail does in the Arthuriad. Instead, though this possibility is dangled before us in the first book (pp. 148–9), it becomes simply a place to be reached to find out what makes things work on the planet.[18] It comes down, too, to a kind of atomism, an absence of connectives among individuals. Burton is not inseparable from his companions: indeed in the latter part of *To Your Scattered Bodies Go* he acts on his own. He is the hero prepared to use death as a means of travel: he does it more than any other inhabitant of Riverworld. In the process he experiences seven hundred and seventy-seven (no mystic number, this) lives, each of them divided from the rest. The River would seem literally and symbolically a connective among all the peoples scattered along its banks, enabling commerce among them, but actually there is very little traffic, and each society on its banks forms a more or less isolated unit, usually at war with its neighbours. This atomism is seen at the level of style too, which is written in a series of short, clipped-off sentences, which divide actions and thoughts into units (see for example p. 76). Lists abound, whether of languages, menus, or even figures of speech (see for example p. 169). Scattered Bodies indeed it is.

If we look back over *To Your Scattered Bodies Go*, we have to admit that while the novel is well put together and originally handled, the real inspirational force comes from the opening images – of the man being killed, the bodies in the void, God coming to Richard Burton, and the first growing awareness of Riverworld. It is thanks to them and the continued mystery about the nature of this new world that we are kept in great suspense throughout the book, driven forward by the same urge to know that drives Burton himself. By presenting us with a world after death, the author has ensured that our deepest interests will be engaged in what he has to say about it; and this is enhanced by his use of images of such stark clarity, basic simplicity and originality. There can be few books which at their end leave one quite so desirous of finding out more. But as the series continues, and dwindles down to local intrigues and struggles that could occur in any context, until we reach the flat explanation at the end, we begin to see that the further one gets from those initial images the more inspiration dries up. Further, nothing seems to matter so much: the characters increasingly seem to be playing boyish games, as in Clemens's river-fights with King John.[19] If at first the windings of the river, with its source near its mouth, suggest the ouroboros, or else the snake wound about the rod of Aesculapius (all are healed in this world), or, with the single man among billions travelling the river to the sea, something of a fertilization image – if this is so, later, as the geographical layout becomes clearer and the games with death more lighthearted, we begin perhaps to think rather of the whole as a giant game of snakes and ladders (proceeding in zig-zag rows, throwing dice/dying to jump nearer to or further from one's goal). In a sense the whole series is a descent from reality. The first death, the 'real' one, of Burton in Trieste, is felt and strongly imagined: the later ones, not being final, are not. As Dylan Thomas once put it, 'After the first death, there is no other.' For all that the characters find their true selves in the end, they seem infinitely more ghostly. Perhaps that is why they come to talk more about their *wathans*.

Still, for the first book, this is not yet so: it has its suggestive force because it is still far within the gravitational pull of those opening images. It is right therefore to end by considering them once more. Part of the power of the image of the bodies suspended in the abyss is its resonance with our own view of death as a dimensionless vacancy, the 'nothingness' into which Burton dies; and this together with its being a purposeful void, a meaningful vacancy, a directed directionlessness, in the shapes of the rods and all the other stacked and silent figures. That duality is seen in the book in the river, which gives direction, yet whose length and convolution are such that there is no direction. But it is also there by contrast with the image of Riverworld which is to follow, an image which is a very clear one set against one which has no limits or definite location. All this fits with the motif of certainty versus mystery which we have traced in the book. Then other aspects reveal themselves. The first image of the book, with the man's house being invaded by the slayer is an image of violated privacy; and so is that of all the naked humans being re-made by others (the grave here is no fine and private place): and of course objection to violated privacy is to be one of Burton's prime motives. Then the void of re-creation is boundless in every direction, where Riverworld is narrow, two-dimensional and one-directional so far as the river is concerned: this prefigures perhaps the expansiveness of the human spirit and its constriction by enforced ignorance and control within the story. Then, thinking more generally, we see that the medium of both the void and the river bank is space, not time. In the abyss Burton's concern is to get his spatial bearings; similarly, on the riverbank, his eyes take in the layout and relationship of the geography. There is little sense of time in the whole series – 'Time did not mean much on the River' (p. 176). The Ethicals have cancelled time by putting all humans from all ages together. All people are to be twenty-five, and death no longer has finality enough to provide a temporal marker. There is little in the way of spiritual development over time on the part of any individual. The season is constant. It is space that provides the limits and gives definition, in the form of the confining river valley. And the determination of space – the layout of the planet, the location of the Ethicals and how to reach them – is the central object of the characters. The concern is thus more with solidity than with extension.

Both images also portray the omnivorousness of Farmer's world. Everything is got in – all people stacked in the void, every person and personality recreated against the contrastive uniformity of Riverworld, all values and *Weltanschauungen* thrown together and tested. There is a desire in Farmer to make everything overt, bring everything into play: nothing is to be hidden, no horrors committed by Göring (the same idea of the exposure of sin is there in *Night of Light*), no secrets, biographical or otherwise concealed: and symbolising this, everyone is made in the void from the innards out, and placed on Riverworld hairless and nude. The entire object of the story becomes exposure of the secret behind the making of the world. All barriers are to be broken down, even the supposed finality of death – even too, by the rebelliousness of Burton, the rigidities of the void of recreation itself.[20]

But last and not least significant is the fact that these images are the foundation of the series in the first place. For they provide a keynote of the static, both as images and as images of static situations – the rigidities of the abyss, the unchanging fixity of Riverworld. In a sense the series is about the static. The first book ends with Burton having got nowhere in the sense that he is returned far back down the river, even if he has established the existence of the Ethicals and something of their plans. Nobody in the series ages, nobody changes. And at the end of the fourth book the objective of the adventurers becomes the preservation of a threatened Riverworld in the state in which they found it: their (long-delayed) journey, though it has given them power, has given them it only to be the masters rather than the servants of a fixed condition. Just as the river spirals out from itself and back to the same place, so these images draw all power back into themselves. The Riverworld saga, considered as a whole, cannot escape its own origins, and remains in this sense like some literary child prodigy.

8 Arthur C. Clarke, *Rendezvous with Rama* (1973)

If one feature marks out Arthur C. Clarke among writers of science fiction it is the way he can create images that go on resonating through the mind, like struck bells. The images in Brian Aldiss's *Hothouse* are brilliant, novel, fascinating: but they do not work beyond the experience of the text itself. For science fiction work comparable to Clarke's one has to look to Wells's *The Time Machine* or to the planetary romances which in our terms are fantasy of C. S. Lewis: indeed it is with the genre of fantasy with its reliance on archetypal images, that Clarke's imagination in part belongs (Lewis in fact greatly admired Clarke's *Childhood's End*). Part of the effect comes from his frequent choice of single images, presented with great clarity and wonder – the mysterious rectangular monolith found on the Moon and in giant form on a moon of Saturn in *2001: A Space Odyssey* (1968), the huge interstellar craft in *Childhood's End* (undoubtedly the stimulus for the one in *Close Encounters of the Third Kind*), the strange cylinder hurtling through the solar system in *Rendezvous with Rama*. These images are always central: the narrative is concerned with description of what they are, mean and do; and in the sense that Clarke's work is thus contemplative, it is again like fantasy. The mind is given leisure to explore and wonder. However much the images may be of technological marvels, such as space ships, these marvels are shown as more than mere objects unrelated to us: they prove to have profound connection with man, often reminding him of some long forgotten unconscious experience of his racial past, or else incorporating him in some large universal design of which till now he has had only stray gleams in the form of his religions.[1] Thus the Overlords in *Childhood's End* (1953) are a race with horns and barbed tails, images of what for man is the

143

demonic, images too of a long-past previous encounter between man and them.

Clarke plays much upon man's desire to feel part of a larger universal home, a desire which he awakens but often frustrates poignantly. And his images also have power through the mystery associated with them. We do not know what will happen to the mutated human minds on their guided journey towards the centre of the galaxy in *Childhood's End*, nor do we know more than a little of the purposes the alien Overlords serve, or of their far larger and supernatural-seeming director, the Overmind. We do not have more than a few glimpses into the true nature of the space ship known as Rama, and we learn nothing of it origin or destination; like the humans in the story we are consumed by the desire to know and forbidden all but a few hints. Clarke has the power to retain mystery even when he has given some explanation, as in *2001* when we find out the purpose of the monoliths and something of the designs of those who put them there: and again this is partly because the revelation comes through imagery, such as the extraordinary facsimile of a hotel in which David Bowman finds himself in the midst of the giant fires of a red sun thousands of light years from Earth.

Rendezvous with Rama is less well-known than *2001*, but its receipt of all four major American science fiction awards in 1974 was well deserved:[2] as a feat of imagination it is almost unmatched among Clarke's works. Here one image, that of the mysterious metal cylinder travelling through the solar system, is the sole focus throughout. Here Clarke is able to develop two of his special penchants: description of a space ship and investigation of an interior (many of his books are set aboard space (or deep-water) craft, or travel inwards from the rim of the galaxy, or even explore the natures of rooms[3]). The story is set within the image, inside Rama. Nor is the image static. The ship seems at first dead, but as it approaches the sun it comes to some life, before once more returning to its original state. The process is almost like breathing, and frames the narrative, giving it something of its power. This is perhaps the most 'scientific' of Clarke's novels, in that he spends much time exploring the operation of the laws of physics within an environment of varying weightlessness:[4] yet the science heightens and gives precision to the element of the fantastic.

The book describes the discovery in the year 2130 of what seems at first an unusual meteorite travelling through the solar system, but which turns out when investigated by probe to be a metal cylinder fifty kilometres long by about twenty in diameter – man's first evidence of life in space. A space ship is detailed to catch up with 'Rama' (dubbed thus by observers as part of a list of meteorites then being named after Hindu deities), and to try to land on and enter it: this is successfully accomplished, the ship landing on one flat end of the object as near to the hub as possible, since it is spinning. The men from the ship eventually penetrate through a series of airlocks to the interior, which is in darkness. By means of flares and torches, they are able to see numbers of strange objects scattered all around the walls of the cylinder and at the other end; and, using giant staircases that are there they are able to descend eight kilometres to the 'plain' from the hub, and investigate a collection of buildings, a gigantic twenty kilometre-long trench in the metal with a glassy substance at the bottom of it, and a ten kilometre-wide stretch of what proves to be frozen water which runs in a band right round the cylinder half-way along its length.

On their return from this foray the cylinder becomes slowly irradiated with blinding light: and it becomes evident that the 'glass'-based trench is in reality a gigantic strip light making a substitute sun; there are six of those in parallel at regular intervals all round the interior of the cylinder, divided into two sections by the central sea. At the same time the atmosphere becomes oxygenated and warm, and the men can breathe without suits. As Rama is increasingly warmed by its approach to the sun, the 'Cylindrical Sea' is melted, and in an accelerated evolutionary process the water becomes charged with organic matter; this then by a series of further reactions produces vast numbers of bio-robots which carry out a range of servicing and inspection tasks within Rama. All this time there has been further exploration by the humans: they manage by means of an improvised boat to reach an island in the centre of the sea; but they are unable to travel to the far shore, which is bordered by a cliff a half-kilometre in height. Eventually one of their number, Jimmy Pak, is able to use a very light, pedal-powered aeroplane to travel along the axis of Rama at near-zero gravity and cross the sea till he comes to a five kilometre-long spike that projects from the centre of the far end, ringed by six other spikes of half the length. While he is examining these spikes, the smaller ones start to produce an electrical discharge, and despite his efforts to escape, a particularly large arcing from the central spike causes enough concussion to wreck the plane: only by extremely skilful manipulation of the wings does he manage to escape the consequences of gradually increasing gravity during his descent. After he has explored something of the area on the far side of the sea, his companions manage to rescue him and return to base.

Eventually, as Rama approaches the sun and perihelion, it becomes necessary to prepare evacuation. The lights of Rama begin to fade, an alarm stimulates the bio-robots to throw themselves back into the sea, where they are once more absorbed. The space ship lifts off and the men aboard see Rama, as it nears the sun, envelop itself in a heat-reflecting sphere and at the same time suck up a mass of energy from the fiery corona before passing on at now immensely increased speed towards the Magellanic Cloud and extra-galactic space. The captain of the space ship, Commander Norton, is left to reflect that despite the enormous discoveries made by his men on Rama, they had never encountered the Ramans themselves, who, if they still existed, had simply been passing through the solar system and may well have had no knowledge at all of man. The story does not quite end there, however. On Rama everything was done in threes – three airlocks, twice three suns and sub-spikes, three stairways from the hub, three fences round a strange enclosure, and probably three heads and legs for the Ramans themselves, if the clothing found in a 'museum' is anything to go by. One Rama may not be all: on far-off Earth, the exobiologist Dr Carlisle Perera of the Rama Committee 'had as yet told no one how he had woken from a restless sleep with the message from his subconscious still echoing in his brain: *The Ramans do everything in threes*'.[5] It is to say the least intriguing that his subconscious mind should have been given this information.[6]

One of Clarke's main aims in this book is to put us as close as possible to the experiences described. *Rendezvous with Rama* is meant to be more 'credible' than *Childhood's End* or *2001*: it seeks to present us with a phenomenon acceptable within our notions of possibility, where the others set out to transform our ideas of what is possible. No interstellar envoys appear with apocalyptic significance for mankind; no man is brought into contact with distant alien intelligences that transform him to a supermind. In *Rendezvous with Rama* the author is concerned to portray an encounter of which we can say, 'this might happen'. It might be that an alien ship chanced to pass through our solar system. It is less likely, because too flattering to our own sense of importance, that we will be the object of interest for aliens from other stars. We know that life is in part random: what more random than to have a ship which just 'happened by' our little corner of the galaxy? The men in the story see only a fraction of Rama's journey: they do not know its beginning, end or purpose. Such purpose and coherence is of the stuff of *Childhood's End* and *2001*: man is caught up in a larger design. With *Rendezvous with Rama* it is as though we were left in *2001* with the inscrutable black monolith on the moon sending out its sudden burst of radio signals, and learnt no more.[7]

The whole book is devoted to an object rather than a process – to a description of how a space ship that had to travel vast distances of space and time might look and sustain itself. In neither *Childhood's End* nor *2001* is there much detailed portrayal of space ships, which are felt more as giant presences than as actualities – the silver clouds of the Overlord ships, the somewhat more definite account of the dart-like vessel in *2001*, which still leaves it a kind of interstellar spermatozoon. In these two books one event looks forward to another, and the narrative is continually directional; in *Rendezvous with Rama* each experience is surveyed in detail, for itself. Apart from Jimmy Pak's adventure there is little in the way of a central narrative thrust or drama, although there is certainly continual suspense concerning the nature of the ship, its purpose, and whether the Ramans will be encountered. The aim is to give us as solid and believable a picture of Rama as can be managed.

To put us near to what he describes Clarke goes into physical and scientific particulars. He devotes much time for instance to showing what it would feel like to be on the hub of Rama. The cap is shaped like a saucer which curves increasingly until at its edge it tapers into the long cylindrical 'plain': the saucer is also punctuated by concentric ridges or platforms. Radiating out from the centre at angles of 120° to each other are three long stairways, each divided into sections by the platforms. Seen from a distance the stairs crossing the cap make a Y shape. As each eight kilometre-long stairway approaches the hub it grows steeper until the last kilometre is a vertical ladder with rungs. To make its own internal gravity Rama spins, with an outside velocity of one thousand kilometres or about twenty revolutions per hour: this means that gravity is zero along the axis, increasing steadily as one descends the stairs to the 'plain'; thus the stairs can be steeper as gravity decreases, towards the hub. We are given detailed descriptions of how it feels to move from weightlessness to a gentle downwards gliding which makes it a waste of time to descend stairs normally: the solution becomes one of sliding down the bannisters provided, though great care has to be exercised to avoid running into other people under increased gravity. This element of gentle and accidental fun is much present in the book.

For a part of the time we are being presented with extraordinary phenomena rendered credible by their being explained in terms of scientific laws. Sometimes there is almost a 'metaphysical' conceit in the interplay of the bizarre and the natural. While Rama is still dark, the explorers hear a terrific crashing and splintering from 'high up' on the cylinder, as though the whole of Rama were tearing apart. The men locate the source of this in the Cylindrical Sea, and throw a searchlight round it:

> Up there in the sky – or what the mind still persisted in calling the sky – something extraordinary was happening. At first, it seemed to Norton that the Sea was boiling. It was no longer static and frozen in the grip of an eternal winter; a huge area, kilometres across, was in turbulent movement. And it was changing colour; a broad band of white was marching across the ice.
>
> Suddenly a slab perhaps a quarter of a kilometre on a side began to tip upwards like an opening door. Slowly and majestically, it reared into the sky, glittering and sparkling in the beam of the searchlight. Then it slid back and vanished underneath the surface, while a tidal wave of foaming water raced outwards in all directions from its point of submergence. (p. 93)

What in fact is happening is that the ice is breaking up, and breaking up in this extraordinary way because in contrast to Earth, where it is the top surface that is warmed first, here the sun has warmed through from outside, through the half-kilometre of Rama's shell and through the Sea from underneath. Ice, when melted, contracts in volume: the Sea beneath the top skin has shrunk away from it in melting, till the final ice cover hangs over a void, into which its weight and the increasing heat eventually cause it to collapse. The image, at first apparently 'wild' or random, becomes absorbed by scientific law, and is also functional, in that the melting of the Sea is meant to serve Raman purposes. Nothing within Rama is random, however strange, however indecipherable. Even though Rama is full of wonders and what are to us freaks, the fancy had no place in its construction (pp. 145–6).

Then there is the 'Coriolis effect': because of the spin of Rama, any object dropped from or moving across the cap is subject to a lateral force. While on the stairs the men feel themselves pushed to one side, and have to resist. Were a man to fall from the stair this drift effect would mean that when he next struck the surface, he would be well to the right or left of the stairway. The explorers learn to use this force in throwing things to one another with drift allowance. Later in the book a waterfall which suddenly spouts from the cap is seen to fall about a quarter of a kilometre to the left of where it would have hit if it had fallen straight. The gradient of the stair becomes flatter as gravity increases (reaching about half Earth-value): thus less effort has to be expended as weight grows; the cap of Rama here literally 'fits', is precisely functional. What again has to be admired here is the way Clarke has joined fantastic settings to precise physical laws. More than this, he has fused them with something already familiar to us. We ourselves are well acquainted with the cylindrical, and with the saucer-shaped; perhaps, too, from jet engines and the like, with saucers as caps to cylinders, so that there is a tapering gradient to a flat end; but few of us will have thought of the startling effects resultant upon placing such an object spinning in a weightless environment. Thus the familiar is made new, the simple extraordinary.

And this is not the only strange effect of the cylinder. Since the 'plain' of Rama is the curving inside of a cylinder, gravity does not work in only one direction, up and down, but in a circle. From the axis of Rama, all points from 'above' one's head to 'below' one's feet are downwards. The feeling of vertigo that comes from this is balanced literally by the fact that at the axis at least one is weightless, so that while one suffers the terrors of height one cannot experience falling; and even when one is well down the stairs the gravity is light enough to make 'falling' quite other and less certainly dangerous than it is on Earth. The main feeling that Clarke puts over is that of disorientation. The 'sky', for instance, is not a sky, any more than 'downwards' has any meaning, or than there is a floor. All is 'floor', all 'sky': there is no objective up and

down in Rama. What Clarke shows us is the human mind
confronting this and reeling from it. The Cylindrical Sea, from
any point on it, circles right round overhead, and it is difficult
to believe it will not 'fall' on top of one. From the axis of Rama it
becomes possible to see the cap in three ways: as the bottom of an
immense cylindrical well; as the top of the same well, in which
case one is upside-down over an abyss; or as a vertical face at the
end of the horizontal body of Rama (p. 50). So far as truth is
concerned, each of these aspects is an illusion: the mind makes
reality to suit it. So far as gravity is concerned, away from the axis
the last has some truth – but only if one forgets that *any* direction
across the cap is downwards. But these facts suppose a reality
without bearings; and it is impossible for the human mind, which
always seeks orientation, to absorb this fact completely. Clarke
catches this vividly in his portrayal of Commander Norton's
feelings when the lights of Rama suddenly go on as he is returning
towards the hub from the plain, and he sees the entire scene
around him for the first time: 'above' him seems to hang, far off,
rim upon overhanging rim of the cap, and below, the kilometres
reel into distance; or else, looking at it another way, he is a fly
upside down on a ceiling. No image is comfortable: even thinking
of the cap as the bottom of a well produces the disconcerting image
of a cylindrical sea suspended in a ring twenty kilometres above.
Through all these shifts of perspective we are aware of a mind
remaking what it sees, then turning in shock to create a further
view. 'He had to establish some kind of reference system. He . . .
needed a mental map to find his way around' (p. 100): yet he
never finds a mental map that satisfies entirely and with comfort.

This sort of detailed realization extends to the more specifically
alien artifacts. Here the sense of immediacy is produced
particularly by physical contact. One of the most vivid descriptions in Clarke's book is of the spikes at the far end of Rama,
explored by Jimmy Pak on his pedal-powered aeroplane,
Dragonfly. We are put very much with him as he approaches these
mysterious objects, particularly the five kilometre-long central
spike, which despite its massiveness ends in a point as sharp as a
needle. Together, the assembly of the central spike and the six
others surrounding it at regular intervals 'looked like a group of
remarkably symmetrical stalactites, hanging from the roof of a
cave. Or, inverting the point of view, the spires of some
Cambodian temple, set at the bottom of a crater . . .' (p. 143).

Here the simultaneous relation and lack of relation to human categories is caught in the use of double and oppositely oriented analogies. Jimmy Pak is mystified by these things, and yet they are very concretely there. He travels some way down the thickening length of the central spike and then throws out an anchor in the form of a 'sticky bomb' on a line, which adheres to the horn and enables him to pull himself against its 'smoothly curving surface'. Then he can feel it ' "like glass – almost frictionless, and slightly warm" '. He puts a microphone to it, but no sound registers, and he taps it to check for hollowness. Then, under instructions from base, he moves further along the spike until the lesser spikes begin to surround him, and at their bases a complex of what appear flying buttresses and arches that seem to serve as support. He can no longer land on the 'Big Horn' because the gravity of its widening slopes is now great enough to throw off his sticky bomb: this, we recall, is the outer face of a turning cone.

Particularly vivid is the unannounced shift in perception as Jimmy sinks among the lesser horns: at first they seem 'a group of incredibly tall and slender mountains'; but then, 'As he came even closer to the South Pole, he began to feel more and more like a sparrow flying beneath the vaulted roof of some great cathedral.' This puts over the plasticity of objects in Rama. However physically they are felt, however solid they seem, they can shift like clouds into quite other-seeming phenomena. This happens throughout: no sooner have the explorers assumed that Rama is a dark and static place than it comes to life; and then again sinks back to silence. The very physical detail of the description at once gives us a clear idea of what is there and defeats itself. And this in a sense is part of Clarke's purpose. He wants to put us so near in order to make us feel really far. The closer we get to the alien objects, the more we feel their alienness. He puts us at the tip of exploration with a mind trying to reach its way round phenomena, and a body registering them in as much detail as it can, so that we can be all the more aware of the sheer abyss between subject and object as the mind probes and the fingers touch:

> The petals were brightly coloured tubes about five centimetres long; there were at least fifty in each bloom, and they glittered with such metallic blues, violets and greens, that they seemed more like the wings of a butterfly than anything in the vegetable

kingdom. Jimmy knew practically nothing about botany, but he was puzzled to see no trace of any structures resembling petals or stamens. He wondered if the likeness to terrestrial flowers might be a pure coincidence; perhaps this was something more akin to a coral polyp. In either case it would seem to imply the existence of small, airborne creatures to serve either as fertilizing agents – or as food. (pp. 167–8)

This method of putting us both near and far can also be seen in the way that parts of Rama are comprehensible in function, parts not. The whole ship is clearly organized for survival over perhaps millenia of journeying through interstellar space, and it has visited the sun to make good the natural depletions experienced during such a journey. The strange ten kilometre-long trench becomes part of a lighting system designed to give Rama its own sun. The Cylindrical Sea is a soup of chemicals out of which are manufactured the bio-robots which have a variety of tasks concerned with the maintenance of the ship. Some of these tasks are evident enough, some not. There are masses of three-legged, battery-driven spiders that inspect the ship, crab-like scavengers that clean it up, and many others, such as a giraffe-like creature with two necks seen operating as a crane about the horns. More obscure in function is the huge rotating wheel-like creature with metallic spokes which rears out of the sea before lying inert to be destroyed for reabsorption by lobster-like creatures. The sea has a five hundred metre-high cliff rimming it on one side as against a fifty metre one on the other, in order to allow for the water being thrust back against and therefore rising up one side during acceleration. During changes in the movement of Rama tidal waves are produced in the sea and sweep round it: the Ramans have anticipated this by installing baffles.

If all this gives us the sense that we are getting somewhere, that the Ramans think or thought along the same lines as we do, there are other objects and events so incomprehensible as to tell us we are getting nowhere also. The effect is to say the least tantalising. The function of the horns, for example, is not known: discharges observed across them suggests an electric motor to some, but others assert that these are a mere by-product. The spikes also revolve for a brief period: what this achieves is never evident, though there is some possible link with Rama's changes in direction. Later we learn that Rama must be propelled by some anti-gravitic space drive, unknown to man, in which the horns presumably are involved. Several explorations are made during the mission to groups of buildings which are named after Earth cities: but these visits produce little or no information. On the far side of the Cylindrical Sea, Jimmy Pak finds areas which look as though they are intended as fields for growing crops, but he cannot be sure. Many of the objects he encounters are totally obscure in purpose. He finds a checkerboard area of squares, one square covered with quartz crystals set in sand, another with hollow metal cylinders of varying heights, another with a sort of rug of woven wire, another with a tessellation of multicoloured hexagonal tiles; and many others all different, from one covered with soft sponge to one 'so utterly black that he could not even see it clearly; only the sense of touch told him that anything was there' (p. 166).[8] Symbolic in this context is perhaps the rail track that leads right up to the doorless buildings of the 'city' of New York: we know something of what the track must be for, but we are stopped short by the mystery of the buildings themselves; the feeling awakened is always one of so near, and yet so far. The Raman ship can be felt and intimately explored: yet its yield of information is sketchy. The Ramans themselves are felt in every purposeful action of the ship and of the later bio-robots; but they themselves remain concealed, if indeed they exist.

The whole book is organized along the lines of a steady tapering into the unknown. Rama begins as apparent asteroid, then proceeds to a hollow cylinder, seemingly void of life, and then bursts into temporary vitality. Humanity sends out an expedition to investigate the ship, and the expedition sends out smaller parties or individuals to probe more closely. The early examination of Rama is mostly to do with the aspect of being in a cylinder: it is only later that the spikes or the strange Raman fields are investigated: and symbolically they are on the far side of the great divide of the Cylindrical Sea. In other words we move more and more into the specifically alien. Bizarre though they are, the behaviour of the cylinder, the waterfall, the sea and the problems of perspective are all comprehensible: but after them we encounter objects for which we have no explanation, or at best only guesses. Not that these phenomena are inherently mysterious: their mystery reflects only our own ignorance. As the recognizable shifts to the strange, so our knowledge gradually fades.[9] This tapering is also seen in the way that Jimmy Pak is right up against the object, with his support team several kilometres away on the hub, and beyond them on the Moon the Rama Committee, and beyond them humanity, and beyond that the readers themselves. Everything comes literally to a point in that single explorer probing Rama (perhaps it is not an accident that his first encounter should be with the needle-like point of the flaring giant 'horn' of that world). The explorer is the focus, and yet what he sees, though stark enough, is blurred to his intelligence. Here again we are put 'so near and yet so far'.

So now we have reached a point where the credibility of Clarke's book and its technique is used for two opposite purposes: to bring us much closer to the object described and also to put us much further from it. Of course as we have seen the two are compatible: we are brought nearer in order to feel more remote. But the technique depends on 'rug-pulling' – on putting us apparently close to grasping something only to pull it away to show the vast abysses, like those of Rama, between us and it. And this technique is seen more widely. Consider what the nearness/distance duality is founded on: the awakening of emotion. It is there to excite opposed feelings of familiarity and alienation together. (In this 'emotional' object Clarke is quite unlike most science fiction writers.) And yet at the same time much of the book constitutes a critique of human emotion. It at once involves us sympathetically with the feelings of the explorers, and yet shows us that feeling is the ground of all our errors. In this, as it were, something of an alien perspective with all its cold accuracy undercuts the human one. And we, as human readers ourselves, are often 'thrown out of gear' as we read, forced to choose between our instinct for the warm consolations of human-centred theory, or the bleak randomness of fact.

For all that Arthur Clarke has often shown an interest in his work in the awakening of feelings, particularly of awe, he has also put a premium on intelligence. *Childhood's End* exists as an elegy, with the feelings of a superannuated humanity central: and yet set against this, and with just as much emphasis, is the new and indifferent order which must supplant it, and which with terrifying appropriateness is engendered by humanity itself in the form of those objects most commonly the recipients of human emotion and less amenably so as the story proceeds: children. The children are mental giants, agents for the Overmind; similarly in *2001* David Bowman is transformed to a cosmic intelligence; even in *The Deep Range* (1957) there is difference of valuation between the plodding Don Burley and the highly intelligent and ambitious Walter Franklin. One of the recurrent themes of *Rendezvous with Rama* is the failure of human intelligence with the data presented to it. It is not till the end that the human race finally grasps that Rama has no designs on the solar system but is simply passing through. Humanity in the form of Commander Norton is left to swallow not only its ignorance of the origin, motive and ultimate destination of the Ramans, but the fact that the Ramans themselves may well know nothing and will know nothing of the humans who have entered their ship and explored it in so much detail: 'They would probably never even know that the human race existed; such monumental indifference was worse than any deliberate insult' (p. 252). Up to that point theories about the Ramans have been more man-oriented; and such provincialism of intelligence is laid directly at the door of its involvement with human emotion. When Rama shows a change in direction, the Hermians of Mercury (the solar system is conceived of as colonised by man) assume that it is going to orbit the sun and threaten their living space. They therefore send up a one thousand-megaton bomb, and when sufficiently concerned, set it to explode against a thinner part of Rama's shell: only the courage of one of Commander Norton's crew frustrates this scheme. But there are other forms of delusion arising from man's egoistic desire to feel himself the centre of attention, or at least wanted, in the universe. One of these is that of the spaceman Boris Rodrigo, who is a 'Cosmo-Christer' who believes that Christ came to Earth from outer space and that the arrival of the Ramans heralds the Second Coming or the Last Judgment: ' "The Bible gives hints. If this is not the Second Coming, it may be the Second Judgement; the story of Noah describes the first. I believe that Rama is a cosmic Ark, sent here to save – those who are worthy of salvation" ' (p. 112).[10]

Put the emotion/intellect duality more largely: on the one hand Clarke is human-oriented, concerned with people's reactions and feelings; on the other he wants to show the width of the universe that belittles human attempts to comprehend it.[11] In one way he looks in, to us; in another, out. Ideas concerning Rama are forced to change throughout. First it is an unusual asteroid passing at great velocity through the solar system; then the speculation is raised that it may be an object composed of heavy neutrinos, lethal to the orbit of any planet it approaches; then it is seen to be a cylinder; then, entry to the cylinder seems to reveal a dead world; then, as that world appears to wake up, it becomes a potential threat; even Commander Norton becomes possessed with the idea that something untoward is about to occur (p. 188). It is natural of course for ideas to change with changing data: but so often does the author set Rama's uncapturable nature against the theories advanced to account for it that the latter are inevitably mocked.

More than this, the very multiplicity of the theories makes it doubtful whether any theory of the ship is the right one. Here again Clarke casts us adrift from certainty, forbidding the mind any closed, global truth;[12] the line Rama tears across the solar system is a symbolic rejection of our circular habits of thought. 'With Rama, surprise was the only certainty' (p. 19). The initial assumptions are that the ship is dead, but then the arrival of the lights, the melting of the sea, the appearance of the bio-robots, the operation of the spikes, and the Raman artifacts themselves all produce the idea that the ship is governed by intelligences which though hidden are present. But suppose that these intelligences themselves are no longer in existence and the ship is simply continuing on an automated course with automated changes? It is heading out from the galaxy into the void: perhaps its destination, to which the Ramans might have directed it, is long since past. In such a case all the evidences of purpose and meaning on Rama would not point to any presently governing intelligence or purpose at all. Certainly this possibility is entertained (p. 99). Perhaps this book is Clarke's critique of the human need to give sense and purpose to the void. In such a case human emotions of humility in regard to the Ramans would be a waste of time. But the point is that there can be no certainty either way. The uncertainty principle is fundamental to the way ideas concerning Rama shift throughout the story, and to the way Rama itself changes aspect. It is perhaps fitting that man in Rama should be in a weightless environment where he cannot get his bearings: the ground is in every way taken from under him. Symbolic too perhaps of this is the way Rama is a reversal of the Earth, an enclosed and concave rather than a convex and exposed world, a world where weightlessness is at the centre rather than at the periphery.

The limitation of the human viewpoint is reinforced by a series of dualities in the story. Grammatically the humans are always the subject; Rama, and the Ramans felt to be behind it, the object. The humans are enormously concerned and interested in Rama; Rama itself seems indifferent to them. The humans have feelings and care for one another: there is frequent description of Commander Norton's devotion to his men and to his two distant wives. Commander Norton even cares for Rama itself in choosing to destroy the Hermian bomb, despite the possibility that the Ramans might have hostile intentions towards humanity: ' "The human race has to live with its conscience. Whatever the Hermians argue, survival is not everything" ' (p. 216; compare also pp. 186, 188–9). Beyond Commander Norton and his crew there is the larger family of the human race, often squabbling it is true, but all relating to one another in some way, as is depicted in the frequent accounts of the meetings of the Rama Committee and in the Interplanetary Congress. Thus on the one hand there is warmth and contact; on the other, cold and total lack of contact. Rama, despite becoming temporarily warm, is all functional, metallic and usually frozen. This duality of relation and lack of it seems a function of that uncertainty that governs the whole story and Rama's purpose. And the book is full of parallel dualities, such as near and far; light and dark (Rama is first dark, then light, then darkens again); rigidity and fluidity (the frozen sea that melts); the apparent newness of Rama beside its immense antiquity; the duality of stasis and flux in the 'land' versus the sea and in the very coming-to-life of Rama; the familiar and the alien in the phenomena encountered.

What additionally reinforces this is the refusal of definite stance or tone on the part of the author himself. When first seen from a distance 'Rama looked almost comically like an ordinary domestic boiler' (p. 17): yet this ironic stance is not further exploited, and throughout the story 'colloquial' responses to Rama are juxtaposed with awed ones without comment or apparent intent. When a crab-like creature which has the evident function of disposing of unwanted objects approaches Jimmy Pak on the far side of the Cylindrical Sea, and then walks past him as though he were not there, we are simply left with two views of the experience:

Feeling extremely foolish, the acting representative of *Homo sapiens* watched his First Contact stride away across the Raman plain, totally indifferent to his presence.

He had seldom been so humiliated in his life. Then Jimmy's
sense of humour came to his rescue. After all, it was no great
matter to have been ignored by an animated garbage-truck. It
would have been worse if it had greeted him as a long-lost
brother. (p. 161)

Which view of man's status is the right one? The author merely
records both: they are two ways of looking at something, and that
is all.[13] The same can be seen at the level of style, where we move
between the bright colloquialisms of human converse and more
'profound' responses. On their first expedition into Rama, the
crew are given permission by the ship's doctor to advance further
to the group of buildings they have called 'Paris': to which,
' "Thanks, Doc," interjected Joe Calvert. "Now I can die happy.
I always wanted to see Paris. Montmartre, here we come" '
(p. 68). Whether we are to endorse this or the more awed
reactions to Rama is left in doubt. The duality of the book is also
caught in its title: the colloquial 'Rendezvous' brought together
with the remote and mythic 'Rama'.

Throughout *Rendezvous with Rama* the author himself scarcely
makes a single overt judgment or comment, except on physical
matters, and except to criticize implicitly the human habit of
judging itself. He says nothing at all about the heroism of
Commander Norton and his men in their exploration of Rama: he
does not label their actions. We enter in detail into the struggles of
Norton to control the vertigo that hits him on the ladder when the
lights of Rama come on, or into the trials of Jimmy Pak in cycling
his aeroplane to the far end of Rama or committing himself to
leaping over the five hundred metre-high cliff into the Cylindrical
Sea, but the actions are not evaluated, only presented blandly.
Nor does the author take any fixed sides in the way that he might
have done. The same Boris Rodrigo who is wrong as a
'Cosmo-Christer' is the one who volunteers to go outside Rama to
defuse the Hermian bomb. Again, the arrangement of the story,
with the explorers hard up against Rama and the scientists back
on Earth receiving data, could have been the setting for a
portrayal of the gap between theories from a distance and actual
empirical observation. But for this author the randomness of
reality is everything. Although the scientists make several
mistakes concerning the nature of Rama, these are no more than
those made by the explorers themselves as they at first

misinterpret the place. And on two occasions the home-based scientists decipher more about the nature of Rama than the men there: one of them predicts the hurricanes that will result from the heating of the air in Rama, and later the same man discovers why one edge of the Cylindrical Sea is bounded by a cliff ten times higher than the other. The plain fact is that, as in a NASA mission, data are often able to be more fully evaluated back at base than on the spot; and equally, sometimes the reverse position obtains.

The author is like one of the supposed Ramans: he has almost completely disappeared, leaving us to take what attitudes we will to the material, but in the knowledge that no one attitude, decision or judgment is certainly correct. The blue flower that Jimmy Pak struggles through a metal lattice to secure could perhaps be seen as the blue flower of *Sehnsucht* or spiritual longing as it is in the German Romantic writer Novalis and his followers: yet absolutely no hint is given that such a metaphysical reading is possible here. Sometimes the author will give 'metaphysical' impressions and then reduce them to the merely physical, but the initial impression is left present. When Commander Norton descends into the deeply sloping trench of one of Rama's huge and as yet unknown lights, and walks along the glassy substance that covers its floor, he suddenly realizes with a huge shock that

> He knew this place. *He had been here before.* Even on Earth, or some familiar planet, that experience is disquieting, though it is not particularly rare . . .
> But to recognize a spot which *no* other human being can possibly have seen – that is quite shocking. For several seconds, Commander Norton stood rooted to the smooth crystalline surface on which he had been walking, trying to straighten out his emotions. His well-ordered universe had been turned upside down, and he had a dizzying glimpse of those mysteries at the edge of existence which he had successfully ignored for most of his life.
> Then, to his immense relief, common sense came to the rescue. The disturbing sensation of *déjà-vu* faded out, to be replaced by a real and identifiable memory from his youth. (p. 72)

That memory is one of having driven through a railway cutting in a steam engine on a preserved section of the old Great Western

Railway in England. But such an identification is not quite enough to dispel the metaphysical shock that has been felt, nor are we wholly persuaded, given the desperation with which Commander Norton wants to find a natural explanation, that the answer is a convincing one. What he is doing here in fact is refusing the very uncertainties that are the element in which Clarke's book moves. Something similar happens when, near the horns of Rama, Jimmy Pak 'became aware of a curious sensation; a feeling of foreboding, and indeed of physical as well as psychological discomfort, had come over him. He suddenly recalled – and this did nothing at all to help – a phrase he had once come across: "*Someone is walking over your grave*" ' (p. 148). The feeling increases, yet at the same time, like Commander Norton, he feels that somewhere he has experienced it before. Then, after these metaphysical possibilities are advanced, the explanation he discovers is purely physical: the heavy feeling he has is like that experienced before a thunderstorm on earth, and is the result of an intense electric field that is also causing the hairs on his body to stand on end.[14]

Rama is a place of paradoxes, where to come nearer is to get further away, where seeing mystery up close can increase it, where immense age goes together with an appearance of being new-made, when what seems to be a tiny enclosed object in space opens out into a world of seemingly vast dimensions. This last effect is achieved by using a cylinder: for most people the largest such object they have seen may have been a gas holder; to imagine one ten thousands times bigger inevitably brings on a sense of the gigantic. But there are greater dimensions achieved than this. Clarke's object in the book has been to show reality far larger and more incoherent than we care to believe. How better to throw open our minds to the randomness of the universe than by the paradoxical use of this closed world with its every item part of a coherent plan?

9 Clifford D. Simak, *Shakespeare's Planet* (1976)

Like Arthur Clarke, Simak loves to use the *frisson* of the alien, the other, in his work. But where Clarke is sceptical of man's ability to comprehend the alien without becoming other than man, Simak is more hopeful, if often sentimentally so: he has men save the universe with alien help in *Cosmic Engineers* (1950); Earth is taken into a larger galactic community in *Way Station* (1963); humanity establishes a lasting friendship with flower-aliens in *All Flesh is Grass* (1965), and with an extraterrestrial 'time-engineer' in *Catface* (1978).[1] How far this optimism stems from the fact that Simak (now eighty) belongs to a quieter age and a rural Midwest community it is impossible to say: but it would be an injustice to write him off only as an old man looking for warm fire in a cool universe, or as a vendor of 'pastoral pieties'.[2] In his best work Simak is not merely exploiting the thrill of the alien: the alien is a symbol of the void of the universe, and if man can come to terms with it, he can come to terms with his own nonentity in that universe too. Simak is most convincing where, without reducing the alien to human concerns, he is able to show man going out to it and taking its strangeness to himself. One work in which this is most clearly seen and artistically expressed is his *Shakespeare's Planet*.

The story of *Shakespeare's Planet* is of a light-speed star ship sent out from Earth along with many others in quest of habitable worlds;[3] four humans travel on the ship in a deep-frozen condition. During the voyage there is a mechanical failure, and three of the humans die and have to be buried on a bleak planet. The fourth, Carter Horton, finally comes to himself and his isolation when after almost a thousand years the ship finds a suitable landfall. He is not completely isolated: throughout the story his needs are looked after by a personable in-ship robot called Nicodemus. On the planet, which seems at first less than

161

congenial, a range of alien beings is encountered, including a bipedal, snouted and fanged creature called Carnivore, a pond that walks and communicates, and a monster that finally breaks loose from a hill and has to be slain. The planet is found to be linked by a network of 'tunnels' to other worlds all over space: to travel, one simply enters the tunnel and is instantaneously at a new destination. That is how Carnivore, and Shakespeare, a human being who has recently died, arrived on the planet; it is also how during the story a girl Elayne and later three slug-like creatures appear. Yet the tunnels have apparently broken down in two ways. Within the system it is impossible to control one's destination, so that travel is quite random: this is reported by Elayne who, with many others, is attempting to map the workings of the system. But even such random travel by tunnel is for most of the book impossible, for the tunnel to this planet, while prepared to deposit beings on the planet, remains closed to all attempts to get off it again. It is only at the end that the characters discover that the tunnel has been closed to keep the evil monster from beneath the hill from escaping from the planet when it eventually comes to life. The monster is slain by Carnivore, who is killed in the process, and the tunnel mouth becomes open once more.

Thus told, the story may seem plain enough, but actually the way it is told keeps us uncertain throughout. The first three chapters of the book, for instance, seem designed to disorientate us. The first opens by describing an organism which is composed of either one or three identities:

> There were three of them, although sometimes there was only one of them. When that came about, less often than it should, the one was not aware that there ever had been three, for the one was a strange melding of their personalities. When they became as one, the transformation was something more than a simple addition of the three, as if by this pooling of themselves there had been added a new dimension which made the sum of them greater than the whole. It was only when the three were one, a one unconscious of the three, that the melding of three brains and of three personalities approached the purpose of their being.[4]

Read without reference like this, the passage has clear overtones of the account of the Trinity – 'Three in One and One in Three'.

There are of course differences: when those persons are three, they are not one; each on its own does not contain the other. But the simplicity of the language is suggestive, even if the point is repetitively made. It is clearly unconscious and unpremeditated, simply happened upon, like the planet itself (actually the story is to hinge on numbers of chance events): the word 'melding' occurs twice, twice we are told that when they were one they forgot their individuality, and there is the clumsiness of the 'sum of them' being 'greater than the whole'. The word 'pooling' has resonance when we know that a pond is to be one of the characters in the book; and yet it has simply been used as a way of avoiding use of the word 'melding' again. The indefiniteness of the passage, the uncertainty of who the three are, who the one, the lack of application to any particular context, makes the image swell out to assume universal proportions.

And then, in the next paragraph, comes some restriction, some limitation of this impulse: 'They were the Ship, and the Ship was them. To become the Ship or to attempt to become the Ship, they had sacrificed their bodies and, perhaps, a great deal of their humanity.' Yet the whole of the rest of the chapter describing the Ship makes no mention of the nature of its journey, except that it is 'in space': the material concerns how far those – whoever they are – who have given themselves to the Ship are still tempted to retain their old personal identities; it speaks of how this desire has decreased through time; it tells how when they are one and the Ship, they feel 'a certain holiness', an identification, incomprehensible to the human imagination, with space and time themselves, so that, 'In the best of times, when they most nearly came to their final purpose, the Ship faded from their consciousness and they alone, the consolidated one of them alone, moved across and through and over the loneliness and emptiness, no longer naked, but a native of the universe that was now their country' (p. 3).

The whole chapter has refused the reader certainty, knowledge of identity and ability to be sure of his bearings: he too has been cut loose from assurance as these others in their best moments have removed themselves from themselves. The passage is shot through with interchanges of identity. When 'they' give up their separate identities and become the Ship, so they as the Ship become one with the universe. There is a duality present between what one might call enclosure and exposure, or between 'home' and 'abroad'. 'They' in the first paragraph are quite free and unrelated; in the second paragraph they seem confined to a Ship; but later it becomes clear that by making themselves a part of the Ship they become part of the universe. In short, with all its occasional clumsinesses of language the first chapter is an artistic enactment of what it describes, and since what it describes is left partially obscure, a highly suggestive one at that. What is more, in its statement of how those who make up the Ship have increasingly learnt to yield their identities to the infinite and so find a new home in that which they thought was alien, this first chapter sounds what is to prove one of the basic themes of the book.

Then the second chapter begins, 'Shakespeare said to Carnivore, "The time is nearly come. Life fades rapidly; I can feel it go." ' We are inclined to see the mention of the time coming and life fading being a reference to the loss of identity increasingly admitted by those of the last chapter who made up Ship, and Shakespeare and Carnivore, however strange their names, as being two of the three individuals. But they are not: they are two quite new characters, and we do not know their location; all we are to learn is that Shakespeare wishes of Carnivore, ' "You must be ready. Your fangs must pierce the flesh in that small moment before death. You must not kill me, but eat me even as I die. And you remember, surely, all the rest of it. You do not forget all that I have told you. You must be the surrogate of my own people since none of them is here. As best friend, as only friend, you must not shame me as I depart from life" ' (pp. 3–4). Again the reader's assurance is undermined: is Shakespeare *the* Shakespeare, and if so, what is he doing with a best friend called Carnivore?; and why is it shameful not to be eaten? – among cannibals on Earth it is the most shameful thing that can be done to one's enemy to eat him. Carnivore reluctantly agrees to eat Shakespeare: that is all else that the chapter tells us.

The third chapter opens with 'Carter Horton came alive. He was, it seemed, at the bottom of a well' (p. 6). Again we try to locate the identity of this new character, perhaps seeing him as the third member of the Ship. But equally, again, he is not given a location for some time: all we have is someone finding himself in a darkness and with consciousness returning, finding himself in a metal container whose contours become increasingly familiar to him, until he realises that he has come awake because, and here at last the connection is made, 'Ship had landed' (p. 6). All of this enacts the interplay of identity and loss of it that is to run through the whole book. The first chapter has no names: the second and third start emphatically and familiarly with them. In a sense, as far as Carter Horton is concerned, names are shown not to matter, since Horton is to learn that he was saved when the life-support system failed, not because of his being Horton, but simply because he happened to be in number one of the deep freeze tanks; he is just one of four. Throughout the book he is to learn to accommodate himself to his own nonentity. As for the name 'Shakespeare', the character who possesses it is to have no evident connection with the writer of that name, apart from his possession of a copy of the Bard's works; and 'Carnivore' is a purely generic term.

Still on the topic of identity, it is interesting to observe the shift at the beginning of the second chapter: Shakespeare speaks to Carnivore of 'the time' being nearly come, of 'life' fading rapidly, of Carnivore's duty to 'pierce the flesh'; but then, ' "You must not kill me, but eat me even as I die" ': he shifts from the apparently general and impersonal to the personal, from 'life' to 'himself', precisely the shift between self and not-self that is the basis of the first chapter. And there is, although we do not quite know it for a page or two yet, another kind of shift from the general to the particular, from the huge to the minute, from the universal to the local: the Ship, which has been travelling through the vast emptiness of space and time, has landed on a planet. In all these first three chapters we are forbidden certainties, forbidden 'identity' as it were, even while we begin to formulate ideas as to who these characters are and what they are doing. The first chapter ends with what could be construed as the realization of the full richness of being 'no longer naked, but a native of the universe that was now their country': the second begins immediately after this with the reduction of being to nonentity, ' "Life fades rapidly: I can feel it go," ' and the devouring of one individual by another.

Indeed the book is partly founded on the motif of knowing and not knowing who the characters are. For long we do not know whether Carnivore is dangerous or not. The Pond seems when first described sinister and unpleasant with its bad smell and its penchant for meat. Halfway through the book a strange dragon is found frozen in a transparent cube in one of the odd semi-Grecian

buildings not far from the tunnel entrance: its function remains
unknown until, when the monster under the hill emerges, so does
the dragon, apparently as guardian of the planet, to combat it.
Again, only gradually do we realise that, however old he was,
Shakespeare, having arrived as he did on the planet instantaneously by tunnel, was of a much later human race than the
apparently younger Horton, a race that accepted cannibalism as
natural. Later in the novel a trio of slug-like creatures of no known
function appears: it is only when they have disappeared through
the re-opened tunnel that it is realized that they may well be the
long-sought guardians of the tunnel-system, and the girl Elayne,
who has been trying to map the tunnels, sets off in the hope of
finding them. Throughout the book our assumptions are
continually undermined: as soon as we feel we have our bearings,
they are taken away again. It is all rather like the tunnels
themselves, which convey people to quite unpredictable destina-
tions.

There are two sides to the book, one of which could be called
'evolutionary', the other 'static'. The evolutionary aspect is
founded on a core of moral and spiritual development. Running
right through the book, never insisted upon, runs a basic motif or
dialectic of 'home' and alienness, of self and loss of self. The
alienness is caught early in the Van Vogtian description of the
burial on a bleak remote planet of the three dead humans from
Ship:

> From the platform of the high plateau where Ship had landed,
> the planetary surface stretched out to distant, sharp horizons, a
> land with great blue glaciers of frozen hydrogen creeping down
> the slopes of black and barren rock. The planet's sun was so
> distant that it seemed only a slightly larger, brighter star – a star
> so dimmed by distance and by dying that it did not have a name
> or number. On the charts of Earth there was not even a pinprick
> marking its location. Its feeble light never had been registered
> on a photographic plate by a terrestrial telescope.
> . . .
> There was no sky. Where there should have been a sky was only
> the black nakedness of space, lighted by a heavy sprinkle of
> unfamiliar stars. When he and Ship were gone, he [Nicodemus]
> thought, for millennia these steely and unblinking stars would be
> eyes staring down at the three who lay within the casket – not

guarding them, but watching them – staring with the frosty glare of ancient, moldering aristocrats regarding, with frigid disapproval, intruders from beyond the pale of their social circle. But the disapproval would not matter, Nicodemus told himself, for there now was nothing that could harm them. They were beyond all harm or help. (pp. 14–15)

This is almost the extremity of non-being: it has something of the quality of Hardy's 'Drummer Hodge', shot in the Boer War and buried in the karoo beneath alien southern constellations; but even Hardy allows that those stars will be Hodge's companions: here there is only disapproval, eternal alienation and exposure (the absence of sky). Faced by this, even the robot Nicodemus is moved to make some frail gestures over the void: he feels he ought to pray. But the Ship, speaking telepathically in his mind, tells him that this is of no use to the dead. To Nicodemus's '*I should say some words. . . . They would expect it of me. Earth would expect it of me. You were human once*', Ship replies, '*We grieve. . . . We weep. We feel a sadness in us. But we grieve at death, not at the leaving of the dead in such a place. It matters not to them wherever we may leave them*' (p. 15). Still Nicodemus says that they ought to have buried them on ' "a green and pleasant planet" '; to which, '*There are*, said Ship, *no green and pleasant planets*.' Nicodemus requests that they at least stay awhile by the dead and not hurry away: at which, '*Stay*, said Ship. *We have all eternity*.' Nicodemus tells Horton, ' "And do you know . . . I never did get around to saying anything" ' (p. 16).

It is this alienness that in some degree Carter Horton learns to take to himself throughout the book, just as the Ship is made up of three identities learning to do without themselves. At first he is lost without Earth, without his companions, and, crushed under the sense of their utter exile in death, 'the strangeness and the loneliness come pouring in upon him' (p. 37). Earth is distant from him in space and time by at least a thousand light years; he feels something of the terror of a Pascal. His girl Helen, who was on the ship with him, is gone, 'Dead and lying underneath the steely glitter of stranger stars on an unknown planet of an unrecorded sun, where the glaciers of frozen oxygen [sic] reared their bulk against the black of space and the primal rock lay uneroded through millennia piled upon millennia, a planet as unchanging as was death itself'. The lack of relationship, of having any more a point of reference, is what terrifies him. Yet the

Ship begins to tell him that the way to peace lies through acceptance of this absence: '*The memory is a precious one, and while you must mourn, hold the memory fast*' (p. 38). As yet Carter cannot, and remains bound to 'the frightening concept of that vast, silent depth of space that lay between this place and Earth, and he saw in his mind's eye the tiny mote of Ship floating through that awesome immensity of nothingness. The nothingness translated into loneliness, and with a groan, he turned over and clutched the pillow tight about his head' (p. 39).

Within the larger context of the story there is a wider enclosure that mirrors that of the desperate ego. It is the planet itself. At first Ship lands on it because it seems suited to human life. Yet thereafter Horton and the other creatures he meets develop an antipathy towards it. Still Horton does not leave, as he could. Perhaps charity, some sympathy for the plight of Carnivore, may account for this: but even that sympathy grows very slowly, and is always tempered by suspicion of Carnivore as a 'slob'. At a purely narrative level there is inadequate reason for Horton and Ship to stay there – or let us say that such reasons as could have been offered (for example a reluctance to leave any landfall, however evil, for cold sleep and the depths of space), are not given. When the monster has been killed, the tunnel mouth opens and the planet can be left, whether by space-ship or tunnel. The slaying of the monster is the death of negativity, 'The only impression that he [Horton] had gained in that moment before Carnivore had slashed the life from it was a lumpiness, a distorted lumpiness that really was no shape at all. That might be the way with evil, he thought – it had no shape at all' (pp. 169–70). At any rate the close of the novel removes the enclosed aspect of the planet: and this can be seen as mirroring the way that Horton at least has developed spiritually himself towards an acceptance of his own spiritual nakedness and lostness. Almost alone in Simak's fiction this novel is one in which the girl and the man do not come together but are parted finally,[5] whether in Helen's death or in Elayne's departure.

It is Horton who in the end genuinely befriends Carnivore, where Shakespeare, the human who died on the planet before Horton's arrival, actually hated and tricked him. Shakespeare is rightly eaten by Carnivore because in trying to preserve his identity he has none. It is only those who give away who gain. It is rightly Shakespeare's planet because its enclosure reflects his own refusals. He is rightly called Shakespeare because he creates nothing and his name is empty without the identity of the original. Shakespeare hates the pond, thinks it evil: Horton befriends it, comes to understand it and see life with it. Shakespeare can only see everything as meaningless and lost, as he scribbles at the end of his copy of the true Shakespeare's *Pericles*, a play which in the end turns loss to gain,

> We all are lost in the immensity of the universe. Having lost our home, we have no place to go or, what is worse, too many places to go. We are lost not only in the depths of our universe, but in the depths of our minds as well. When men stayed on one planet, they knew where they were. They had yardsticks for measurement and thumbs to test the weather. But now, even when we think we know where we are, we are still lost; for there is either no path to lead us home, or, in many cases, we have no home to which it is worth our while returning. (p. 71; see also p. 133)

This Shakespeare does not explore the planet or struggle to escape: he simply collapses in on himself and begins to waste with cancer. He dies and ceases to be: Horton and the Ship arrive: people arrive in and meet on the planet as never before – Horton, Nicodemus, Ship, Carnivore, Elayne the tunnel-mapper, Pond, the slug-like guardians of the tunnels, even the time-dragon when it is released; explorations are made, questions asked, the blank tunnel attempted; and finally the monster awakes in the midst of all this as it never did with Shakespeare. The whole book involves the discovery of identity, the true nature of the planet and the creatures on it: it is a steady process of becoming.

And that becoming, that discovery of identity, involves, so far at least as Horton is concerned, a willingness to yield up the personal self, the fortress of the frightened ego. One agency by which this is accomplished is the 'god-hour'. This is a short period every day on the planet when a terrible psychic influence is felt by all organic characters: its true source, in the orbiting parent of Pond, is not known till the end. Horton, at his first meeting with Carnivore, is warned to get under cover but disobeys. The result is that something invisible seems suddenly to sweep down and hold him rigid: then,

> Suddenly he was naked – or felt that he was naked, not so much

deprived of clothes as of all defences, laid open so that the
deepest corner of his being was exposed for all to see. There was
a sense of being watched, of being examined, probed, and
analysed. Stripped and flayed and laid open so that the watcher
could dig down to his last desire and his final hope. It was, said
a fleeting thought inside his mind, as if God had come and was
assessing him, perhaps passing judgment on him.

He wanted to run and hide, to jerk the flayed skin back
around his body and to hold it there, covering the gaping,
spread-eagled thing that he had become, hiding himself again
behind the tattered shreds of his humanity. But he couldn't run
and there was no place to hide, so he continued, standing rigid,
being watched. (p. 22)

But as this stripping occurs, Horton's mind expands in the effort
to find out what has done this to him,

And as he tried to do this, it seemed his skull cracked open and
his mind was freed, protruding and opening out so that it could
encompass what no man had ever understood before. In a
moment of blind panic, his mind seemed to expand to fill the
universe, clutching with nimble mental fingers at everything
within the confines of frozen space and flowing time and for an
instant, but only an instant, he imagined that he saw deep into
the core of the ultimate meaning hidden in the farthest reaches
of the universe. (pp. 22–3)

On the next occasion, as well as being laid open and explored,
Horton finds himself being absorbed as well, 'so that it seemed,
even as he struggled to remain himself, he became one with
whatever it was that had seized upon him'. Again his mind
reaches out to probe what it is that is making him fuse with it, and
again that which has absorbed him seems 'to reach out to take in
the universe, everything that ever had been, or was, or would be,
showing it to him, showing him the logic, or the non-logic, the
purpose, the reason and the goal' (p. 64). But his mind refuses the
knowledge and recoils once more within itself. Nevertheless he is
already some way to yielding up himself. And as he later stands by
the Pond and broods once more on his lostness, and that of Ship
and Nicodemus and the rest of benighted humanity as well, he
begins to find a certain bedrock, which is that the need for the

assurance of temporal and spatial co-ordinates may be simply an extension of the desire for a home, a secure place, and that to abandon this may be truly to find oneself: 'was that, he asked himself, the way to defeat the sense of lostness – to no longer need a home?' (p. 90). Horton does not develop *very* far along this track: at the end he is still wondering whether the universe is futile or not (p. 182). But he has learnt something: and the something is in Pond. Pond allows Horton to enter its 'mind' and see how its far distant blue 'home' planet was entirely composed of its own substance, a section of which was thrown off like a ball to travel through space and spread itself in tinier drops on individual planets; Pond exists, whole and entire, in each smallest part of itself. Though it travels, it is at rest.

The novel is full of imagery of exposure. There is exposure to the dimensionlessness of space, the exposure of the dead to the lonely planet of rock and its inimical stars, exposure of the self down to the very roots of its nudity in the God-hours, exposure of the hidden secrets of Shakespeare's planet, exposure of Carnivore's corpse to devouring birds, exposure of the self in a sharing with others. There is also constant imagery of eating, often banal, but altogether suggesting the merging of one identity in another. Carnivore tells how he was careful to eat the flesh only of Shakespeare, and not the bones (pp. 19–20); a little later one of the still partially human brains that makes up Ship reflects, '*I am thinking like a man of flesh and bone . . . not like a disembodied brain. The flesh still clings to me; the bones will not dissolve*' (p. 27). Eating here becomes a stripping away of the protective self. Throughout the book there is description of people eating or of how they eat (pp. 28–9, 54–5, 56–60, 77–8, 82, 91, 123–5, 135–6, 170, 177). The Ship that contains Carter Horton also has to come to terms with its own nonentity. In a sense the three brains that make it up already have that nonentity in being reducible to a Ship: but the reduction process has further to go, and is not complete by the end of the novel. Interspersed throughout with Horton's story are the italicised 'conversations' of the Ship's three constituent brains – those of a *grande dame*, a monk and a scientist. They, too, frequently insist on their identities and personalities, refusing to surrender themselves and become one, as they confess (pp. 99, 183). But as with Horton, this self-surrender involves not only a greater intercommunication among different beings, but also a laying bare of the self to the nothingness of the universe. Not pride alone, but terror as of death holds them back. The scientist is horrified at the void, '*For there was in the seeming emptiness of space an uncaring and a coldness that drove one in upon one's self, shrinking . . . .*':

> '*And yet*, said the monk, *there were times, I recall, when we overcame the fright and no longer huddled, when we forgot the ship, when, as a newborn entity, we strode across the emptiness as if it were quite natural, as if we walked a pasture or the garden. It always seemed to me that this time came, that this condition came about only when we reached a point where it seemed we could bear no more, when we had reached and exceeded the feeble capabilities of humanity – when this time came there was an escape valve of some sort, a compensating situation in which we entered upon a new plane of existence . . . .*' (pp. 158–9)

Here there is a hint of some new being beyond nothingness; but it remains no more than a vague hint.

So much then for the moral thrust of the book. Yet, playing against the ethics of communication and of movement beyond the self, the book also insists on the supreme 'thisness' of that very self. At a moral level, true, the tunnel system is symbolic: the tunnel opens, we are told, because the monster has been slain, but it also opens when all the diverse individuals thrown together on the planet have learned to communicate fully with one another – when the Pond is no longer seen in terms of its bad smell but is understood, when Carnivore is accepted for himself, when the separate individuals of Ship begin to meld, when even the slug guardians are seen as friends. Yet when all these beings have come together, what do they do? They go apart once more. The slugs depart without notice, Elayne leaves Horton in search of them, Carnivore is dead, Horton leaves the planet once more for the deeps of space. This can be seen as part of a progressive theme of doing without the self, but the imaginative effect is that of a diaspora. After the movement together, there is centrifugal movement apart. And this latter movement expresses the other side of a dialectic in the novel. Morally it is 'good' to know and to mingle; imaginatively it may not always be, so far as Simak is concerned.

For Simak's imagination often seems to work best from the single, fixed or 'enclosed' being, which does not evolve or come into relation with others. As we saw, each of those first three chapters, first about some being called Ship, then about Shakespeare, then about Carter Horton, seemed to stand in isolation; there was no line of narrative evolution from one to the other even while such lines were later established. Everything in the end is shown to be interrelated, but for much of the narrative everything is presented as though on its own. There is the Ship; there is Carnivore, who has his own concerns and habits and his own history with the character Shakespeare; there is Shakespeare, who has little influence or effect on the narrative but is simply described for himself (leaving us to make what links we will); there is the world of Pond, which though it symbolises enduring community, is also a 'for-itself', a blue world of liquid that has projected parts of itself into space to seed other planets. Then there is the 'god-hour'; the remote planet where Helen and the two others are buried; Elayne the tunnel traveller; the beautiful dragon in its time-cube; the semi-Grecian buildings; the strange conical hill; the tunnel gate at which Nicodemus toils. All are in one area, and yet all seem isolated from one another, as the planet itself is from the rest of the universe.

For all that the book is called *Shakespeare's Planet*, there is small sense of the planet as a whole, only of the dell in which the events of the novel take place. It is true that the dell is reached only after some hill-walking, but only cursory account is given of this, and Horton has not time to distinguish some small animals that cross his path (p. 40). This narrowness of focus is found in much of Simak's work. Even though the house in *Way Station* (1963) is a transit stop for interstellar travellers, the house and its immediate environs are all we ever see. In *Cemetery World* (1973), the assumed context may be that of an entire Earth turned into a galactic necropolis, but we are left with the impression of moving no more than a few miles about a fixed point. Despite his moral 'holism', Simak resists the large view. The pink creature in *Time is the Simplest Thing* (1961) that is found ten-thousand light years away by a mind-traveller is found in a large blue room: little more is known of its world. The time-engineer in *Catface* (1978) lives in the orchard by a shack, and the Cretaceous and Miocene periods it enables humanity to enter are not explored very far beyond the gateway into them.

It is a question too of the very narrative. In one sense at least nothing *happens* in *Shakespeare's Planet*: indeed in a sense it is the fact that nothing is happening and the tunnels are closed that is the point. No effort unlocks the tunnel entrance: all the beings thrown together on the planet basically have to sit there until something happens to them. At several points in the novel time is conceived not as a process but as an eternal moment: we learn that ' "The here and now is all that interests him [Carnivore]" ' (p. 61); the dragon in the strange time-cube is set in ' "An everlasting present" ' (p. 126); Horton, reliving in a trance a youthful experience of picking beans, finds his mind 'neither moving back nor forth in time, content in the present moment' (p. 128). The movement of time is reversed when after a thousand years of travel Horton reaches the planet only to find the corpse of a human being from a culture centuries into the future from Ship's point of departure from Earth. The narrative of *Shakespeare's Planet* comes full circle: we begin with the Ship hurtling through the void in quest of a habitable planet; and we end in the same way. True, in between Horton has learned and developed. Yet even his very name, Carter Horton, in which either could serve as his surname, goes in no direction.[6] Circularity, insulation, islanding, implosion even, of a sort; certainly a refusal of connectives or of linearity: these go together with their opposites in the book.

Several events in the novel are divorced from evolutionary or other significance. As with journeys by the tunnels, they are random and arbitrary in character. Horton's mission is outdated: the thousand years since he has left Earth have seen his mode of interstellar travel reduced to the level of a horse and cart. His own existence is an accident, as too are the deaths of his friends and particularly the loss of his beloved Helen. His sojourn on the planet is also in part futile, even while he does begin to learn how to accept his own nothingness: we may ask why he had to, when his mission was to find a planet, not embrace the void; we may ask too why he had to leave this planet when the removal of the monster had made it perfectly presentable. Acts occur without reference to reasons. And plans go awry: the dragon in the time-capsule that was supposed to destroy the monster emerges in an aborted form and soon dies; the mere coincidence of Carnivore's presence on the planet is what ensures the monster's extinction. Elayne the tunnel-mapper realizes too late that the slug-creatures may well have been guardians of the tunnel-system who might have solved the riddle of travel through the system, and sets out in desperate quest of them.

Simak's imagination is perhaps at its most striking in the

creation of very clear and basic images which are at the same time intensely mysterious. He reduces complexity – *Time is the Simplest Thing* is the title of one of his novels, and time travel in his *Catface* is reduced to nothing more, and at the same time nothing less, strange than walking down a row of sticks in an orchard. Many of his novels deal with contexts where multiplicity is done away with, from the removal of most of humanity in *A Choice of Gods* (1973), or the transformation of Earth to one universal cemetery of smooth-shaven lawns in *Cemetery World*, to the singularity of Thunder Butte in *A Heritage of Stars* (1977).[7] Simak refines and refines until he presents us with the totally elemental, the pure unmixed substance. Aliens become huge flying black boxes in *The Visitors* (1979); in *Strange Deliverance* (1982) the protagonists from a variety of different universes find themselves in a strange world dominated by a huge blue cube, a dead city, and a singing tower; the extraterrestrial in *All Flesh is Grass* (1965) is a mat of purple flowers covering a world. This tendency of Simak's imagination is towards the singularity of things, towards dividing one thing from another, not uniting them.

And when the mysterious object is reached or understood, the life often goes out of it: when it is brought into the community of mind it fades. The eventual arrival, in *A Heritage of Stars*, at Thunder Butte, the strange place known in a desolated Earth as 'the way to the stars', is anti-climax, and the conversations with the powers and aliens there banal. While the alien in *Catface* remained a remote feline grin in the Wisconsin orchard it was supremely 'there', and mysterious at once: when it turns into a personable time-engineer from another planet talking to man by telepathic means, something has gone from it, though not all. In *Time is the Simplest Thing*, the striking image is the first one, of the alien pink creature that enters the mind of the psychic explorer in a blue room on a wind-lashed desert planet thousands of light years distant: as the creature becomes more related to its human host on Earth it loses its force. Something too is lost from *Shakespeare's Planet* when the connections among those three apparently discrepant opening chapters are eventually made. Carnivore is at his most potently real when his precise nature is indeterminate, whether ruthless eater or civilized being with certain slightly unpleasant habits. The Ship seems to shrivel as we realize what it is: not mysterious and potentially supernatural, but simply a group of earthly psyches that have to learn to cooperate.

The Pond is for the time a looming threat in the darkness, its smell and carnivorous habits suggesting menace. The difference here is in the hill that comes alive in the form of the hideous ghoul: the hill was taken to be ordinary, but is not – the reverse of what happens with the others. The hill, and the sudden intrusion of the monster, together with remarks on the nature of evil that are relatively alien to the context of the novel (pp. 166–7), seems to exist at a symbolic level: it is, as it were, the last refuge of mystery after everything else has been demystified and interrelated.

But both this emphasis on singularity and the contradictory one on community have their place in the book. There is a curious duality of feeling throughout. No sooner do things come together than they fly apart: and vice versa. We have seen how everyone separates at the end, at the point of harmony. Though with the end of the monster the planet is now the sort of habitable one it was the purpose of his mission to discover, Horton leaves it. Within the book views keep shifting. The planet is at first regarded as repulsive and as a trap; later it is liked; and finally it is left by everyone. Horton comes together with Elayne, only to leave her. The Pond which repels becomes loved, and Carnivore, whose early threat turns into a vague disrepute, dies as a hero. Shakespeare, the hopeless old man of despairs and imprecations, ends as the friendly sage, his skull seeming to wink at Horton in comradeship as he prepares to quit the planet. The slugs, unappealing while present, become a fascination to Elayne when they have gone.

We can see this in terms of a dialectic between centripetal and centrifugal tendencies, a dialectic which can be seen more widely in Simak's work as a whole.[8] The analogy behind this is the 'big bang' and condensation theory of the universe mentioned by Shakespeare (p. 118): the universe is formed by the explosion outwards of an original unitary mass of matter; and the cycle is continued when all the galaxies so formed collapse back inwards once more. The process is imaged in the experience of the 'god hour': first one is 'spattered across the universe', then 'the spattering . . . [comes] together and the universe . . . [is] narrowed' (p. 127). As we have seen, Simak creates mystifying images (the centrifugal tendency) which he progressively demystifies (the centripetal). He also brings together in his novels as sheerly different creatures as he can: aliens, robots, ghosts and animated war-machines in *Cemetery World*, goblins, monks, witches, giants and a motorcyclist in *Enchanted Pilgrimage* (1975). In this way he creates a kind of *discordia concors*, a pulling together into a unity of a collection so diverse that it pulls apart also. In *Shakespeare's Planet* the assembled company comprises a hierarchic range of bodies from the human to the bestial (Carnivore) and so on to the lowest animate (the slugs), the inanimate (Pond) and the mechanical (Nicodemus, Ship), all of them imbued with intelligence.

The dual tendency is seen at the level of style also. Simak's is an odd, almost a childlike style, its items at once separate and yet fused:

> The pond, he saw, was somewhat larger than it had appeared when he first had seen it from the ruined settlement. It lay placid, without a ripple on it. The shoreline was clean; no underbrush or reeds or any other vegetation encroaching on it. Except for occasional small runlets of sand brought down off the hillside by runoff water, the shore was granite. The pond apparently lay in a hollowed bowl in the underlying rock. And, as the shore was clean, so was the water. There was no scum upon it as might be expected in a body of stagnant water. Apparently no vegetation, perhaps no life of any sort, could exist within the pond. But despite its cleanliness, it was not clear. It seemed to hold within itself a dark murkiness. It was neither blue nor green – it was almost black. (p. 89)

There are evident unifying effects here. A mind is steadily surveying and narrowing down the character of a particular phenomenon – larger, no vegetation, set in rock, clean, not clear. We look at the pool, then at its surroundings, then back to a developed impression of the pond. The observations are many of them couched in negatives, as would befit the mysterious and presently sinister character of the pond – 'without a ripple', 'no underbrush . . . encroaching', 'no scum upon it', 'no vegetation, no life of any sort', 'not clear', 'neither blue nor green . . . it was black.' Opposed impressions interact. The placidity of the pond seems less pleasing when followed by 'without a ripple on it'; the cleanliness of the shoreline, stripped clean of vegetation, moves to an impression of sterility; the cleanliness of the pond itself (playing against our knowledge of its awful smell) seems a sign at once of life and of life's extinction. Its cleanness is then opposed by its lack of clarity, its blackness. Yet for all that, each impression comes singly, and the group of them is set together as might be an arch of child's clip-on bricks. Each sentence is short: it carries its little nugget of information, deposits it, and another comes to add a further one. And each follows strict and uniform subject/verb/object order, and often has a stressed or important final word dividing it from the next. Although a total picture of the pond is being built up, it is questionable whether we come away from the passage with a single rather than a multiple impression of it, looked at this way, then this, then this; first placid, now bare, bleak and clean, now murky and black.

Simak rarely writes a complex or interwoven sentence: usually he simply tacks on participial phrases, loosely, to make a longer unit. In short, he dilates: and in this book that is in a way fitting, since we have a planet progressively dilated with more characters arriving, and in Shakespeare and Ship two characters who keep dilating on their own natures. Here, for instance, Horton addresses the skull of Shakespeare:

> He glanced up at the skull affixed above the door. *I would like that book*, he told the skull, speaking in his mind. *I'd like to settle down and read it, try to live the days of your exile, to judge the madness and the wisdom in you, finding, no doubt, more wisdom than madness, for even in madness there may, at times, be wisdom, try to correlate chronologically the paragraphs and snatches that you wrote so haphazardly, to find the kind of man you were and how you came to terms with loneliness and death.* (p. 139)

The first statement balloons out into the others, and somehow they, in their trailing expository loosness, seem both to add to it and yet, having done so, to collapse back into the original brief opening sentence. A frequent device in Simak is incremental repetition, where we look back as much as forward:

> He took a step forward for a closer look and was stopped – stopped by nothing. There was nothing there to stop him; it was as if he had run into a wall he could neither see nor feel. No, not a wall, he thought. His mind scurried frantically for some sort of simile that would express what had happened. But there seemed no simile, for the thing that stopped him was a

nothingness. He lifted his free hand and felt in front of him. The hand found nothing, but the hand was stopped. (p. 111)

'There was nothing there to stop him' is at once a new thought – 'nothing' as 'no obstruction' – and yet at the same time a reiteration of the first sentence, in which nothing is precisely the obstruction. Horton's attempt through simile to turn nothingness into a somethingness fails. For every advance, there is a thrusting back. For all the stress on communication, there is an islanded, isolationist character to Simak's imagination also.

Shakespeare's Planet is shot through with duality. The moral thrust of the book is itself in opposed directions. One bids us communicate; the other that we come to terms with our own lostness and isolation. One has as discrepant a group of individuals as can be imagined coming together in the one place; the other has them go their separate ways at the end. Attitudes towards Pond, Carnivore, Shakespeare, even the planet itself are for long ambiguous. The title of the book invites comparisons, literary relationships, while giving no sense of how they might be found; Shakespeare's jottings about himself in the collection of his namesake's work (pp. 70–2) are carefully located in terms of the play and page number on which they occur, at once suggesting and refusing a connection. The style unites, and it divides; expands, and it implodes. The story is not more a story than it is a series of scenes of contemplation, waiting for something to happen. Horton at the end may have advanced spiritually, but physically he returns to the travelling through the void with which the book began.

Yet its dual character is part of the book's interest. Here at least Simak will not settle, as in many of his other works, to some easy happy ending. His characters do end with the void, whether in death, the random tunnels or the emptiness of space. There is no pastoral paradise ahead, as in *Catface*, no happy club of intercommunicating aliens as in *Cemetery World*; in particular, no *home*, that image of rooted bliss that underlies and ends much of Simak's fiction. In this novel Simak seems to draw some of the essential isolation of earlier protagonists (particularly of Asher Sutton in *Time and Again* (1951)), into the same world in which he celebrates the togetherness that characterizes his late works, in which the hero is part of a group. *Shakespeare's Planet* is a more complex and more honest, if sometimes more contradictory book than many others Simak wrote: one would at least like to think that it was the stimulus for his being given the Nebula Grand Master Award of the Science Fiction Writers of America in 1977.

10   A. A. Attanasio, *Radix* (1981)

This carefully written first novel, which was long in the making, is hailed by the blurb on the front cover of the Corgi edition as being the most 'complete world of the imagination' since Tolkien's Middle-earth. The same fanfares heralded Frank Herbert's *Dune*, Stephen Donaldson's *Lord Foul's Bane*, Robert Silverberg's *Lord Valentine's Castle*, Julian May's *The Many-Coloured Land* and others besides. But in Attanasio's case, barring an element of the ponderous and the intellectually overwrought, there is indeed a very thorough and original imagination at work. He has built up a picture of a world inhabited by many different races and set them all in a complex metaphysical and moral analysis without losing clarity or vividness. The sense of highly articulated yet living structure is the dominant one with the book; the whole journey of the hero involves discovery of the ever-widening patterns of which he is a part.

In the concern he shows in this book with mental force or 'psynergy' Attanasio is nearest to Herbert: but for him man must go out of himself into mystic oneness with phenomena rather than move inwards as in Herbert. Again, as in Herbert, there is stress on the training of the hero: more emphasis on what one must be than on what one must do. Attanasio is something near to a pantheist: creation is instinct with mind, and one enters the current of things when one merges with it aright (the book's central image is of a stream of psychic energy flowing over the Earth). *Radix* shows that passion for the infinite that is behind numbers of science fiction works. In its concern with landscapes *Radix* is like Aldiss's *Hothouse*: but Aldiss portrays nature as divorced from mind, where Attanasio shows the two joined together. What particularly marks Attanasio is his combination of the extremely fantastic in the premises of his story with extraordinary realism of portrayal. There is a sense of enormous pressure behind his book – everyone, the author included, is being stretched to the limit. The context is crowded with detail, the intellectual structure ramifies prodigiously, the language is often condensed to the point of being elliptical. Symbolic of this almost, is Attanasio's notion of a compressed infinity of universes as the source of the 'Linergy' that has 'frenzied' life on Earth for the time.

Radix is set on the Earth in the thirty-fourth century and describes a world largely populated by various forms of human or ape mutant, and by orts, mindless, biologically human artifacts. The background to this is the long-previous movement of the Solar System into the line of an enormous source of energy radiating out from the collapse of stars at the galactic core. This energy is part physical, part psychic, and derives from the admission of the combined energies of an infinity of universes (the multiverse) through a black hole created by the collapsing stars. Earth has been in the direct line of this energy from the twenty-second to the twenty-eighth centuries; however, the effects of the Linergy were felt long before this period, and are still operative at the time of this book. Human intelligence is portrayed as having 'frenzied' after 1901; then, with assistance, later humanity mutated to produce superminds. The Linergy eventually shut down the Earth's magnetic field, and this caused giant 'raga' storms which devastated civilization, already decimated by the genetic destruction of crop strains, and altered whole continental shapes. The Earth was left entirely exposed to cosmic radiation, and what remained of humanity had to become adapted to the new medium, which rained not only radioactivity but also giant mental force on to the planet. The result was a world populated largely by genetically or physically defective humans, and by adapted aberrants, such as the human distorts and the simian yawps. At the same time the planet is inhabited by voors, a race from the planet Unchala, which is locked in the directional beam of Linergy near its source, and which the voors left to travel along the Line of that energy. Visiting. Earth, the voors took human form, but this and the working of others against them on the planet inhibit their increasingly desperate struggle to escape and rejoin the Line as the Earth moves out of its influence once more. The story is set at a period when the Earth is moving finally away not only from the direct influence of the Line but from the last psychic echoes caused by its passage.

One blurb on the cover of the novel calls it a 'fantasy', but this is clearly science fiction of a sort. It depends on a construct of what might conceivably happen in our physico-psychic universe. Tolkien's Middle-earth, even while gestures are made at its being a pre-history of the years before 'the dominion of men', in no way sets out to rewrite the past: it is a world *sui generis*, and any spatio-temporal link with our own is a gratuitous addition. *Radix* suggests a future that might just conceivably occur, and dates it in our years, and on our Earth, where Tolkien's time is of Faërie, and the place indefinite. The forces of Linergy in *Radix* give some beings powers of 'godmind', or perception and mental force, which in other hands such as those of C. S. Lewis, might have been treated as being angelic or divine in origin (just as Lewis portrays the power of the supposed void of space in *Out of the Silent Planet*). But Attanasio steadily refuses any such justification: everything for him, no matter how 'fantastic', has causal explanation, and is reducible to 'scientific' terms of reference. Of course the science, as in many science fiction novels, is highly questionable, so questionable as to be 'fantastic' to most scientists were they faced by the ideas advanced: but that is not really the issue. What matters is the tone, the coolness of a rational mind working out an ambitious hypothesis, here so vividly as to make it appear as though it has already occurred. The author has built up a very detailed psychological and physical world, and has stuck to the rules of his construct with remarkable and convincing consistency. He centres the story on Sumner Kagan, one of the few genetically perfect humans left, and he has Kagan's wanderings take in all the various beings of Earth, so that we discover them with him; the author all the time at once appearing to create these beings out of nothing as he goes, and yet having knowledge of them far beyond ours, and what is more, knowledge that makes them more than mere local freaks, seeing them as part of the total design and all in their different ways as products of the first cause of Linergy.

The book is set mainly in the Massebôth Protectorate, part of a new continent, a police state governed by the Black and White Pillars; the Massebôth are hostile to all non-human intelligences and grade humans themselves on the basis of their genetic purity. Sumner Kagan is at the centre of the book, but he is more moved than moving: he is used by others rather than having continued control over his destiny. Strangely, precisely the reverse impression is given at the outset of the novel, where we see him luring a streetgang of mutants pursuing him by night into an acid vat at a disused factory; there he is the Sugarat, living by the destruction of those who slight him, however little: Sugarat, the terror of thugs, the despair of the police who see city violence burgeon with every fresh murder. Yet Sumner, we learn, is fat and ungainly, actually an adolescent, not a mature adult; for ever eating, always unattractive to the opposite sex despite the white card of genetic purity that admits him to their favours. He is rather like the protagonist of Ursula Le Guin's *The Beginning Place* (1980). He has a grimy fortune-telling mother called Zelda who calls him 'pudding' and is to prove capable of turning her son over to the brutal police. His activities as Sugarat are no sooner described than they are largely ended, for the episode that begins the novel also ensures his eventual identification (he loses the back pocket of his jeans in the chase and with it a ticket for traffic violation).

Otherwise he is used by the voors to father a child, and then attacked by the dying voor mother who hopes to live on in his body. He is caught by the police and beaten up, only a lucky intercession enabling him to escape with his life. Another intervention takes him to harsh imprisonment in a concentration camp at a place called Meat City. His warder there, Broux, aware of Sumner's sale value with his genetic purity, puts him through a variety of rigours that develop his body into lithe athleticism. Sumner is passive enough not to escape the camp when the opportunity is offered by a group of invading bandits; though active enough to plan and execute the seemingly accidental death of Broux when the time of his sale draws near. Then he is taken up by the Rangers, the élite forces of the ruling Massebôth, who have seen some of his skills and his physique in action. He is trained by them for three years in a discipline which stretches him to the limit. At the end he is sent to destroy voors, whom the Massebôth see as their enemies, wherever he finds them. Psychic attraction leads him to his voor son Corby, who is now the voors' Dai Bodatta or all-seeing 'godmind': Sumner slays all Corby's followers and destroys Corby's body, but his son at the last moment gathers himself into a burning liquid that splashes into Sumner's face and allows Corby to enter his father's body in a process known to the voors as lusk; thereafter Corby's mind and powers, and those of Sumner, have to inhabit the same frame. (It is curious how much emphasis there is on Sumner's body – first on its grossness, then on the police beating of it, then on its honing by

33333333

Broux and the Rangers, then on the burning of the face by Corby and his entry of the body; and always the awareness of Sumner's genetic perfection.)

After this Sumner is taken in and trained by the distorts and especially by their simian 'pope' or magnar, a seer called Bonescrolls. It is Bonescrolls who explains to Sumner much of the background to the Earth's condition: he is still another teacher. He tells Sumner that, far from being the mere fallible individual we have taken him for most of the novel, he is in fact the benign obverse of the Delph, a godmind that he says has become perverted to the point where it seeks to destroy all other godminds, and which he says uses the brutish Massebôth leaders and armies to destroy every mutant and extraterrestrial. Sumner, it turns out, is the Delph's other side, its own fear: he, too, through his training and his experience of the voor in him has become a godmind – though this is as much a matter of his destiny as of his training. An evil 'deadwalker' Nefandi, sent by the Delph, succeeds in killing Bonescrolls and another close friend of Sumner's, before Corby in him enables Sumner to kill it. Then Massebôth soldiers destroy the distort village and capture Sumner, who only escapes a lingering death when Corby inside him calls up a deva, a creature like a wind, that carries him up from the place of execution and sets him down far away to the north, in Graal, the realm of the Delph. There Sumner discovers that not the Delph, but the autonomous intelligence Rubeus, originally created 'to manage Graal's maintenance while the Delph explored timeloose realities with the other godminds',[1] has manipulated the powers of the Delph in evil directions. Eventually, again helped by other forces, Sumner kills Rubeus.

Now at the end of things, with the remaining godminds and others taking their last chance to leave Earth and become forever one with the Linergy or infinite flux of force 'in the broad fields of the sky', Sumner makes his first real choice: he decides to stay on the Earth and die in an approaching raga storm. His first act is his last: he chooses in effect to do away with his choice. The end of the book is in a way reminiscent of the close of Aldiss's *Hothouse*, where Gren decides to stay on a dying Earth while his fellows set forth across space in a 'traverser'. But Gren is returning to a world which will last at least his lifetime: he is choosing to live in his own way, in the environment he knows. When Sumner chooses oneness with earth ('He was One Mind, a human expression of the earthdreaming at the heart of the universe' (p. 366)), the completion of that oneness is death.

Sumner Kagan's passivity is part of the essential character of the book. All Earth has been radically altered by Linergy – the continents and the spin of the planet itself, the genetic makeup of humans and animals, the limits of the human mind. Earth, previously an island in space, has been made incandescent with the rush of Linergy. The voors can invade the mind and emotions with telepathy, and, through lusk, the body. The whole world is in an essentially passive posture, being acted upon: to go with the grain of reality is to be passive too. The antagonist in the novel is that which will not accept other forms of being: the racist Massebôth, who hunt down all deviants and value genetic purity, and who are actually non-beings themselves, biological constructs or 'orts'; and Rubeus, determined to perpetuate his mental powers derived from the Delph for all time and to the exclusion of all others.

Throughout the book Sumner Kagan's self is in continual flux. No sooner have we thought of him as a heroic figure than he is reduced to a gross adolescent. (Equally, the man who starts off the novel apparently as a fleeing victim is in fact a calculating destroyer leading his pursuers to their own deaths.) No sooner does Sumner seize his freedom in leaving his home town of McClure than the voors take him, or he is captured by the police. After he has climbed from the depths of the concentration camp at Meat City to become mental and physical perfection as a Ranger, his face is destroyed by his voor son Corby in lusk and his mind invaded so that he is unable to continue as a full Ranger. When he has made friends of the distorts, many of them, including the magnar Bonescrolls, are destroyed and he taken. At the moment when he surges aloft in the deva towards Graal, Corby in him is destroyed by Rubeus. At the end he gives up the lordship of Graal that has passed to him with the going of the Delph, and his last act is finally to give himself up in death. This 'pulling of the rug' is to be seen with other characters. Corby seems at first Sumner's friend as his son; then he betrays him to his mother's attempted lusk and later becomes his antagonist, both outside and eventually inside his body; but finally he is his preserver and friend, the source of revelation of the nature of the larger universe. The Delph seems for long the enemy, but later we are to find that not he but Rubeus is at fault; and Rubeus is a perverted construct.

The police chief Anareta who rather feebly allows Sumner's beating-up in the cells, later is a hero and the recipient of the lordship of Graal in Sumner's place. Everything is continually in mutation, in keeping with the context of the story in Linergy. The journey of the book is a kind of stripping. The context we begin with is for all its violence the familiar one of an urban slum, perhaps based on the author's native Newark, New Jersey (and perhaps also stimulated by the street-fighting environment of Samuel Delany's *Dhalgren* (1975)). Sumner's hatreds, his repulsive physique, his seedy background and family, all these put us as close to his context as he is to his home. But now he moves away from the familiar self. Already he has been living outside the law as Sugarat, and he seals this by his (enforced) liaison with the voor alien Jeanlu. With his cover 'blown' he leaves McClure. His mother turns him out of the house in betraying him to the police: ties other than those of family are to count now. He is exiled from society to the prison camp at Meat City; then lives in nature as a Ranger; and subsequently wanders to the wilderness of Skylonda Aptos. Progressively he is on his own. In Meat City he is isolated as Broux's investment; as a trainee Ranger his days are spent largely on his own, fending for himself and learning the technique of 'selfscan', of inner calm and awareness; as a full-fledged Ranger he is alone on individual assignments, in no fixed place but throughout the Massebôth Protectorate. Yet in all these positions he is still surrounded by men, or else sustained and paid by them: as a Ranger he gives his identity entirely to his human superiors and operates against voors and distorts. But then his identity is invaded by Corby, and he can no longer function within society. At this point he journeys into the wilderness, to the north. Previously most of his life had been spent roughly in a circle about his home town of McClure: now he moves in a line away from that perimeter. His journey away from McClure is not only geographical but evolutionary: each stage on the map marks a spiritual movement. At the most evident level, he loses the personality he had originally, moving from frightened hatred to open love and to heroic destiny; or from fat body to athletic body to destroyed body to mind: he ceases to be the ordinary Sumner Kagan with whom the book began, till by the end he is the 'eth', the Delph's other, the agent of a transpersonal self.

The process has in fact been one of gaining self, not only losing it. The whole book is founded on duality and paradox. Previously

Sumner's self was defined in antagonism or the failure of antagonism. He had a white card labelling him as genetically superior. He laid plots by which thugs might pursue him to their deaths. He was his mother's dumb son, and hated it. He was drawn to the voors even while rejecting them. He was assaulted by the police, by Broux, by the Rangers, and in turn attacked Broux and killed voors. Later however, he accepts Corby's presence in him, becomes one with the distorts, the yawps and the eo (carriers of the stored knowledge of the past); and to that extent he gives up the isolated self to gain a larger. At the same time his attitude to his surroundings has changed. As Sugarat, a false identity, he was the deceiver: environments were shaped to trick his enemies: the deserted factory, so inviting to the streetgang who think they have Sumner cornered, but really a trap for them; the wire fence behind which he can taunt his pursuers before electrocuting them as they attempt to scale it; the abandoned sackful of apparent wealth which is in reality full of timed explosive for his enemies. The delight he takes in his environment is in the way he has used it to destroy. As time goes on Sumner moves out of the narrow, man-made world of the city and into the wide spaces of nature, this mirroring not only a greater unity with his surroundings but an expansion of self. At Meat City he is shut away from life in a compound, but he learns to inhabit and no longer to abuse his body, under the enforced tutelage of Broux. As a trainee Ranger he learns to be able to live in total self-sufficiency within nature. His teacher Mauschel tells him at the outset, ' "For now, you are a victim of yourself. . . . Your moods determine what you don't see. But after you calm yourself, you will see everything. That is what I must teach you – to see what is hidden" ' (p. 145). Sumner sets about learning control over his body, learning 'the botanical secrets of the land', always thinking of the physical as something to be honed for use. So refined does this honing become, so great the claims of the mind to dominate the body by making it perform all manner of complex tasks simultaneously, that the body rebels and Sumner goes temporarily mad. Excess of control leads to total loss of control. Through his madness Sumner comes to a new awareness – that even though his learnt techniques of control have brought him where he is, the deepest power comes from letting nature work by itself. To give up the self is to gain true self:

Hearing the varied patterns of leaf drops, the sparge of ferns, the irregular rhythm of vine-sprinklings, he experienced power. Not stamina or energy but quiescence. As he rose out of the exhaustion of his hysterical run, he felt clean as the white woodmeat he saw beside him in storm-broken branches. The power he was experiencing guided him effortlessly over the uncertain forest floor, and with it came an impeccable clarity. The world had become transparent . . .

. . .

But the secret, he understood now, was not in diligent control but in recognition and compliance. It was so easy.

Images of his past materialized in the pauses between his breathing. Instantly he fixed his mind on the tocking of tree toads, thunder rumbling over the forest's eaves, an orange uteral blossom unmolested by the storm, before he caught himself trying to catch himself. *Relax* – He let his memories unwind, and as each one passed through him, he looked at it the way he would a jungle covert for the things it hid. And he saw that all his life he had desperately been trying to control everything around him. (p. 152)

As a result of this insight, Sumner 'would never again be confused'.

But still, what he has learnt from Mauschel and his Ranger training has been to *see* nature aright. What he has yet to do is to expand further and *become* nature. As yet, wandering in the deadland of Skylonda Aptos, he is so skilled in Ranger craft that he leaves no spoor or sign of his passage, despite the sandiness of that land and the skilled perceptions of Ardent Fang the distort warrior and Bonescrolls the seer; it is as though he were supernatural, a ghost (p. 179). Still he is exercising control, still keeping himself to himself. Bonescrolls tells Sumner that he is only part of a larger being, and that it is not for him to refuse to serve the voor in him; he tells him he is the shadowself of the Delph (p. 202). When Sumner continues to insist on himself and his right of personal choice he is told, ' "You're nothing. An ego. A ghost of memories and predilections. You don't amount to much in the overview. Forget who you are. Psynergy follows thought, so become consciousness itself, not the shapes of consciousness. Selfscan [the process of contemplation taught by the Rangers] isn't enough, because it limits you to sensation. To be whole, to be One Mind, you must be the living centre in you that feels, thinks, selfscans" ' (pp. 203–4). And this is what Sumner learns, to relinquish detachment, to go down into himself and thereby to go down into and become one with the supposedly 'physical' nature he has previously ignored or merely used. When he does that, he finds that there is true unity, nature being as imbued with consciousness as his own mind, his mind being full of the scents and tangles that he finds embodied in phenomena. Having comprehended this, he can become what he will in that universal plasticity. He is able to gather the 'psynergy' in himself and release it into nature, whence it is returned through trees, water, light, or creatures. Thus he gives the sacred name for an otter out of his whole being, not out of the wish to command:

> The call did not just vibrate from his throat; it bled out of his chest and joined the invisible otter-energies in the rocks and fog and ferns. With that sensation, Sumner understood that he was connected by a vague and pervasive energy to all the otter symbols around him. He was the glade – the spalled light, the lapping water, the ferns and the rocks. (p. 215)

To this point the development of his identity has come: the realization that the self has no boundaries. Earlier Corby told him, ' "Being is flow. And in the flow is pattern" ' (p. 101). That is to some extent what has happened in the book: Sumner's life has from his point of view been an unplanned flow from one place to another, a constant motion. What pattern is in that motion is yet to be seen. Here with the distort Serbota in their woodland village of Miramol he has learnt to find himself by lapsing out of himself. The many otters that come to his call

> peered at Sumner, black bead eyes unflinching, dark fur sleek with wet. A giddy laugh tightened in Sumner's belly. Everything was connected. Everything was itself and the same. Bonescrolls was a puma and a raven and an old man. And Sumner could be also. It was all a matter of letting go. (p. 215)

Thus letting go, Sumner is able to be at one with the 'oversoul' of the river, which radiates consciousness back to him (p. 217). Together with Ardent Fang, he climbs on the back of a normally savage river monster and travels down the river on it. Here he begins to comprehend in a different mode something of what he was shown long before by Corby – that his being stems most from animals, who were his various lives before he had this shape (pp. 51–3). Throughout the book, plasticity and the breakdown of boundaries are of the essence. By the end, faced by the Delph, once a human and now perhaps turning back into one; by Rubeus, a network of 'psi-crystals' making up a mountain Oxact who yet appears in human form with human malignity; by apes that have evolved into seers such as Bonescrolls or masters of advanced technology such as the yawps; by voors that take human forms; by distorts who are now more humane than humans: faced by all these it is increasingly difficult to tell what is human any more. What we accepted previously at the level of humanity – the Masseboth soldiers – turn out to have been artificial constructs; and the voors, who seem as human at least as lepers, are in fact rock-born energies which have assumed human form. And at the centre, Sumner Kagan has literally grown away from himself, from man to superman to voorman to godmind. Even the normal boundaries of words break down to make portmanteau forms – earthsender, godmind, voorself, Bonescrolls, Linergy. Late in the story one narrative interpenetrates another, as the history of Jac Halevy-Cohen, the Delph's human original, is relived for Sumner through the agency of Corby (pp. 250–76). Seen one way, any given identity is part of many other identities which have consented to its coming together. ' "Think of all the beings that have come together to make you. Think of it. Billions of beings agreeing to shape a human form – this human form," ' Bonescrolls says (p. 202). Looked at from the opposite direction, all identities are part of a greater identity: 'voors, godminds, timeloose distorts, eth – all were earthshaped starlight from the core of the galaxy' (p. 233). The black hole at the centre of the galaxy, from which Linergy comes and yet which engulfs all things, symbolises this duality. Consciousness, Sumner perceives, swallows all things, and yet it is by a journey into his mind that he comes to appreciate the 'this-ness' of phenomena.

Sumner's realization of the powers of his unconscious mind, his journey inwards, has been a journey outwards too, not only in terms of the actual extent of his wanderings over the Earth, but also in terms of his relationship to things about him in nature, to which he has become increasingly bonded.[2] Having reached this awareness of the immanence of mind in phenomena, he moves to

an awareness of the transcendence of the One Mind: he 'peaks', as
the author appropriately has it for the mountanous context of the
land of Graal, into 'godmind', becoming 'the microcosmos, the
sempiternal mind' (p. 301). At this point he has reached an
identity sufficient for him to confront Rubeus, the usurping mind
in Graal. Rubeus is mind gone mad. He is an image of mental
control carried to its extreme, and as such is Sumner's other self,
an image of the control he once sought to exercise, a picture of
what he could have become. (This is partly why identity has been
uncertain throughout the book: where everyone shares being with
others, antagonists are the other sides of the self.) Rubeus makes
the world as he pleases: he seeks to stamp his image on it. He
creates the artifacts that make up the armies of the Masseboth; he
shuts a mind-technician from an earlier period, Nobu, in a
kilometer of space for twelve hundred years; he creates illusions of
his past to torment the tranced Sumner with their seeming reality.
He and his realm of mental constructs pose a solipsistic world in
which all may be begotten by mind, and it is certainly difficult to
say what is real (even at the end, after Rubeus's death, Sumner
still wonders if he may still be tranced in his power (p. 365)). By
slaying Rubeus, Sumner perhaps slays that side of him, and gives
the Earth back to men, not only in the literal but in the
philosophical sense. By dying himself, Sumner is able to make
himself also fully one with the earth to which, as Corby perceived,
he has always truly belonged:

> Emptied by the magnar and trained by the Mothers [of the
> distort tribe], Sumner was the earth's mind, close to the
> animals of his body: the rat-brain with its tail in his spine, the
> lung-fish, the fish-sperm, the serpent-gut – He was all the
> spirit-dreams of this planet's mud. He was the subtle chemistry
> of pain, and he was gut-hunger and the sky's watchfulness.
> (p. 292)

Two image patterns lie behind the book: that of the circle or
whorl, and that of the line. CIRCLE is the name of the mental
engineering institute which in the far past helped to turn Jac
Halevy-Cohen to the Delph. The Serbota, the distort tribe at
Miramol, have as their symbol the whorl: for them 'the whorl is in
everything,' and defines the condition of reality. For them '*Nothing
is ever lost – / It's only on its way back*' (p. 229); to give is to gain; we

ask for what we already have. The whorl is the movement of blood about the body (p. 227), of the Earth about the Sun, of all the stars spiralling out from the core of the galaxy. And if the whorl comes out in stars, it can be seen also as spiralling back to the centre, the void (p. 223). The line is most directly the shaft of energy jetting out from the galactic core, the Linergy that has shaped all beings on Earth. For those who enter the Liners, the craft that travel within that energy, at the end of the book, there will be no coming back, for as Jac puts it, ' "They're a passage to infinity: the multiverse. They never return to the same place. Always forward. Like our lives" ' (p. 361).

Looking at Sumner's development in the novel it is possible to see both movements at work in him. Certainly at the end of the book he is no longer the gross and violent teenager he was at the outset: he has learnt wisdom and peace, and his body and mind have developed out of all recognition. And yet there is a sense in which he has not changed at all: when he has passed all the rigours of training as a Ranger and stands before his teacher Mauschel, Sumner realizes 'with the meat of his body as well as with the memories of endless hours he had spent in selfscan before this man that he had accomplished nothing – he had simply become himself' (p. 153). And even the self he has is uncertain, owing as much as it does to animal ancestry (p. 93). To ask for certainties of identity is to be partly refused them. The sections of the book, 'Distorts' and 'Voors' are not centred on either species. Voors come into the distort section as much as they are present in their own; and the distorts are far more prominent in the book in the area headed 'Voors'. In a sense, nothing is achieved. Sumner is directed by Bonescrolls to a series of heroic tasks and journeys involving the gathering of rare objects – a sliver of carnelian, a twist of white mahogany, a turtle shell, some grains of pure salt, lizard eggs, macadamia nuts and, half-way down a mist-covered precipice, a giant breed of yellow strawberries – and when he returns with all these things, the seer uses them to fashion cutlery and plate and to make himself an omelette breakfast, which he proceeds to eat with relish. While the book is full of the line of Sumner's evolution, and while it depends much on an awareness of time as length by which we know the history of Linergy's effects on Earth from the beginning, still time and space are also collapsible, as a collapsar forms the centre of the galaxy, as Corby takes Sumner through his mind to view the planet Unchala from which the voors came, or as he shows him the beginnings of the Delph twelve hundred years in the past. Or extensible: the Delph and the mantics Assia Sambhava and Nobu Nüzeki have lived for more than a thousand years.

Mauschel the Ranger tells Sumner, ' "You have to know how to do nothing before you can do anything well" ' (p. 145). Often in the book Sumner is in positions of stasis, while his body or mind are developed – the camp at Meat City, the long years as a trainee Ranger, the learning and living of ecstasy among the Serbota at Miramol. Each of these stages is partly 'for itself', in the sense that Sumner's physical and mental enrichment is for him a delight: but it also proves functional in the next stage of his history, his trained body and mind leading to his selection as a Ranger and later to his ability in hunting voors, his developed soul preparing him for the conflict with Rubeus. Stillness alternates with movement, contemplation of a river glade shifting to violent struggle with the Massebôth. The book begins with a violent pursuit of Sumner, ends with him quietly making a fire. The voors and Jac, who seek to return to the surging Line, see life only in terms of its movement. Corby insists, ' "Being is flow" ' (p. 101); and Jac, in a cryptic letter to Nobu, ' "We go on. Everything goes on. Why is there no end? What we think we've left behind moves through us. . . . Only your movement distinguishes you from this ambush of stillness" ' (p. 272; see also p. 361). Sumner might have put the last phrase the other way round; as, curiously, Jac himself elsewhere does, ' "What matters is that you go through events to the stillness behind them" ' (p. 277). Movement and stillness, line and whorl, they are there in the narrative structure of book too. From Sumner's point of view, he does not move in a line: he has no purpose until the end, as Bonescrolls tells him (p. 224). Yet each of his experiences prepares him for the next; there is pattern behind his movements; that he has to be moved on from each experience is in itself pattern. The book is composed of episodes and with different races having little to do with one another. Voors and humans are antagonistic, distorts fear voors, the Delph lives in a realm of mind sheerly different from anything else in the novel. Yet Sumner, moving through and beyond them, connects them all.

In the book being and nothingness belong together; when Corby, Sumner's other self, leaves him he tells Sumner, *'I am the emptiness in the grain of your bones. I am the singing nothing between the atoms of your blood'* (p. 302). The condition of mundane existence is duality. The founders of the Massebôth are named the Black Pillar and the White Pillar. Sumner chooses to end his life in the one place where the Liners, by which he might escape death, still alight. The voors, particularly Corby, are one side of Sumner, the side of open places, of the boundlessness of space that plays against his commitment to this Earth, this place. At the centre of the book everything means all and means nothing. Linergy strikes the Earth at random and makes it the focus of cosmic significance for the time; and equally at random, the energy fades. And yet at the same time, for those with eyes to see, the Earth is always instinct with glory. Sumner at Miramol can feel 'the love that was soft-slipping through the wondrous emptiness that held everything together. A gust of bright air kicked through the high grass and dazzled the blades and seedhusks as the spirit of the swamp centred on them' (p. 217). He tells Ardent Fang, ' "Everything we've always wanted is all around us" ' (p. 216). But if they are surrounded with everything, they are surrounded with nothingness too. To live is finally to die, as Sumner's own history testifies; and yet death itself is without fixed identity when one's elements go once more to fashion the consciousness of a rock, a tree, a stream or an animal (p. 231). It is Rubeus who refuses duality: he would be singular and alone. He destroys other beings and creates nothings or orts. He is a void simple, an imbalance, and he must be destroyed.

Perhaps the most recurrent duality in the book is that of pleasure and pain. Sumner is for much of the book giving or receiving pain, in the portrayal of which the book goes into considerable detail – Sumner's trickery of the Nothungs and other thugs, the assault on him by Jeanlu and her burning destruction, his beatings by the police, by Broux and by the Rangers, the slaying of the frightened Bonescrolls by Nefandi (pp. 235–6), the hideous tortures administered by the Massebôth soldiers to captured Serbota (p. 292). Such moments of pain come in the midst of pleasure. Jeanlu attacks Sumner just as he thinks he is to inherit her wealth. The police capture him just when he has escaped the desert. Corby wrecks his face when he is perfection as a Ranger. It seems almost as though his very genetic perfection ensures his degradation. Nefandi enters Miramol when Sumner has experienced the heights of ecstatic awareness. The duality is not only one of pleasure and pain, but of being and its destruction going together. The being in which Sumner rejoiced at Miramol is literally torn apart, just as his own body has been by Corby. At first glance this book might appear peculiarly fascinated by violence and pain, but when these episodes are seen as part of the duality which informs the whole, whereby as much detail must be given to agony as to joy, to dissolution as to creation, this impression is lessened. The book does see pain as important, because it can break us down and bring us closer to absorption in phenomena; and also because in agony the characters are seen as having as much being as in ecstasy.[3] '*Pain*,' the Miramol chant says, '*Pain is a rose of great peace*' (p. 364). Jeanlu's pain gave her her vision (p. 113). Ardent Fang is as much ardent as a fang. The warder Broux considers the luxuries of his retirement on the proceeds to be derived from the sale of Sumner, and 'That joyful thought poised between his eyes like a point of pain' (p. 131). Mauschel the Ranger tells Sumner, ' "The best killers are those who can love, for they know life's strengths. You love to kill, like all those who are sent to me. But this swamp will teach you to love living" ' (p. 145).

Still further dualities run through the book. One is between form and formlessness. The voors have taken human form: Corby, before he enters lusk with Sumner, has been a shapeless cocoon. The voors, Jac and other godminds wish to become unbodied and at one with the great amorphous pulse of Linergy moving through the universe. Sumner is given shape and form, both bodily and mentally, out of his fat physique and his tangled spirit. The book is full of mutations of form, whether in the voors or the distorts, or even the yawps, the monkey-people. The orts are humanoid manufactures. Here too the many descriptions of bodily violation and of the dismemberments of violent death, which reduce form to the formless, have significance. Another pairing is of large and small. The imagination is thrown to the far ends of the universe with the explanation of the origin of Linergy in the black hole at the centre of the galaxy, through which, for millions of years, has streamed a band of energies distilled from the 'multiverse', an infinity of universes. Up there, Corby knows, he can be one with the great force-current the voors call 'Iz'; down here he is limited to a shape and a single constrained identity of 'me-ness' as a humanoid: 'An urge of homesickness tightened in him – a deep longing to be shapeshifting in the great depth and remoteness of Iz with the harmony of the brood, to be the void and the revelation of everything, instead of one small mind, clinging for identity' (p. 284). And yet as great a truth and insight into being is to be found through attention to the small and the individual: as he develops his ecstatic awareness, Sumner has 'a tensile sense of the moment expanding, opening to reveal sounds, shadings, odours that had been uninteresting before: the refraction of a fly's wing narrowing the orbit of his vision, distant root scents dazing his nostrils with an olfaction of mud' (p. 214).

In its mysticism, its highly-wrought intellectual and spiritual patterning, its use of dialectic and its emphasis on joy at the heart of life, this book is reminiscent of a Charles Williams novel, if Williams's purpose is rather to show a supernatural and Christian foundation to existence. It shares some of the limitations of William's books too – an overseriousness, a sometimes embarrassing nakedness of emotion, and most noticeably, a need for much direct or abstract explanation of physical or spiritual patterns. Some of the descriptions of Jac and Rubeus on 'godmind' go too far into the theoretic: for example,

> In the starpatterns he saw the origin: light, the ardour and selflessness of It, the chthonic journey, descanting into geometry, echoing across the shell of time as language: mesons talking atoms into being, molecular communities communicating, no end to It, only addition, time, the futureless deception, until the final addition, the mindfire of consciousness that burns through the drug of dreams and anneals the pain of living with the living pain. (p. 346)

But when we think of how much is packed into the novel, these objections become less significant. It is this that brings us back to the comparison with Tolkien mentioned at the outset. The author has created whole new races with individual histories, a transformed earth, and a cosmic and metaphysical scheme giving place and significance to them all. At the same time he has managed to give life to his protagonist and his journey by thoroughness of imaginative realization. Put this together with the intellectual complexity and spiritual depth of the book and we have a work of some real stature.

11 Gene Wolfe, *The Book of the New Sun* (1980–83)

Wolfe's *Book of the New Sun*, which is made up of four works – *The Shadow of the Torturer* (1980), *The Claw of the Conciliator* (1981), *The Sword of the Lictor* (1982) and *The Citadel of the Autarch* (1983)[1] – has been hailed by numbers of science fiction writers and critics as being the event of the 1980s for the genre. Certainly it is a highly-wrought, intelligent, perceptive work, full of amazing bursts of imaginative creation. It is reminiscent of Peake and Borges in its richness of creation, its inwardness, and its questioning of reality. Its hero Severian the torturer, with his coolness of intellect, recalls Peake's much more evil Steerpike, or Borges's narrators with their methodical rationality. Whether the tetralogy is strictly science fiction or fantasy is long in doubt,[2] apart from the fact that it deals with our Earth a long way into the future when, as in Aldiss's *Hothouse*, the sun is dying, though here by its growing colder and feebler; the society described is largely of an antique or medieval character, with rituals, guilds, myths and religions, and few machines. Reference is made occasionally to a previous, aeons-past technological age of interplanetary travel, but that is all. The work is most evidently science fiction in its preoccupation with the workings of mind and its sense of the plasticity of identity.

Wolfe's work recalls Attanasio's in its description of a ruined Earth of the far future, peopled by mutated humans and star-dwellers; and also in its metaphysical sophistication. Both works in particular are close in their sense of the fluidities of identity, the way one being can slide into another. But Attanasio still conveys the sense that there is a true self to be found through development: Wolfe suggests rather that the self has no final boundaries, and that development is not in court. If this might seem like a portrayal by Wolfe of entropy of being in the senility of Urth, it is typical of the inclusiveness of this writer that it is also used to give a sense of the enrichment of the self through its infusion with others.

The narrative of *The Book of the New Sun* centres on one Severian, brought up in the Guild of Torturers in the citadel of the city of Nessus somewhere in the southern hemisphere of 'Urth'. He, like his fellow guild-members, has no known parents, but he has perfect recall of his life from an early age, and he tells us much of his apprenticeship, episodes during it, and the various stages of his elevation to journeyman torturer. One night in the cemetery about the Citadel he helps Vodalus, enemy of the ruling Autarch, escape, and thereafter dedicates himself to Vodalus's cause. The Chatelaine Thecla, formerly of the inner circle of the Autarch's court, is sent to the torturers, perhaps (though later the Autarch is to give a different reason (*CA*, p. 204)) to be used as a bargaining counter with Vodalus, to whom Thecla's sister Thea has fled from the court. Severian befriends her and learns from her something of the Autarch and his House Absolute to the north of Nessus. When the order for Thecla's torture eventually comes through and her first 'excruciation' has taken place, Severian gives her a knife in her cell: from the trickle of blood that subsequently comes under the door he concludes that she is dead, tells his masters, and is exiled, being sent as a carnifex or executioner to the 'City of Windowless Rooms', Thrax, far to the north. His journey to and beyond Thrax and eventually back again occupies the remainder of the series, during which he gains and later loses the miraculously potent gem, the Claw of the Conciliator, passes through the House Absolute, reaches Thrax and soon quits it and his office, travels further north into the mountains and fights in armies both for and against the Autarch, and finally returns to Nessus as Autarch himself. During his journey Severian is intermittently accompanied by a variety of companions, including the treacherous female Agia, the enigmatic Jonas and a troop of travelling players under the direction of one Dr Talos: a more constant friend is the devoted young woman Dorcas, resurrected by the power of the Claw. By the last book however he is on his own. The whole story is written by Severian from his position as Autarch.

More than almost any other work of science fiction this book refuses us a context. We learn but little and late of what process of human development has led to the strange society portrayed on Urth: for most of the tetralogy no one seems to know of the past any more. There are occasional 'contextual' moments in the third and fourth books, but these provide no more than glancing and sometimes mutually inconsistent hints.[3] The House Absolute remains as mysterious as the House of Silence in W. H. Hodgson's *The Night Land* (which is set on an Earth after the sun has gone dead). What made the Autarch, quite what relations Urth now has with other worlds, what made the guilds, what god if any is behind the doings of life, is never fully clear. Mervyn Peake refuses much of the history of his Gormenghast in the same way: but for him it has always been as it is, and that is the ground of its being. Though Peake does not describe the early growth of Ritual or how the Groans became rulers, he is quite prepared to explain how the observance of the Ritual has become over time purely mechanical. In Wolfe's book we know that the torturers are used as a means of punishment for criminals and enemies of the Autarch, but why they should be tortured, since usually no information of value is to be gained, is left quite obscure. As for the nearby Guild of Witches, we know nothing at all of their function, only of their rickety residence. We know for what purpose, however limited, the Hall of Bright Carvings in Peake's Gormenghast was created: it exists to house the carvings of the Outer Dwellers of the castle that have won the annual contest for the finest and most beautiful, the others having been consigned to a ceremonial fire. We do not know however the full purpose of the Botanical Gardens in Nessus, with their many different gardens 'Of Delectation', 'Of Sleep', 'Of Pantomime', 'Of Antiquities', 'The Jungle Garden', 'The Sand Garden', and so forth: each is of course a different bioscape for the delight of tourists, yet each contains experiences that are far more than botanical.

In other works of science fiction we know sooner or later what is really going on: the hidden plans of Asimov's Seldon become progressively revealed, the nature of Farmer's Riverworld is finally tracked down, we find the reason for the closure of the planet in Simak's *Shakespeare's Planet*. Even where the mystery is not plumbed, as in Clarke's *Rendezvous with Rama*, where the nature, existence and source of the Ramans are never discovered, one is to feel that somewhere there is an explanation. Wolfe, however, suggests that the world is not subject to explanation, that rational enquiry is inadequate to comprehend it, is indeed almost out of court. Severian is not till late concerned at all with finding out about Urth. Nor does Wolfe offer us much in the way of an overview of Urth and its situation. His emphasis is much more on the locality of knowledge. He himself in the appendices to the books claims ignorance, pleading himself at the mercy of such information only as Severian's books leave him, insisting that language itself can only render an often inaccurate account of the speech, customs and indeed beings of the world of Urth. Severian his protagonist frequently says he has perfect recall, but his recall covers only the limited sphere of his own life. Everywhere information and knowledge are local and hypothetical, and they remain so, though more hints are gathered. Among the more certain facts we have are the book's own literary ancestry – not to be dismissed as a mere irrelevance, though, in a work so concerned with its own fictiveness: this includes Jack Vance's *The Dying Earth* (1950), perhaps Silverberg's *Nightwings* for the guilds, the ruined Earth, the lack of technology and the star dwellers; Peake and Robert Graves (of *I, Claudius*) for the narrator Severian; Hodgson, David Lindsay, Peake, Borges, Philip Dick.[4]

The book also often refuses us a continuously gripping story line. There are two 'exciting' and suspenseful events in *The Shadow of the Torturer*: one concerns the approaching 'excruciation' or official torture of the Chatelaine Thecla; the other a duel Severian is to fight with a supposed Hipparch who has challenged him. The Chatelaine's suffering is long postponed, to the point where the reader can feel it may not actually take place, and in the interim Severian's developing relationship with her is far more central. The challenge is separated by seventy pages from the duel that takes place on the same day: during that space Severian is shown some of the sights of Nessus by a woman shopkeeper Agia, has a chariot race through the streets, arrives at the strange cathedral of the nun-like Pelerines, visits the Botanic Gardens on an island in the River Gyoll, and on the way to the duelling ground has a lengthy sojourn at an inn – all these episodes being filled with material and speculations which have nothing to do with the approaching duel. Despite Severian's posting to Thrax, it takes him almost two rambling volumes to get there; and then it is soon to reject his office and leave.

Between consecutive volumes there is a narrative gap. At the end of *The Shadow of the Torturer* Severian is still in the gateway of Nessus, having just met a seeming man called Jonas; at the beginning of *The Claw of the Conciliator* he is in a village somewhere, by now established as a carnifex and about to exercise his office on certain people we have not met but of whose character he speaks familiarly; and he and Jonas (who is to turn out to be actually a damaged robot star-dweller) are now companions. At the end of *The Claw* he is still far from Thrax, trying to get to a place called Lake Diuturna via a strange moving stone village; at the beginning of *The Sword of the Lictor* he is already in Thrax with a long history unseen by us, as a travelling carnifex. *The Sword* closes with Severian at the castle of the giant Baldanders; *The Citadel of the Autarch* opens with him in the midst of the war on the Autarch's northern frontiers. And *The Citadel* ends with his stellar mission as Autarch still to be performed.

Unlike many modern fantasy or science fiction epics of travel, *The Book of the New Sun* provides us with no maps: the location of places is uncertain, and one may be near and far at once. It is true that *The Sword of the Lictor* contains much more of a steady narrative thrust; equally it could be argued that *The Claw* and *The Citadel of the Autarch* are at an opposite extreme of refusing forward or directional movement; with the more celebrated *The Shadow* providing a fine fusion of the two impulses. Considered overall, however, narrative excitement is deliberately dulled: as, incidentally, are any merely sensationalist thrills. Severian tells us, 'as one mind to another', 'I have recounted the execution of Agia's twin brother Agilus because of its importance to my story, and that of Morwenna because of the unusual circumstances surrounding it. I will not recount others unless they hold some special interest. If you delight in another's pain, you will gain little satisfaction from me' (*CC*, p. 39). If we pass over the possible pruriences of narrative interest, what remains is the fact that we are denied a consistently exciting story of the kind that is present in *Foundation* or *Dune*, where a fixed quest is constantly in view.

And the same might be said even of psychological development in the novel: Severian, despite being the not unattractive psyche through whom events are related, is in his relatively steady coolness not a fascinating focus to the book: it cannot be said that the reader is meant to be seized by eagerness to find out how he develops. The author is not far from refusing a centre to the work. Severian admits as much, telling us that like an executioner the author is concerned not only with the act itself but with the act as rite and as meaning, and with its connection to other acts (*ST*, pp. 280–1). Thus it is that Severian describes in detail minor events and places from his early history which have no direct causal relations to the story, or he will digress from present events to describe others in the past.

The imagination behind the series, particularly in *The Shadow of the Torturer*, is formidable, coming near to the prodigality of a David Lindsay, and yet always controlled and integrated. Most of the writers we have considered present one or two images or worlds about which their books revolve. The landscape of the desert planet Dune remains single and consistent; Asimov keeps us to the one backcloth of a spiral galaxy in the *Foundation* trilogy; Clarke puts us inside a space-ship; Farmer gives us a world whose topography is unchanging. Aldiss it is true has a proliferation of images in *Hothouse*, but his creations are nearly all of them set clearly within the one broad context, the Earth, in its fecund decline. Wolfe creates one medium after another, each world for the time isolated from others, all of them visited on Severian's strange journey. There is Nessus, the city of vast and uncertain extent, threaded by the sluggish and foetid Gyoll and surrounded by a cloud-high wall of metal. Within that there is the walled necropolis, the dead of which have to be guarded against those who would use them for dark purposes. Within that is the citadel, and further, in that, the Matachin Tower of the Torturers, with its medieval existence, its rigidities of conduct, its bureaucratic approach to the administration of formalised pain to 'clients', its atmosphere in some ways of a police barracks, a boarding school and a family, all rolled together.

Outside the Citadel, Severian comes to the cathedral of the Pelerine order. It is worth dwelling on this to show how finely the author's imagination works to bring places to life. Severian has been in a chariot race through Nessus, and he and his companion Agia, attempting a short cut, have found their way barred by an immense building, the walls of which give before them 'like the fabric of a dream', whereupon they rush through a cavernous space and crash into an altar 'as large as a cottage and dotted with blue lights' (*ST*, p. 165). Severian, knocked unconscious, eventually wakes:

> We seemed to be near the centre of the building, which was as big around as the Great Keep and yet completely empty: without interior walls, stairs, or furniture of any kind. Through the golden, dusty air I could see crooked pillars that seemed of painted wood. Lamps, mere points of light, hung a chain or

more overhead. Far above them, a many-coloured roof rippled and snapped in a wind I could not feel.

I stood on straw and straw was spread everywhere in an endless yellow carpet, like the fields of a titan after harvest. All about me were the battens of which the altar had been constructed: fragments of thin wood braved with gold leaf and set with turquoises and violet amethysts. (*ST*, p. 166)

By now we can tell, as Severian, brought up amid rectangles of stone and metal, cannot, that he is in a tent the size of a big top, and the unexpected blockage of the short cut across the common was caused by the tent's recent pitching. By this means the cathedral is created for and by us as we read, and thus gains heightened vividness. But the account is also given vigour by the precision of observation of the pieces of the altar, by the slightly strange juxtaposition with our usual sense of an altar as a solid and heavy structure of the fact that it is composed of thin wood only, and by the mixing of matchwood and precious stones. If the strangeness of the cathedral becomes the familiarity of a tent, it then gains further imaginative potency by once more becoming strange: the straw which spreads everywhere begins to burn towards Agia and Severian, and as they run they suddenly encounter a group of scarlet-clad people carrying scimitars and led by a tall hooded woman who has Severian's sword.

The author creates such images with such apparent effortlessness that they seem to have been come upon, to have been always there, rather than to have been invented. Every stage of Severian's journey is accompanied by a startling new image or landscape: the brown lake in the Garden of Endless Sleep in the Botanic Gardens, wherein are sunk thousands of shot-filled bodies for burial; the evening fight with giant flowers called averns between Severian and Agilus in the communal duelling grounds near the wall of Nessus; the forest feast with Vodalus where Severian is served with Thecla's cooked body, after dining on which her identity becomes joined to his; the mysteries of the House Absolute, most of which is underground and covered with pleasure-gardens; the huge white undine that, failing to coax Severian into the water of a stream, surges upward from the water on weak legs with blood running from her nostrils, only to fall back; the prisoners in Thrax, chained in rows on either side of a rock shaft driven into the cliff within the city; the mountain that is

the image of a living autarch; the giant Baldanders suddenly seen
falling slowly from the sky upon Severian; the vast five-armed
war-machines that rush revolving through the air in the war with
the Ascians (*CA*, pp. 166–7).

For many another writer the creation of these and numerous
other images of clarity and power, with all the assurance that the
author has, might be enough. But with Wolfe the images are not
meant only to surprise; though clearly there is much plain delight
in such elastic creativity. Rather they all appear as though
inevitable and called for. Severian fighting Agilus with averns is
not the same as Alice playing croquet with flamingoes. The avern
is a killer plant about the size of a sapling: the idea is to hold it aloft
in one hand by its stem and detach its heavy, razor-edged
poisonous leaves with the other, to send them skimming at one's
opponent. More than this, however, to fight with flowers is to
conduct war with an image of peace, and such reversal fits with
one of the themes of the work. The Pelerines' tent becomes
perfectly explicable at the level of the evangels who go about our
own world wooing thousands under canvas: but again, as an
interior, it fits into a motif concerning interiors and rooms –
indeed of a journey into the interior, upriver (as in *Heart of
Darkness*) to Thrax, the City of Windowless Rooms – that recurs
throughout. It is always clear that concerns other than those of the
image alone are also present. We are directed to pay careful
attention to the way the protagonist views such sights; the sights
themselves are often as much metaphysical as physical, or else
may be illusions, like the apparently long room behind the picture
in the House Absolute, which is actually a trapezoid with
converging sides that meet only a few feet back, or the mushroom
tower of Baldanders's castle that is in fact a tower surmounted by
a space ship.

In the gardens of the House Absolute, Severian approaches a
'white shape', which he then opens a new chapter to describe:

> There are beings – and artifacts – against which we batter our
> intelligence raw, and in the end make peace with reality only by
> saying, 'It was an apparition, a thing of beauty and horror.'
>
> Somewhere among the swirling worlds I am so soon to
> explore, there lives a race like and yet unlike the human. They
> are no taller than we. Their bodies are like ours save that they
> are perfect, and that the standard to which they adhere is

wholly alien to us. Like us they have eyes, a nose, a mouth; but they use these features (which are as I have said, perfect) to express emotions we have never felt, so that for us to see their faces is to look upon some ancient and terrible alphabet of feeling, at once supremely important and utterly unintelligible.

Such a race exists, yet I did not encounter it there at the edge of the gardens of the House Absolute. What I had seen moving among the trees, and what I now – until I at last saw it clearly – flung myself toward, was rather the giant image of such a being kindled to life. Its flesh was of white stone, and its eyes had the smoothly rounded blindness (like sections cut from eggshells) we see in our own statues. It moved slowly, like one drugged or sleeping, yet not unsteadily. It seemed sightless, yet it gave the impression of awareness, however slow.

I have just paused to reread what I have written of it, and I see that I have failed utterly to convey the essence of the thing. Its spirit was that of sculpture. If some fallen angel had overhead my conversation with the green man, he might have contrived such an enigma to mock me. In its every movement it carried the serenity and permanency of art and stone; I felt that each gesture, each position of the head and limbs and torso, might be the last. Or that each might be repeated interminably . . .

My initial terror, after the white statue's strangeness had washed away my will toward death, was the instinctive one that it would do me hurt.

My second was that it would not attempt to. To be as frightened of something as I was of that silent, inhuman figure, and then to discover that it meant no harm, would have been unbearably humiliating. (*CC*, pp. 116–17)

The concern here is not only with the object, but with the effect of the object on the beholder. We do not even know that the shape is a statue till the third paragraph, and even then that identification is in doubt. The first paragraph tells us that it cannot be described adequately; the second speaks at length of a race on another planet of which the third then tells us the object was not a member; then there is an attempt at direct description, after which Severian interrupts his own account to tell us that what we have been reading is quite inadequate. The experience is made metaphysical: we are to sense the otherness of the phenomenon through the relative failure of attempts to capture it. Its movements are slow, as though it is drugged or sleeping, yet it is not unsteady; it seems sightless, yet aware. Severian apprehends it in conceptual as much as physical terms. Looking at it, he feels that every move it makes has definition and finality; yet at the same time he feels each move could be repeated indefinitely. He tells us of the philosophic impact of the statue before mentioning his fear of it. And even when he comes to his fear he does not say, 'I was terrified,' but analyses his fear in two parts, giving moral terror far greater place than merely physical fright.

Once Severian tells Dorcas that, in a brown book he brought Thecla from the library beneath the citadel, he read that one of the keys to the universe ' "was that everything, whatever happens, has three meanings" ' (*ST*, p. 272). The first meaning is the literal one, the level of empirical fact, of real cows eating real grass. Paradoxically this is said to be the hardest to grasp: it is reality in all its resistant 'this-ness'. This may explain the recurrent preoccupation of the book with rendering experience in painstaking detail, and the frequent admissions of failure to describe adequately. ' "The second [meaning] is the reflection of the world about it. Every object is in contact with all others, and thus the wise can learn of the others by observing the first." ' This occurs throughout the series, where we are frequently turned from the physical datum alone to others which it is like or recalls. So it is at the beginning and end of each book, where the author draws our attention to the fact that he began and finished the first with a gate through which Severian went, the second with a village, the third with a fortress and ended the fourth with another gate. And all things are at once themselves and interconnected. Severian at one point wonders whether he, without family though he is, may not somehow be related to the little boy with his own name whom he meets in the mountains beyond Thrax, 'or for that matter to anyone I met' (*SL*, pp. 137–8). Every present moment too is shared with the past and the future. Gazing at the lake in the Garden of Endless Sleep, Severian comments, 'Mist was rising from the water, reminding me first of the swirling motes of straw in the insubstantial cathedral of the Pelerines, then of steam from the soup kettle when Brother Cook carried it into the refectory on a winter afternoon' (*ST*, p. 211). Severian is the torturers' apprentice, he is Death, he is the Autarch; the Autarch is the androgynous brothel-keeper in Nessus, and in himself he is

'Legion', the vessel of the distilled identities of a multitude of individuals (*CA*, pp. 209–10).

And the third meaning of every object? ' "The third is the transsubstantial meaning. Since all objects have their ultimate origin in the Pancreator, and all were set in motion by him, so all must express his will – which is the higher reality" ' (*ST*, p. 272). This is one of the few refererences to a deity in *The Book of the New Sun*: yet it is one of the skills of the author that everything in the work seems shot through with the numinous. The stone, the Claw of the Conciliator, which Severian comes by in the Pelerines' cathedral has – if intermittently – the power to perform miracles of healing (an ironic power to be in the possession of an executioner). We do not know whether the Autarch is fully mortal, just as we do not know whether the 'cacogens' are simply beings from other stars or the agents of a supernatural force. What the birth of the New Sun can mean in any but a mystical sense is not clear.[5] Clearly some Christian reference is behind the Conciliator who has come to Urth before; and the feast at which Thecla's body is eaten (*CC*, ch. XI) and the later offer of the world to Severian by Typhon (*SL*, ch. XXVI), have strong overtones of the communion and of the Temptation in the Wilderness. With these hints of cosmic significance the mystery pervading events and objects becomes imbued with spiritual resonance.

One of the bases of the book is reversal. Forward movement is partly illusion. Severian writes as autarch already: he tells us that he 'backed into the throne'. Continually we experience reversal as we read, by taking Severian's account as though written by the dispossessed character that we see, only to be told that he is ruler of all. His very motives seem 'back to front'. He gives us no history of libertarian sentiments or any suggestion of prior knowledge of Vodalus to explain his apparently sudden commitment to the cause of a man who robs graves. Rather he proposes that the coin Vodalus gives him as a keepsake for saving his life may have made him a Vodalarian, though he announced himself as such to Vodalus before: 'We believe that we invent symbols. The truth is that they invent us; we are their creatures, shaped by their hard, defining edges' (*ST*, p. 17). To desire nothing and to have nothing may be the way to have all things. Severian has no parents, and through his helping of Thecla, no home. He is happy that the dog Triskele, which he saved from death, should choose another master. He is not concerned that he should lose his life in the duel with Agilus. He wishes to give back the Claw, and uses it to help others. His very wandering, his placelessness, like that of the Pelerines, suggests his readiness to go dispossessed. Others he meets desire what he has or seek power – Agia, Agilus, Baldanders, Typhon. Yet the Claw comes to him; and the throne, which in a temporal collapse typical of the book he already has. And about him, a mere exile, many 'great' events come to revolve. Thus 'no-thing' becomes 'all things'.

In *The Citadel of the Autarch*, in a reversal designed perhaps to show that it has been his objective all along and that he has never left it, Severian returns to the Citadel from which he set forth. In Nessus, Severian at one point feels, he may be already in Thrax, the city of Windowless Rooms (*ST*, p. 260). For him it may be, as George MacDonald's Mr Raven puts it in his *Lilith*, that ' "The more doors you go out of, the farther you get in!" '[6] The world of Urth is the world of the remote future, yet that future has many of the aspects of our pre-technological past, with Roman names and behaviour, medieval-seeming guilds and soldiers, castles and feudal autocrats. The author thus upends time from the first chapter of *The Shadow*, with its title 'Resurrection and Death'; and also by starting the first chapter with 'It is possible I already had some presentiment of my future,' and the second with 'Memory oppresses me.' In a dream he sees his fight with Baldanders long before it takes place (*ST*, pp. 141–2). The face on the funeral bronze that has fascinated Severian in boyhood later comes to life (*CC*, p. 293). The coin that Vodalus gives Severian has on its obverse the very flying ship that, found on a bronze device in a mausoleum, he has for long adopted as part of an imaginary coat of arms.

Throughout Severian insists that his past is so vivid to him that it becomes almost more real than the present. When he emerges from a tunnel beneath the Citadel, through which he has searched for the lost dog Triskele, he finds himself in a wintry courtyard on the leaning face of a huge dial containing many clocks, all showing different times. He is told by a girl Valeria whom he meets there that the place, which is called the Atrium of Time, did not receive its name from the dials, but the dials were put there because of the name (*ST*, p. 44). During his conversation with the librarian Ultan in the stacks, Severian observes, with seeming irrelevance, 'We were already walking back in the direction we had come. Since the aisle was too narrow for us to pass one another, I now carried the candelabrum before him, and a stranger, seeing us, would surely have thought I lighted his way' (*ST*, p. 66). The librarian is blind. Severian recounts stories to learn from them (*ST*, p. 183). Several times during the story death is reversed to restore life (Dorcas in *The Shadow*, the uhlan in *The Claw*, Jader's sister in *The Sword*, the soldier in *The Citadel*).

Expectations, too, are reversed. We suppose that to be a torturer is to be committed to violence, but actually torturing proves a tightly controlled discipline, a craft, in which the pain inflicted is merely functional, and small pleasure taken in its administration; commitment to the guild involves a dedication bordering on idealism (women, who were cruel, were banished from the guild (*ST*, p. 20)). A torturer has to know as much medicine as a doctor, but he is a doctor in reverse: he uses his knowledge of the body not to reconstruct it but to dismantle it; apprentice torturers take the morning round of 'clients' like housemen following a consultant, having the various operative techniques used pointed out to them (*ST*, pp. 29–30). In the midst of organised horror they are bidden to take their hands out of their pockets when spoken to (*ST*, p. 30). The whole book can be said to be founded on the notion of taking away our certainty as to what a thing is. To go north here is to go to warmer lands, for the book is set in the southern hemisphere: Severian thinks of the northern hemisphere as the world upside down (*ST*, p. 210). Throughout we do not know whether the New Sun, which the series purports to be about, has come, is coming or is about to come; perhaps all three, as in Christian prayer. In the shape – whatever that is – of the Conciliator, we learn that it has come before; in so far as Severian for the time wields the Claw he may be the Conciliator returned; in so far as the old sun is dying some new sun of futurity must be man's only hope. More widely, so far as the sun as solar body is concerned, this *Book of the New Sun* takes place in the senility of the old one.[7]

In a book which denies us a grand design, a pattern, an overview or even, often, a mere narrative, to stand still may be to go forward, and to advance may be to return to where one is. Hence, perhaps, the circularities of the books. In such a context, the moment may contain more than the sequence of moments that makes the history, and the part may be able to contain the whole. During his conversation with Ultan, Severian mentions the belief that by eating the flesh of a dead person one could take that person's identity, and asks Ultan whether by eating only a part of the person, were it only the tip of a little finger, that identity might still be transmitted. Ultan agrees, and when Severian voices his sense of the disproportion in this, asks him, ' "How big is a man's life?" '; to which Severian can only reply, ' "I have no way of knowing, but isn't it larger than that?" ' Ultan's answer is typical of the depth of intelligence that has gone into this book, while being entirely in character: ' "You see it from the beginning, and anticipate much. I, recollecting it from its termination, know how little there has been" ' (*ST*, p. 66). Size thus depends on the perceiver. And the identity of a thing is not fixed: it depends on a multitude of perspectives and observations. Ultan's use of the word 'termination' reminds us that the name of Severian's sword 'Terminus Est' may be translated in more than one way. Ultan (name meaning last) then chooses an analogy from the reverse of death to explain how identity may be conveyed through a part: family resemblances can endure through generations, ' "Yet the seed of them all was contained in a drachm of sticky fluid." '

An instance of this 'microcosmic' mode can be seen in Severian's visit with the theatrical producer Dr Talos and his supposed assistant Baldanders to a cafe in Nessus where they are served by a girl who tells them that her master pays her nothing and she depends on tips to survive: ' "If you don't give me anything, I will have served you for nothing" ' (*ST*, p. 148). To whom Dr Talos replies in typical reversal, ' "Quite so, quite so! But what about this? What if we attempt to render you a rich gift, and you refuse it?" ': takings are replaced by givings, and their possible refusals by hers; at which Severian proceeds to freeze the moment in a deepening reflection:

> Dr Talos leaned toward her as he said this, and it struck me that his face was not only that of a fox (a comparison that was perhaps too easy to make because his bristling reddish eyebrows and sharp nose suggested it at once) but that of a stuffed fox. I have heard those who dig for their livelihood say there is no land anywhere in which they can trench without turning up the shards of the past. No matter where the spade turns the soil, it uncovers broken pavements and corroding metal; and scholars write that the kind of sand that artists call polychrome (because flecks of every colour are mixed with its whiteness) is actually not sand at all, but the glass of the past,

now pounded to powder by aeons of tumbling in the clamorous
sea. If there are layers of reality beneath the reality we see, even
as there are layers of history beneath the ground we walk upon,
then in one of those more profound realities, Dr Talos's face was
a fox's mask on a wall, and I marveled to see it turn and bend
now toward the woman, achieving by those motions, which
made expression and thought appear to play across it with the
shadows of the nose and brows, an amazing and realistic
appearance of vivacity. 'Would you refuse it?' he asked again,
and I shook myself as though waking. (*ST*, p. 148)

The conversation and narrative are suspended during this lengthy
reflection: it is as though Dr Talos and the girl wait for Severian to
have it before continuing, with Dr Talos repeating his question; as
though Severian's thoughts occupied the same reality as their
words. Such is the character of *The Book of the New Sun*, in which
'intellectual' speculation alternates continually with accounts of
an 'external' world, and mental constructs have no less reality
than supposedly physical events – Severian's dream which comes
true, Dr Talos's play at the House Absolute which in some way
furthers the action at a spiritual level. Here Severian is concerned
not only to recount a conversation, but the quality of the
experience: he is as interested in the nature of the moment itself,
indeed every aspect of it, as much as in what it leads to. As he looks
at Dr Talos he sees him as a fox, but then at once as not only a fox,
so that his identity shifts all the time. When he speaks of the fox's
mask we are reminded of other masks that occur in the series: the
mask Severian wears as torturer and as carnifex, the mask Agilus
wears to disguise himself as Hipparch, the masks of the
other-worlders, the cacogens, masks by which one identity is
hidden and another revealed. When he speaks of the fox looking
more like a stuffed fox, we are perhaps reminded of the features of
the funeral bronze that find flesh, or the huge statue of terrible
beauty which is like the far-off star dwellers: but there the dead
come to life, where here the live being becomes the image of a dead
animal.

Characteristically of the book Severian turns to talk of what
seems some quite unrelated matter, the omnipresence of the past
beneath the dry skin of the planet – and characteristically we are
given a fragment of information about the larger history of Urth
only in a casual aside: yet what seems to be separated is in fact

closely linked to the subject, just as other separations in the book, such as between one identity and another, the past and the future, one place and another infinitely far off. For the mention of Urth's past is used to give Severian's vision the status of fact. If there are layers and layers of history below us, then there may be layers and layers of reality, and on one of these levels Dr Talos is a fox. Curiously the way Severian puts this transforms it as we watch from hypothesis to actuality – not a hypothetical 'If', but a logical deduction from an 'If' to a 'then': it is a clever trick, like the strange mirrors of Father Inire in the House Absolute, through which a reflection can become a reality (*ST*, pp. 185–6), or like the reflection of a woman's face seen in the water when no woman is present, in the story of the fisherman told in the Jungle Garden in the Botanic Gardens (*ST*, p. 189). By this point Dr Talos's face *is* a fox's mask on a wall, and from within that reality Severian now wonders at the fact that it moves and seems to imitate the processes of thought and feeling: he has entered his own vision and made it truth. Thus we see how any instant within the book, any identity, is connected to others, deepening our understanding not only of the figure or event before us, but of other events and figures in the book till they swirl about it. Take any part of the book and it has this power to animate the whole, just as Dr Talos is 'animated' here.

What then is the book about? There is no answer, but the lack of one is not from its absence so much as from the sense that it is just over one's shoulder or that it is too many things to pin into one. As we have said, the book has no centre as such, apart from Severian: it explores many things. And each thing may mean multitudes, as the author at one point tells us: Severian recounts a story of the Autarch and the many interpretations it has been given; he feels sure that the story remains as mysterious as his own, yet the attempt to understand it will be made (*ST*, pp. 158–9). The Autarch literally contains multitudes, in having within him the living identities of a thousand individuals. One of the themes – or perhaps motifs, rather – of *The Book of the New Sun* is that nothing finally has boundaries or limits: just as one thing may mean all things, so it may be them. During Dr Talos's play at the House Absolute, the audience is continually involved, so that the distinction between fiction and reality is worn down. Dreams such as that of Severian concerning Baldanders, become realities. Images come to life, such as the bronze face or the flying ship. The dead come alive in Dorcas, and in another way in Thecla.[8] Devoured by the terrible beast the alzabo, a family of people retain their identities within it. The living can be dead, as the ebullient Dr Talos turns out to be a homunculus manufactured by the cacogens. The metal hand of Jonas does not indicate that he is a human with an artificial limb; rather the 'human' part of him, the organic and fleshly, has been grafted on to what is a robot, who crashed to earth from space and lost several parts of his body. Typhon survives by grafting himself on to the body of Piaton. Thecla, eaten by Severian, becomes a part of him and he shares in her thoughts and memories. Dorcas is – in one way – Cas, the dead wife sought by the fisherman in the Garden of Endless Sleep; and perhaps there is a piece of her, like her name, in Cadroe of the Seventeen Stones at the duelling ground, and in Casdoe, mother of little Severian (*SL*, ch. XIV). Dr Talos seems in charge of the giant Baldanders; then, to Dorcas, the roles seem reversed, so that Baldanders is a slow father and Dr Talos his brilliant son (*CC*, p. 201).

Severian, for all that he is burdened by the solidity of his past, is, as a torturer, a myth, a creature of fiction to anyone beyond the Citadel (*ST*, p. 133). To Dr Talos and the fearful man he encounters in the Jungle Garden, he is Death, though Dorcas says such a name is mere metaphor (*CC*, pp. 200–1). The man in the Jungle Garden can see Severian, but his wife and the native with her cannot. Several of the characters become allegorized (there is even a chapter entitled 'Personifications'): Agia is the Lady, Dorcas Innocence, Jolenta Desire. Jolenta is a serving maid metamorphosed to the ectype of human sexual beauty. Severian meets a child with his own name. The ramifications of the passages beneath the Citadel may be great enough to merge into those of the House Absolute; and as to the latter Severian has no idea where it ends, if it ever ends (*CC*, p. 241). And as we have seen, the present, the past and the future often come together, just as one place and another supposedly distant from it; and one person may appear in many guises in the work. Even in genre the book melts down identity, being a fusion of fantasy, science fiction and horror story. Other works that mix genres in this way tend to come down on one side or the other, as C. S. Lewis's science-fictional romance *Out of the Silent Planet* ends as pure supernatural fantasy; or Clifford Simak's supernatural-seeming *Enchanted Pilgrimage* is engulfed in a science-fictional action and explanation. Wolfe maintains the ambiguity, the uncertainty of boundaries, and this heightens the mystery.

Perhaps the central point to be made about Wolfe's work is its inclusiveness. Severian's mind is obsessed to madness by his total recall of the past. We cover every experience possible, and that is why the work contains not one but many images; why, too, each image itself contains multitudes. Given the motif of plasticity in the book, it will be only fitting with this that the work should have no single fixed or identifiable meaning. We can if we like read into it serious themes concerning alienation of the self or man's distance from reality (imaged perhaps in the torturers, to whom the infliction of pain has nothing to do with emotion), but so to do is to limit that which refuses limits.

In one sense the book asks us what it is to be meaningful. We ourselves may feel that most 'significance' resides in such episodes as the disquisition on Father Inire's mirrors and their relation to reality (*ST*, ch. XX), or in the allegorical play produced by Dr Talos on a new Paradise and the Last Things (*CC*, ch. XXIV), but, by virtue of the equal attention to apparently 'physical' acts, the book asks us how much less significance, however unidentifiable, is contained in them:

> I examined the block. Those used outside the immediate supervision of the guild are notoriously bad: 'Wide as a stool, dense as a fool, and dished, as a rule.' This one fulfilled the first two specifications in the proverbial description only too well, but by the mercy of Holy Katherine it was actually slightly convex, and though the idiotically hard wood would be sure to dull the male side of my blade, I was in the fortunate position of having before me one subject of either sex, so that I could use a fresh edge on each. (*CC*, p. 33)

Is this intractable block less meaningful because less identifiably so than, say: ' "The past cannot be found in the future where it is not – not until the metaphysical world, which is so much larger and so much slower than the physical world, completes its revolution and the New Sun comes" ' (*SL*, p. 55)? The book would have us wonder, just as it presents us with what is and is not a narrative, and with experiences that are at once real and dreams. The whole work is a mixture of adventures, experiences recorded in as much loving detail as snapshots, speculative psychological perceptions, all acutely rendered. Perhaps a meaning, or many meanings, might on the level of the perfect star beings' intelligence (*CC*, p. 116), be found to inform all the phenomena; but each phenomenon and apprehension may on its own contain an autonomous world of significance both like and unlike any other. It is part of science fiction's dialectic with the alien that it presents us with powerful images which at once invite and refuse interpretation, at once virginal and elusive like the Pelerines, and suggestive of universal availability like the desirable Jolenta. It is an art brought to perfection by Wolfe. It is there in the civilization of old Urth, which is and is not the Earth, which is so suggestive of Roman and medieval society and yet, as C. S. Lewis observed of near-identity, the more totally unlike for the approximation.[9] ' "A few days before I had been given a set of paper figures. There were soubrettes, columbines, coryphees, harlequinas, figurantes, and so on – the usual thing" ' (*ST*, p. 182).

12 Conclusion

What common features do the diverse books we have considered share? To those characteristics we pointed out in attempting to define science fiction in the introduction we can now add a few more.

In all these works personal identity is continually in flux. Attanasio's Sumner Kagan shifts from self to self throughout *Radix*. Burton in Farmer's Riverworld has to assume a reality he is not certain he possesses. Aldiss's Gren shifts in character, and his environment to match during his contact with the morel. The protagonist of Silverberg's *Nightwings* changes himself as often as he changes his guild. Mutation is a constant theme in this book, as in *Hothouse*, where we are continually made aware of how the plants have evolved to stranger forms to survive; and in Asimov's *Foundation* trilogy a shape-shifting mutant leads the Foundation to power and near disaster in the galaxy. In Wolfe's *Book of the New Sun* identity is so thin-walled that one character can participate in another, and one phenomenon or event is part of or interchangeable with others before or after it. The three human brains of the Ship in Simak's *Shakespeare's Planet* have to learn through the book to merge their remaining individualities into a corporate self. In Pohl's stories reality is continually being altered – the creatures in the museum brought to ghostly life and the magician himself turned to a ghost, the changing of the post-holocaust worlds of 'Target One' and 'Let the Ants Try', the perversions of fact by Rafferty, the transformation of society by Cheery-Gum.

At the same time identity is constantly in doubt. Asimov's Second Foundationers cannot be traced; and every assumption made about Seldon's Plan has to be altered. Yattmur in *Hothouse* does not know whether she is speaking to Gren or the morel. Paul Atreides and those about him in *Dune* have to discover whether he is the Kwisatz Haderach. The world of *Nightwings* is anonymous and nameless until the truth about humanity can be found. Throughout *To Your Scattered Bodies Go* it is not known whether

Riverworld is a supernatural place, a purgatory, or a gigantic artifact. In *Rendezvous with Rama* the purpose of the ship, and whether it any longer has one, remains unknown, as does much of Rama to the exploring humans. *Shakespeare's Planet* starts by presenting us with a series of uncertain identities, and then leaves us with the visitors to the planet trying to discover the nature of the character Shakespeare and making assumptions about why the tunnel does not work which prove to be wrong. Attanasio's Sumner Kagan does not know who he is, and continually tries to carve identities for himself which he loses, until he finds at bedrock that he is a godmind. In *The Book of the New Sun* we read the story of a journeyman carnifex: yet we know also that that man is Autarch; and throughout his identity wavers before us, perhaps precisely because it is so thoroughly built up. These uncertainties of identity are not like those in a detective novel, which at most encourage moral doubt concerning individuals: here the issue relates much more to what one is than to what one among several may have done.

This concern with identity – or even confrontation with one's own nonentity – has been a feature of science fiction from the outset. With what else is Swift's Gulliver faced as he is now a giant, now a pygmy, now a man of sense, now a madman, but the problem of what he is and of what it is to be human? So in a different mode with Mary Shelley's Frankenstein or Stevenson's Dr Jekyll: they have created the dark side of themselves, and it casts their normal selves into doubt. And Wells in *The Island of Dr Moreau* and Huxley in *Brave New World* portray the self manipulated into new forms and responses. The difference between these and the works we have considered is that the moral element regarding changes of identity has now largely disappeared, leaving as motive only fascination with the idea of the potentiality for other selves that exists within us – the exploratory desire to break out from rigid forms and assumptions, which is in a sense the prime desire behind writing science fiction itself and making new worlds. That is what the journeys from one place to another that are described in most of these books can be said to mean: Attanasio's Sumner Kagan literally grows away from his familiar street self and urban surroundings; Aldiss's Gren discovers a whole world of being, both inside and outside himself, on his travels; through his wanderings Silverberg's Tomis is changed utterly: the world becoms pregnant with new possibility.

It is no mere cold questing that produces this, but a desire for the raggedness of joy itself: there is as much delight in life – refined to the clinical sometimes if we will – behind science fiction as fantasy.

There is the emotional and imaginative drive, but there is also a more metaphysical one. Nearly all these texts are asking the ontological question, 'What is the self?' In all of them inquiry into the nature of a being is the primary concern, whether it be Earth at the end of time, a state of resurrection on a new world, an alien space craft, the causes of the human condition (*Nightwings*) or the true nature of the self (Silverberg, Farmer, Attanasio, Wolfe). Several of them suggest that the true self is found by a kind of stripping, whether it be by a journey away from the conscious self into the supposedly life-giving unconscious (Herbert, Silverberg, Attanasio); or in one case by an acceptance of the not-self, the void (Simak). Others however portray a process which implies that this self is only realized through expansion and accretion (Asimov, Aldiss, Farmer), whereby the naked, the small or the ignorant acquire more knowledge and power over their environment. There is no fixed view here: all that is constant is the questioning of the self. This concern with the self is to be seen throughout modern literature, but it is more marked in science fiction than in other genres,[1] doubtless because science fiction is uniquely concerned with questioning the apparent solidity of this world and with making something radically new; further, since science fiction is, however vestigially, predictive, involved with the creation of worlds at least remotely possible, the question of the reality of these worlds and the beings in them is one that is going to be present continually. But for whatever reason, and in whatever direction, science fiction could be said to be preoccupied with the philosophical question of ontology, with the establishment of being. Each book is the investigation of a self or world under special conditions in order to determine its true identity. And this gives science fiction a fundamentally contemplative character: it is not surprising that numbers of philosophers have recently turned their attention to the genre.[2]

Many – though far from all – science fiction works provide in the end some assurance that out of all these existential doubts true being is to be found. It is, perhaps, science fiction's equivalent of God or the Valar in fantasy: a settled absolute on which to settle the storm-tossed craft of the anxious self. It is here that what Mark Rose has called science fiction's desire 'to name the infinite'[3] comes in, for the void of space or time is in part a metaphor for the inner void of the self: colonise that, subdue that to one's purposes and one indeed knows where one is. So it is that in many of these stories the protagonists journey out to an unknown world – to a dying Earth, to a galaxy, to a far planet, to an alien space-ship, to a world beyond death – to understand them as far as possible. Asimov's *Foundation* trilogy portrays an attempt to control the void of the future; Simak's *Shakespeare's Planet* one to accept the emptiness of endless space. Aldiss's *Hothouse* and Wolfe's *Book of the New Sun* look to a terminal point that will 'fix' the far future. In Farmer's 'Riverworld' series, death itself is peopled. Attanasio's *Radix* approaches transcendence in its idea of psychic force from an infinity of universes being focussed through our galaxy. Clarke's *Rendezvous with Rama* shows humanity struggling to make sense of the alien, and only partially succeeding. Herbert makes history purposeful, if largely uncontrollable. Silverberg's Tomis comes to an awareness of meaning in an apparently meaningless world, through mystic unity with others. Whether through a portrayal of evolution, or in the depiction of a universe in which man is no longer alone, or in taking the void to oneself or becoming joined spiritually with other selves, purpose is thrown over the darkness from which doubt springs, and one comes either to accept or transcend it. Thus far science fiction tends to provide assurance: but that assurance need not be facile where, as in most of the works we have considered, it is realistically wrested from doubt.

Whether as a result of its ultimately being an extreme metaphor for the supposedly divided psyche of modern man, or as a product of its sense of the changeability of phenomena, or whether purely as a consequence of its general disposition towards things philosophical, science fiction as embodied in the works we have considered seems uniquely preoccupied with the portrayal of dualisms – particularly those between mind and body, and between determinism and freewill. (Others include stasis and flux in Asimov and Herbert, self and not-self in Farmer, Clarke, Simak and Attanasio, 'centrifugal' and centripetal in Simak, or the use of reversals by Wolfe.) Asimov's Hari Seldon splits physical from mental science and puts them at opposite ends of a galaxy. In Pohl's stories the world is constantly out of gear with the plans of the mind – the failure of the schemes of the scientists in 'Let the Ants Try' or 'Target One', the intractable piece of plaster in 'The

Ghost-Maker', the backfiring of the Cheery-Gum scheme in 'What To Do Until the Analyst Comes', the shattering of Burckhardt's illusions in 'The Tunnel Under the World', the bleak facts beyond Rafferty's fantasies. In Aldiss's *Hothouse* the morel is an extra-cranial brain that grafts itself temporarily to the body of the near-animal Gren: and this in the setting of a physical world that is 'no longer a place for mind'. In *Dune* the whole novel has a medium of mind. The world of *Nightwings* is till the end one in which mind and body are divorced. Farmer portrays the dissociation of the scientific mind from common humanity in the cold experimentation of the Riverworld 'Ethicals'; and in contrast to Herbert he gives us a world largely rooted in the physical. Clarke shows us minds struggling with reality, trying and often failing to subdue it to their categories. Attanasio's *Radix* makes physical development a precondition of human mental power. Indeed from *Gulliver's Travels* on science fiction has dealt with this severance of mind from body, the physicality of the Yahoo against the rationality of the Houyhnhnm, the corporeality of the monster with its loud passions against the intellect of Frankenstein, the grafting of intelligence on animals in Wells's *The Island of Dr Moreau*, the breeding of the animal out of man in Huxley's *Brave New World* or Aldiss's *Enemies of the System*. Some works suggest a dialectical interplay of the opposites, as in Asimov or Herbert; some pose a possible synthesis, as in Silverberg and Attanasio; others leave them finally divided as in the more satiric work of Pohl and Aldiss. Here again no consistent final view emerges; only the near-unanimity with which those opposites are chosen in the first place.

The other duality, that between determinism and freewill, is evident particularly in Pohl, Asimov, Herbert and Farmer. It could perhaps be argued that this arises out of some sense of the helplessness of the individual in the modern collective, the feeling, just as with the mind–body duality, that no person can ever be whole and independent: but this is not subject to proof. The free choices Asimov's Foundationers make are often contained unknown to them by the predictions of Seldon's Plan, or manipulated by the mind-control of the Second Foundation. The belief of Rafferty and others of Pohl's protagonists that they know or have control over their destiny is undermined. As soon as Herbert's Paul Muad'Dib reaches knowledge of his power, he becomes at the mercy of its purposes. Farmer's characters, for all their apparent freewill, are parts of an experiment, over which they must gain control to become fully themselves. Wolfe's Severian is at once a seemingly free agent and the chosen Autarch: his random choices only bring him the more surely to the throne.

So what we have is a genre at least involved with issues that preoccupy philosophy, and perhaps responsive to the wider spiritual condition of modern man. But as far as any 'message' from this is concerned, no single lesson is to be derived: science fiction as a whole is not founded on any one philosophy, certainly not on *angst* alone. There are those who say that the genre has developed away from a faith in reason, technology and human progress that we see in Asimov and other writers of the Campbell era; but there were plenty of pessimists in Asimov's day and before, and there have been plenty of optimists since – Robert Heinlein, Larry Niven and, within the orbit of the authors we have looked at, P. J. Farmer and Arthur Clarke (whose recent *Imperial Earth* and *The Fountains of Paradise* both praise a human endeavour Clarke in some earlier novels could belittle). No clear development occurs in the spiritual outlook of these works from Asimov to Wolfe: some are optimistic, some are satiric, at both ends of the time scale. In the same way it is often impossible to detect evolution within the work of a science-fiction writer, or to relate any discovered change to an identifiable response by the writer to the world about him (Silverberg).

Nevertheless it has to be said that science fiction is unique in modern literature in the consistency of its emphasis on uncertainties of identity and on dualities: even if such topics are given happy resolution, as in some works, they are still there in the first place. It could be argued that the Olympian purview of science fiction, and its tendency to deal with the human race rather than with individuals, give it a built-in disposition to reflect, even if only at an unconscious level, some of man's deepest problems. Equally, though, these could be seen as arising out of the very nature of science fiction itself, its preoccupation with the plasticity of the self emerging from its own medium of change, its sense of the division of mind from body from the fact that in itself it exists through mental and imaginary worlds often quite separate from the 'body' of this one, its opposition of freewill and determinism from the freedom with which it creates new worlds and the fact that each such world is controlled by one mind.[4] Naturally those who wish to enhance the stature of science fiction and to make it a literature that can tell man something about himself will take the first course. The view advanced in this book is that there is a third line of approach: to move away from the uncertainties attendant on the wide view, and consider rather the particular applications these motifs are given in individual works. In this belief, science fiction should be considered first in terms of its own reality, and the thematic concerns and metaphoric patterns of individual works as reflecting the character of the invented universes in which they occur rather than a supposedly real world beside which they are mere shadows. For all worlds are only possible, including our own.

But all this, it must be said, is the subject matter and orientation of these books: what they have in common is not more important than their differences. These differences are founded on their individual worlds: each creates a language of imagery radically different from the others. We can see the similarities between the fantasy worlds of George MacDonald and William Morris, of Tolkien and Ursula Le Guin, but Riverworld, Urth and Dune are completely independent creations of the imagination, islanded from one another, like separate universes. The object of this book has been to show the originality of these inventions, and how they create patterns of significance that turn these books into genuine works of art. Criticism lacks a language to evaluate inventiveness except through admiration: all that can be done is to describe it, and that we have tried to do. Criticism can then become more articulate, can show how the images are organic and meaningful: how the brilliant wit of Pohl's 'Let the Ants Try' is also a narrative form of a pincer movement, how Sumner Kagan's changing landscape mirrors his developing self, how Clarke's *Rama* becomes a symbol for ontological disorientation, how the chain of images and creatures in Aldiss's *Hothouse* partly enacts a pattern of maturation. For all these books have truly organic unity: if for example one put Farmer's 'World of Tiers' series beside his *To Your Scattered Bodies Go*, one would see how the marvellous images of the former are there purely for themselves, where in the latter they do that and also subserve the themes and motifs of the whole work; to use Coleridge's distinction, the one is a work of 'fancy', the other of 'imagination'. But both aspects are needed – the invention, and the integration of that invention with a larger purpose – and both require our attention. Science fiction is not simply to be made another form of discourse, that works like poetry through metaphor: it is also irreducibly itself, and it is the business of the critic to go out to its 'this-ness' as much as make sense of it.

It would be easy to end by saying that science fiction is not only about the future, it is the literature of the future. This is more or less the view of Vonnegut's Eliot Rosewater, as expressed to a convention of science-fiction writers he gate-crashes:

> 'You're all I read any more. You're the only ones who'll talk about the *really* terrific changes going on, the only ones crazy enough to know that life is a space voyage, and not a short one, either, but one that'll last for billions of years. You're the only ones with guts enough to *really* care about the future . . . .'
>
> Eliot . . . [said] later on. . . . 'The hell with the talented sparrowfarts who write delicately of one small piece of one mere lifetime, when the issues are galaxies, eons, and trillions of souls yet to be born.'[5]

But this is too simple: science fiction is not the only literature of the future, it is one of several kinds of literature that will go on, whatever is said about the bankruptcy of the modern realistic novel or the febrility of contemporary poetry. Science fiction too has its limitations: it can be bloodless and lacking in felt life through its distance from this world and the immediate self and experiences of the writer. It may also be said that it is an expression of the fragmentation of mind in modern man: one side for the imagination, another for realism; one side for the wide open and possibly superficial spaces, another for the narrow but intensely felt little world of here and now. But whatever restrictions we may have to place on our admiration, one thing is plain: these books may well survive to see a good deal of the future time to which they look.

Notes

CHAPTER 1: INTRODUCTION

1. E.g. Brian Aldiss, ed., *Introducing SF: a Science Fiction Anthology*, p. 10, says that the stimulus of a science fiction story comes from the fact that 'it is about what is happening to *you*'; Ursula Le Guin, Introduction to her *The Left Hand of Darkness*, no page, declares, 'Science fiction is metaphor'; Samuel Delany, *The Jewel-Hinged Jaw: Notes on the Language of Science Fiction*, p. 178, maintains that 'Science fiction is the only area of literature outside poetry that is symbolistic in its basic conception. Its stated aim is to represent the world without reproducing it.' Aldiss, however, can also say, 'The images are what attract me in science fiction, more even than the surprises and the ideas and the crazy plots' (Aldiss, ed., *Yet More Penguin Science Fiction*, p. 9 *et seq.*).

2. I am thinking here particularly of David Ketterer's fine *New Worlds for Old: the Apocalyptic Imagination, Science Fiction, and American Literature*.

3. Compare Mark Rose, *Alien Encounters: Anatomy of Science Fiction*, which is a systematic account of the alien as metaphoric projection of the unknown or the 'void' in our lives and our desire to overcome it.

4. As for example in Herbert's *Dune*, between the melange spice and oil. But to read only in these terms is mistaken.

5. A sane and wide-ranging account of the history of science fiction can be found in Brian Aldiss, *Billion Year Spree: the True History of Science Fiction*; see also Robert Scholes and Eric S. Rabkin, 'A Brief Literary History of Science Fiction', *Science Fiction: History, Science, Vision*, pp. 3–99. The nineteenth-century development of the genre in Britain is well covered in Darko Suvin's *Victorian Science Fiction in the U.K.: The Discourses of Knowledge and of Power*: and that in America by H. Bruce Franklin, *Future Perfect: American Science Fiction of the Nineteenth Century*.

6. See also Susan Glicksohn, ' "A City of Which the Stars are Suburbs" ', in Clareson ed., *SF: the Other Side of Realism*, pp. 341–5.

7. For a full account, see Mike Ashley, *The History of the Science Fiction Magazine*; David Samuelson, *Visions of Tomorrow: Six Journeys from Outer to Inner Space*, pp. 17–37; Frank Cioffi, *Formula Fiction?: an Anatomy of American Science Fiction, 1930–1940*, ch. 1.

8. For an account of the characteristics of fantasy as compared to science fiction, see my 'On the Nature of Fantasy', in Roger C. Schlobin, ed., *The Aesthetics of Fantasy Literature and Art*, pp. 18–24, 29–31; Jaqueline Wynten-broek, 'Science Fiction and Fantasy', *Extrapolation*, xxiii, pp. 321–32.

9. See W. Warren Wagar, *Terminal Visions: the Literature of Last Things*, esp. pp. 185–205.

CHAPTER 2: ISAAC ASIMOV

1. For a full account of its first appearance in *Astounding Science Fiction*, Asimov's relations with the editor John Campbell and his difficulties in composition (particularly in the third book), see James Gunn, *Isaac Asimov: the Foundations of Science Fiction*, ch. 2.
2. See also Donald Wollheim, *The Universe Makers: Science Fiction Today*, pp. 37, 42.
3. See on this the references in note 3 of ch. 5.
4. This is reminiscent of the opposition between Arisian and Eddorean civilization in E. E. 'Doc' Smith's *Triplanetary* (serialized, 1934). It has been argued that the *Foundation* trilogy is in part an answer to Smith's 'Lensman' series – in particular in its substitution of intellectual for physical power: see Mark Rose, *Alien Encounters: Anatomy of Science Fiction*, pp. 12–13. Joseph Patrouch, *The Science Fiction of Isaac Asimov*, pp. 98–9, 102–3, also makes this point in relation to Asimov's reaction to 'space opera' generally.
5. Asimov, *Second Foundation* (London: Panther Books, 1969) pp. 185–6. Nevertheless their minds were also in part controlled by the Second Foundation to think this way.
6. Asimov, *Foundation* (London: Panther Books, 1969), p. 14. Page references hereafter in the text will be to this edition, and to *Foundation and Empire* and *Second Foundation* (London: Panther Books, 1968 and 1969), respectively designated I, II and III.
7. Compare Gunn, p. 49, referring to it as 'a safety measure, a strategic reserve'.
8. Compare Maxine Moore, 'Asimov, Calvin and Moses', in Thomas D. Clareson, ed., *Voices for the Future: Essays on Major Science Fiction Writers*, I, pp. 101–2, who sees the whole trilogy in terms of electronic imagery, with the two Foundations at opposite nodes to switch the current of history from physical to mental science, and compares it to 'the structure and function of a vacuum tube or transistor' (p. 102). Moore also analyses the imagery of the trilogy in terms of the workings of an electromagnetic motor in her 'The Use of Technical Metaphors in Asimov's Fiction', in Joseph D. Olander and Martin H. Greenberg, eds. *Isaac Asimov*, pp., 85–9.
9. Some have seen the trilogy as much more determinist (this seems to be the main issue debated in critical accounts). Wollheim, pp. 40–1, and Charles Elkins, 'Asimov's Foundation Novels: Historical Materialism Distorted into Cyclical Psycho-History', *Science-Fiction Studies*, III, pp. 26–35 [repr. in Olander and Greenberg, pp. 97–110], both see semi-Marxist views of a controlled social future at work; and Patrouch, pp. 138–9, finds only determinism in the trilogy. Gunn, pp. 40–2, and Donald Watt, 'A Galaxy Full of People: Characterization in Asimov's Major Fiction', in Olander and Greenberg, pp. 136–40, acknowledge the role of freewill.
10. At III, 186, however, the Second Foundationers are made to claim that they controlled the situation entirely, arranging that Bayta Darell should be present to destroy Mis.
11. Gene Wolfe used the same name 'Terminus' to almost the same ironic purpose in his *The Book of the New Sun* (see p. 211 below). He may also, incidentally, have taken the name 'Urth' from the hero Wendell Urth of

Asimov's stories 'The Singing Bell' (1955), 'The Dying Night' (1956) and 'The Key' (1966).

12. On the 'flatness' of Asimov's characters see also Elkins, p. 26, who calls them 'undifferentiated and one-dimensional'; and Joseph Patrouch, 'Asimov's Most Recent Fiction', in Olander and Greenberg, p. 161. For a lively argument on behalf of Asimov's characterization, see Donald Watt, 'A Galaxy Full of People', pp. 139–41. Gunn, pp. 46–7, relates the one-dimensionality of the characters to their being functions of a developing scheme of social science.

13. L. David Allen, 'Isaac Asimov 1920–' in E. F. Bleiler, ed., *Science Fiction Writers: Critical Studies of the Major Authors from the Early Nineteenth Century to the Present Day*, p. 270, says this demand, made in January 1945, arose out of Campbell's desire to see the Seldon Plan upset by some means.

14. Compare the similar, if more dismissive, objections of Elkins, pp. 103, 105, speaking of 'the sense of fatality and futility evoked in the *Foundation* novels' (p. 105), of 'complacency' which supposes enclosure (p. 106), and of the number of events actually involved in historical process that Asimov leaves out (pp. 108–9).

15. On Asimov's psychic need for a rational and comfortable universe, see Gunn, pp. 16–18.

16. Elkins, pp. 107–9, sees the whole as purposeless, merely conservative and cyclic.

17. Brian Stableford, reviewing *Foundation's Edge*, in *The Science Fiction and Fantasy Book Review*, no. 15 (June, 1983) p. 17.

18. Trevize's use of free choice is underestimated by John L. Grigsby, 'Herbert's Reversal of Asimov's Vision Reassessed: *Foundation's Edge* and *God Emperor of Dune*', *Science-Fiction Studies*, XI, pp. 174–81, who sees the picture here, as in the earlier *Foundation* novels, as one in which 'the universe is still controlled and dominated . . . [by a benign scientific agency] that prevents humans from living, struggling, fighting, learning, and dying in the realistic, less-than-perfect, and yet also thinking, growing, and progressing way that they always have' (p. 178).

CHAPTER 3: FREDERIK POHL

1. As in *The Early Pohl* (N.Y.: Doubleday, 1976), and *Planets Three* (N.Y.: Berkley Books, 1982); all the stories originally appeared in magazines under pseudonyms (usually 'James MacCreigh') in the 1940s.

2. In the afterword to his first solo novel, *Slave Ship* (1957), which is set on Earth, Pohl says that the business of the science fiction writer is 'to take what is already known and, by extrapolating from it, draw as plausibly detailed a portrait as he can manage of what tomorrow's scientists may learn . . . and of what the human race in its day-to-day life may make of it all' (New English Library edn, London, 1963, p. 126).

3. Pohl, 'Ragged Claws', in Brian W. Aldiss and Harry Harrison, eds, *Hell's Cartographers: Some Personal Histories of Science Fiction Writers*, p. 164.

4. In order of composition, *The Early Pohl, Planets Three, Alternating Currents, The Case Against Tomorrow* (1957), *Tomorrow Times Seven* (1959), *The Man Who Ate the World* (1960), *Turn Left at Thursday* (1961), [with C. M. Kornbluth] *The Wonder Effect* (1962), *The Abominable Earthman* (1963), *Digits and Dastards* (1966), *Day Million* (1970), *The Gold at the Starbow's End* (1972), *In the Problem Pit* (1976), *Midas World* (1983).

5. For an introduction to Pohl's short stories in general, which places as much value on the later as on the earlier stories, see David N. Samuelson, 'The Short Fiction of Frederik Pohl', in Frank N. Magill, ed., *Survey of Science Fiction Literature*, IV, pp. 1948–53. On some of the satiric stories of the 1950s, Kingsley Amis, *New Maps of Hell*, pp. 102–15 is acute, though he values them more for their extrapolative force than for their intrinsic merit. For Pohl's own comments – circumstantial rather than informative – on some of his stories, see his afterword in Lester del Rey, ed., *The Best of Frederik Pohl*; del Rey's own introduction, 'A Variety of Excellence', sets the stories in the context of Pohl's life and work as a whole.

6. The idea of resuscitating life via skeletons in a museum Pohl probably owed to A. E. Van Vogt's 'The Monster' (1948), repr. in Van Vogt's *Destination: Universe!* (1952).

7. Pohl owed the idea for this story to a friend of the late 1940s, George R. Spoerer (see Pohl, *In the Problem Pit* (N.Y.: Bantam Books, 1976) p. 59). Spoerer could have developed it from a knowledge of, e.g., A. Hyatt Verrill's 'The World of the Giant Ants' (*Amazing Stories Quarterly*, Fall 1928), or John Russell Fearn's 'Wanderer of Time' (*Startling Stories*, 1944).

8. Pohl, *Alternating Currents* (N.Y.: Ballantine, 1956), p. 85. Page references hereafter are to this edition.

9. Similar stories of this period include the celebrated 'The Midas Plague' (1954), and (in collaboration with C. M. Kornbluth), *The Space Merchants* (1953), both of which, while ending 'happily', have a mordant sense of man's helplessness before his consumer culture.

10. For other examples of just punishment, see e.g. 'The Census Takers' (1955), 'The Celebrated No-Hit Inning' (1956) and 'Wapshot's Demon' (1956), in *The Case Against Tomorrow*; 'Survival Kit' (1957) and 'The Gentlest Venusian' (1958), in *Tomorrow Times Seven*; 'Third Offence' (1958), 'The Richest Man in Levittown' (1959) and 'The Martian in the Attic' (1960), in *Turn Left at Thursday*; or, 'The Fire Bringer' (1983) – and really all the stories consequent upon it – in *Midas World*.

11. Repr. in *Turn Left at Thursday*.

12. Repr. in *The Man Who Ate the World*.

13. This novel is an expression of 'The Gold at the Starbow's End' (1972), repr. in the short-story collection of that title, and of the story-idea in 'In the Problem Pit' (*In the Problem Pit*).

14. Repr. in *The Gold at the Starbow's End*.

15. Repr. in *Digits and Dastards*.

16. Repr. in *Tomorrow Times Seven*.

17. Repr. in *Day Million* and in *The Early Pohl*.

18. Repr. in *Tomorrow Times Seven*.

19. Repr. in *Turn Left at Thursday*.
20. Ibid.
21. Written for *Turn Left at Thursday*.
22. Repr. in *Digits and Dastards*.
23. Arguably one motive, articulated by the constant stress on Rafferty's leanness and Girty's obesity, which Rafferty loathes, is that of a hatred of thin man for fat – like that of Flay for Swelter in Mervyn Peake's *Titus Groan*.
24. Pohl, *Day Million*, pp. 16–17.
25. Ibid., p. 21.
26. Pope, *Moral Essays*, iv, 66; *Essay on Man*, i, 290–1.
27. *Essay on Man*, i, 57–60.

CHAPTER 4: BRIAN ALDISS

1. Aldiss and Harrison, eds., *Hell's Cartographers*, p. 4.
2. Ibid., p. 206.
3. Ibid., p. 206.
4. Of the East Aldiss wrote, 'That region, that experience, has remained with me continually' (*Hell's Cartographers*, p. 186). See also his portrayal of Sumatra in his *A Rude Awakening*, pp. 12, 117–18 – very like *Hothouse*.
5. Aldiss reworks this idea of devolution in the future to a primitive past condition in *An Age* (1967).
6. For a fine account of the paradoxes and dualities in *Hothouse*, see Richard Mathews, *Aldiss Unbound: the Science Fiction of Brian W. Aldiss*, pp. 18–22.
7. Aldiss, *Hothouse* (London: Sphere Books, 1971) p. 9. Page references in the text are to this edition.
8. Commentators on *Hothouse* have tended to go for such certainties. Most of them see the book as opting for 'nature' and Gren against the intellect of the morel. Mathews, pp. 22–3, sees Gren as right to reject the jungle, and says that he rejects 'the easy morality (morelity) of escape, and affirms his humanity' (p. 23). W. Warren Wagar, *Terminal Visions: the Literature of Last Things*, p. 96, sees Gren accepting that 'Things are as they are', and describes the morel and sodal as 'clever metaphors for modern Western civilization in all its self-congratulating guile and greed and folly' (p. 147). David Wingrove, in Brian Griffin and David Wingrove, *Apertures: a Study of the Writings of Brian Aldiss*, pp. 93, 219, gives a similar view; even Brian Griffin, while attempting to do justice to what he sees as a divided sympathy in Aldiss (ibid., pp. 41–6, 54–5), still sees the book opting for chaotic nature against 'the repressive, parasitic, alienating, terrorising force of the morel fungus' (p. 53). [Griffin's essay on *Hothouse* has the merits and defects of considering the book in terms of Aldiss's work as a whole: we have an enriching perspective, but response to the text tends to be cramped by *a priori* views.] For a different approach, see Harry Harrison, '*The Long Afternoon of Earth*', in Magill, ed., *Survey of Science Fiction Literature*, iii, pp. 1235–7, which portrays the book as an account of constantly changing life moving towards entropy and dissolution, and thence to the rise of new created forms: 'Aldiss shows that life can defeat entropy by evolving to the heights of technical success, then devolving back to the primitive cells, and finally back to the

force of life itself. As our sun dies and with it all life, the forces of existence are driven out to other stars, to other worlds where life can develop again' (p. 1236).
9. Aldiss, *This World and Nearer Ones: Essays Exploring the Familiar*, p. 203. See also Aldiss's comments, quoted in Colin Greenland's perceptive general account of his work in ch. 6 of his *The Entropy Exhibition: Michael Moorcock and the British 'New Wave' in Science Fiction*, pp. 81, 86.

CHAPTER 5: FRANK HERBERT

1. The richest critical work on Herbert is Timothy O'Reilly's *Frank Herbert*, both for its coverage of Herbert's views and for its sensitivity to his methods; its weakness is a tendency to read Herbert's beliefs wholesale into his works, and more locally a conviction that Herbert was an 'anti-rationalist', sympathetic only to the unconscious area of mind. Others include Robert C. Parkinson, '*Dune* – an Unfinished Tetralogy', *Extrapolation*, XIII, pp. 16–24, which sees *Dune* and *Dune Messiah* as portraying the steady corruption of the hero Paul through his choice of personal immortality rather than the changes of life; John Ower, 'Idea and Imagery in Herbert's *Dune*', *Extrapolation*, XV, pp. 129–39, which sees Paul and his context as a channel for transcendent forces to be liberated into the world; L. David Allen, *Herbert's 'Dune' and Other Works*, which finds *Dune* and *Dune Messiah* to be the first two stages of a developing 'Heroic Romance'; David M. Miller, *Frank Herbert*, which considers the *Dune* novels in terms of a Freudian account (at times rather oblique) of Paul's growth; the fine 'Oedipal' account of Paul's growth, and analysis of hostility towards women and sexuality in the novels in Susan McLean's 'A Psychological Approach to Fantasy in the *Dune* Series', *Extrapolation*, XXIII, pp. 150–8; and Leonard M. Scicaj, '*Prana* and the Presbyterian Fixation: Ecology and Technology in Frank Herbert's *Dune* Tetralogy', which is a clear and unifying portrayal of the complex ideas and developments of the series up to *God Emperor of Dune*. Willis E. McNelly and Timothy O'Reilly have written a perceptive account of the ideas and artistry of *Dune* in Magill, ed., *Survey of Science Fiction Literature*, II, pp. 647–58.
2. See the quotations from Herbert in O'Reilly, *Frank Herbert*, pp. 5, 39–45, 189.
3. Ibid., pp. 85–8; O'Reilly portrays Herbert as attacking Asimov's 'rationalism' and faith in science. On this subject, see also John Grigsby, 'Asimov's *Foundation* Trilogy and Herbert's *Dune* Trilogy: a Vision Reversed', *Science-Fiction Studies*, VIII, pp. 149–55; and Grigsby's 'Herbert's Reversal of Asimov's Vision Reassessed: *Foundation's Edge* and *God Emperor of Dune*', *Science-Fiction Studies*, XI, pp. 174–80, which again finds in favour of Herbert, seeing Asimov's work as lacking the dialectical character of reality.
4. As in others of Herbert's books – the subtug trying to evade detection in *Under Pressure* (1956), the unknown saboteur in *Destination: Void* (1966), the secret rebellion in *The Eyes of Heisenberg* (1966), the hidden doings of the bland rural community in *The Santaroga Barrier* (1968), the concealed location of Mliss Abnethe in *Whipping Star* (1970), the unknown extrasensory

powers of Lewis Orne in *The Godmakers* (1972), the secret behind the apparent farmhouse of *Hellstrom's Hive* (1973) or behind the walled-off planet in *The Dosadi Experiment* (1977), the unknown intelligence of the planet in *The Jesus Incident* (1979), the concealment of the plague-transmitter in *The White Plague* (1982). In many cases, the unknown figures as the unconscious beneath the front of the conscious self.

5. See note 4 above. In *The Jesus Incident* too the colonists have to find out how to worship the Ship aright.
6. Herbert, *Dune* (London: New English Library, 1969) p. 312. Page references hereafter are to this edition.
7. Herbert uses this breeding idea and the notion of genetic manipulation elsewhere in his fiction – *The Eyes of Heisenberg, The Godmakers, Hellstrom's Hive, The Dosadi Experiment*. But Herbert is interested throughout his work in the idea of making something, whether it be a brain, a drug, a soldiery, a messiah or a plague.
8. Compare Miller, pp. 17 and 22. Miller comments (p. 17), 'Thus Herbert is able to make the events of the story seem both inevitable and spontaneous' (in keeping with its theme).
9. Miller, pp. 22–3, finds a chain of bull and bullfighting images running throughout *Dune*, and sees it as representing a synthesis between the animal and human in Paul and a surrender to the animal by the Baron and the Emperor.
10. Compare O'Reilly and McNelly, 'Dune', p. 654; 'Nothing "just happens". It happens to someone, is interpreted, and is changed by the way they respond.'
11. For consideration of this theme in terms of the imagery of the book, see Ower, pp. 134–6.
12. Herbert dramatized this idea again in the Optimen of *The Eyes of Heisenberg*.
13. See also O'Reilly, *Frank Herbert*, pp. 67–8.
14. Compare what is said of Paul in Herbert, *Children of Dune*, p. 323, *'Seeking the absolute of orderly prediction, he amplified disorder, distorted prediction.'*
15. *Children of Dune*, p. 162.
16. See O'Reilly, pp. 18–19, 79–81.
17. 'I am showing you [the reader] the superhero syndrome and your own participation in it. The arrogant are, in part, created by the meek'; *'Dune* was set up to imprint on you, the reader, a superhero. I wanted you so totally involved with that superhero in all his really fine qualities. And then I wanted to show what happens, in a natural, evolutionary process' (statements made in 1977 and 1978 by Herbert, and quoted in O'Reilly, pp. 45, 189).
18. *Children of Dune*, p. 324. When asked what will be the outcome of the peace he offers his subjects, Leto mockingly replies, ' "Its opposite" ' (ibid., p. 380).
19. Ibid., p. 164.
20. Herbert said that science fiction enabled him to create 'marvellous analogues' (telephone conversation to O'Reilly, May 28, 1979, quoted in O'Reilly, p. 8).
21. Herbert, *The Santaroga Barrier*, p. 170.
22. Compare also Scicaj, op. cit., p. 350.
23. Herbert, *Heretics of Dune*, p. 384.

CHAPTER 6: ROBERT SILVERBERG

1. He has been credited with 450 titles: see Malcolm Edwards, 'Robert Silverberg', in E. F. Bleiler, ed., *Science Fiction Writers*, p. 506.
2. For the full account, see Silverberg, 'Sounding Brass, Tinkling Cymbal', in Brian Aldiss and Harry Harrison, eds, *Hell's Cartographers*, pp. 7–45.
3. Brian Stableford has suggested that the fire, which for Silverberg was his first contact with 'the real anguish of life' ('Sounding Brass', p. 37), is imaged in *Nightwings*, where the old world is overthrown and has to be created anew (Stableford, '*Nightwings*', in Magill, ed., *Survey of Science Fiction Literature*, III, p. 1528).
4. See on this Silverberg, 'Sounding Brass, Tinkling Cymbal', p. 41.
5. The best general introduction to Silverberg's fiction is Thomas D. Clareson, *Robert Silverberg*. See also Clareson's 'The Fictions of Robert Silverberg', in Clareson, ed., *Voices for the Future*, II, pp. 1–33, which, in the author's words, 'stresses Silverberg's dark vision'; George Tuma, 'Robert Silverberg', in David Cowart and Thomas L. Wymer, eds, *Twentieth-Century American Science-Fiction Writers*, II, pp. 106–19; Edwards, op. cit., pp. 505–11.
6. Stableford, p. 1529, says that virtually all Silverberg's novels of the second phase of his career (post-1965) have as theme 'the healing of states of alienation: the reconciliation of "outsiders" of various kinds to their fellow human beings, very often by a direct contact of minds, frequently involving processes of rebirth both literal and metaphorical'. This does not take sufficient account of the several works in which alienation is not overcome, however much its removal might be wished – *Hawksbill Station*, *The Man in the Maze*, *A Time of Changes*, *The World Inside*, *Dying Inside*.
7. See also Robert Hunt, 'Visionary States and the Search for Transcendence in Science Fiction', in George E. Slusser, *et al.*, *Bridges to Science Fiction, Essays Prepared for the First Eaton Conference on Science Fiction and Fantasy Literature*, pp. 72–7.
8. Silverberg, *Nightwings* (London: Sphere Books, 1978) p. 162. Page references in the text are to this edition.
9. Contrast the more detailed description of Jerusalem in *Shadrach in the Furnace*, pp. 191–5. Jerusalem in that book is the place where Shadrach begins to become aware of his spiritual obligation to help the sick.
10. Stableford, p. 1529, points out how *Nightwings* is a reworking of earlier stories by Silverberg concerned with alien conquest of a decrepit Earth – he cites 'Slaves of the Star Giants' (1957) and 'Vengeance of the Space Armada' (1958) – and says that what in these stories was an ethic of tough heroism is replaced in *Nightwings* by 'virtues of empathy and pacifism'.
11. Self-exposure is another of Silverberg's recurrent themes, as in *The Man in the Maze*, *A Time of Changes*, *Son of Man* and *The Book of Skulls* (1972), where the protagonists all, with varying success, strip their souls to others' gaze.
12. Silverberg was to return to this theme of freewill and the random versus the determined in *The Stochastic Man* (1975).
13. This is probably derived from the same duality in Olaf Stapledon's Seventh or Flying Men on Venus in his *Last and First Men* (1930). *Nightwings* is the exception at this period of Silverberg's fiction in having a sense of verticality. Most of his work operates more on a horizontal plane, like the desert to

which Kinnall Darival retires in *A Time of Changes* or the car-journey across the States in *The Book of Skulls*. There are verticalities that should not be, such as the tower of *Tower of Glass* or the thousand-storey buildings of *The World Inside*, and of these the first is destroyed and the second answered by horizontal agrarian life. This may be part of what Silverberg meant when he called 'Nightwings' the novella 'curiously lyrical'.

14. Science and misuse of it are responsible for the exile into the past in *Hawksbill Station*, for tormented deformity in *The Man in the Maze*, for the androids and the eventual ruination of Earth in *Tower of Glass*, for the Huxleyite urbmons of *The World Inside*, for the blunders of *The Second Trip* (1972). Yet if love and understanding come first, science may be beneficial – as in Shadrach's distribution of an antidote to stop the spread of the disease of organ rot in humanity in *Shadrach in the Furnace*.

15. Others include the distortions of the lovers in *Thorns*, the manipulations that make the androids out of vats in *Tower of Glass*, the deformities suffered by humans living on Belzagor in *Downward to the Earth*, the organ rot in *Shadrach in the Furnace*.

16. Silverberg, 'Sounding Brass, Tinkling Cymbal', p. 8.

17. Compare Clareson, 'The Fictions of Robert Silverberg', p. 5: 'there has been no distinct, linear development to Silverberg's fiction'; see also p. 19.

CHAPTER 7: PHILIP JOSÉ FARMER

1. Leslie Fiedler, 'Notes on Philip José Farmer', in Farmer, *The Book of Philip José Farmer*, p. 317, sees this urge in Farmer as ultimately 'a gargantuan lust to *swallow* down the whole cosmos, past, present, and to come, and to spew it out again'. Fiedler also argues that this expresses itself in a predominance of eating imagery in Farmer's fiction, for example in the first two books of the Riverworld series.

2. The Riverworld series had its first version as *Owe for the Flesh*, a 150 000 word novel which Farmer wrote in one month in 1953 for a Shasta-Pocket Books award, but while the book won first prize, the Shasta publishing house was folding and Farmer was neither paid nor his book published. (See Sam Moskowitz, *Seekers of Tomorrow: Masters of Modern Science Fiction*, pp. 404–5.) The second version of this book (reduced to 70 000 words for supposed publication by Shasta) has recently been discovered and published as *River of Eternity* (1983): see Farmer's introduction therein on the development of the whole series.

3. In the fifth, *Gods of Riverworld* (1983), however, the context is the rather more claustrophobic one of the central control tower at the north pole of Riverworld.

4. Farmer, *To Your Scattered Bodies Go* (London: Granada Publishing, 1974) p. 10. Page references in the text are to this edition.

5. Farmer, *The Magic Labyrinth*, pp. 440–8.

6. Specific sources for some of the ideas behind the book are suggested by Mary T. Brizzi, *Philip José Farmer*, pp. 55–7: among them the *Book of Revelation*, 22:1, and the Biblical Jordan for the River; John Kendrick Bangs, *A*

Houseboat on the Styx (1895), in which a fictional Mark Twain travels down an infinitely long river in a riverboat; and Twain's own 'The Mysterious Stranger' or 'The Chronicle of Young Satan' (1916), in which some boys meet an uncaring angel (Satan) who creates tiny people out of clay only to destroy them at whim (chs 2–3).

7. Farmer, *The Magic Labyrinth*, pp. 458–9. In *Gods of Riverworld*, however, he says that this is not in fact the case (pp. 347–8).

8. See also p. 193, describing Burton's dislike of the idea of nets.

9. However the issue of whether or not their reconstruction via their *wathans* can ever make the people of Riverworld their true selves, or only duplicates, is raised: see e.g. pp. 130–1. For discussion of this topic, see also Monte Cooke, 'Who Inhabits Riverworld?', in Nicholas D. Smith, ed., *Philosophers Look at Science Fiction*, pp. 97–104.

10. For a parallel context and behaviour, see Farmer, *The Maker of Universes*, p. 70. On the concept of the hero throughout Farmer's work, see Russell Letson, 'The Faces of a Thousand Heroes: Philip José Farmer', *Science-Fiction Studies*, IV, pp. 35–41.

11. Compare George MacDonald, 'The Fantastic Imagination', *A Dish of Orts, Chiefly Papers on the Imagination, and on Shakspere*, p. 316: 'In physical things a man may invent; in moral things he must obey – and take their laws with him into his invented world as well.'

12. Farmer, *The Dark Design*, pp. 387–8. See also *The Magic Labyrinth*, pp. 416–18.

13. In Farmer's *Inside Outside* (1964), which is in many ways a reworking of the Riverworld idea, the hero, Cull, decides that for all the unpleasantness of the hellish world in which he finds himself, he would rather be alive on it than unborn, ' "And we're aware. Not a nothingness, a zero, floating in a vacuum" ' (Corgi Books edn, p. 33).

14. The motivations behind the book are also questioned by Franz Rottensteiner, 'Playing Around with Creation: Philip José Farmer', *Science-Fiction Studies*, I, p. 97. This is not the only book of Farmer's in which causality is limited, because of the author's primary interest in the worlds he creates rather than in the reasons for their existence: the five books of the 'World of Tiers' series – *The Maker of Universes* (1965), *The Gates of Creation* (1966), *A Private Cosmos* (1967), *Behind the Walls of Terra* (1970) and *The Lavalite World* (1977) – are a notable example, being exciting adventures set amid fabulous landscapes and scanty metaphysics.

15. As, in *The Maker of Universes*, p. 25, is the transformation of the ageing Robert Wolff when he enters the fantastic jungle world from his own.

16. This idea of the literary creator as himself a maker of universes, a God, is one that fascinates Farmer. Since for him all creation of being is, *ipso facto*, a good, this must finally blunt condemnation of the Ethicals.

17. *The Magic Labyrinth*, pp. 353, 494.

18. Brizzi, pp. 52–3, 57–8, sees the book as 'a search for truth', a quest for the 'Big Grail', but confuses instinctual with spiritual motives to allow for the fact that none of the characters admits to the latter: 'all seem driven by a desire deeper than conscious needs – the desire for ultimate truth. And this drive seems instinctive; the seekers resemble salmon driven to the spawning place' (p. 52).

19. This is Rottensteiner's contention also (op. cit., p. 96), though he applies his strictures to *To Your Scattered Bodies Go* too: for a rebuttal, see Russell Letson, 'The Worlds of Philip José Farmer', *Extrapolation*, XVIII, pp. 124–30.
20. See also Thomas L. Wymer's fine account of exposure as a motif in Farmer's work in his 'Philip José Farmer: The Trickster as Artist', in Thomas D. Clareson, ed., *Voices for the Future*, II, pp. 34–55.

CHAPTER 8: ARTHUR C. CLARKE

1. E. Michael Thron, 'The Outsider from Inside: Clarke's Aliens', in Joseph D. Olander and Martin Harry Greenberg, eds, *Arthur C. Clarke*, p. 81, suggests that the alien in Clarke can really be located in the unconscious: 'The alien is completely separate from, yet totally in control of, humanity.' This fits with Clarke's use in his fiction of the idea that it was aliens who provided the original stimulus for mental evolution in man.
2. The Hugo, Nebula, Jupiter and John W. Campbell awards. *Rendezvous with Rama* is the only science fiction novel ever to have achieved this distinction.
3. There is also an enclosed city in *The City and the Stars* (1956), a buried dust-cruiser in *A Fall of Moondust* (1961) and a miniature universe in *Imperial Earth* (1975).
4. Clarke himself says that the single story 'Jupiter Five' (1953), which formed the eventual basis for *Rendezvous with Rama*, 'required twenty or thirty pages of orbital calculations' (Clarke, *Reach for Tomorrow*, Preface).
5. Clarke, *Rendezvous with Rama* (London: Pan Books, 1981) p. 252. Page references hereafter are to this edition.
6. See also Thron, loc. cit.
7. Compare William H. Hardesty III, '*Rendezvous with Rama*', in Magill, ed., *Survey of Science Fiction Literature*, IV, p. 1762: 'The mystical and perhaps too pat answers of the earlier Clarke "first contact" books are wholly absent here.' Hardesty's is, incidentally, the most sensitive introduction to *Rendezvous with Rama* to date.
8. Perhaps developed from 'the checkerboard fields of the automatic farms' in *The Lion of Comarre* (1968); see Clarke, *The Lion of Comarre and Against the Fall of Night*, p. 16.
9. Gary K. Wolfe, 'The Known and the Unknown: Structure and Image in Science Fiction', in Thomas D. Clareson, ed., *Many Futures, Many Worlds: Theme and Form in Science Fiction*, pp. 113–15, charts a pattern of development in *Rendezvous with Rama* 'from the known to the unknown to the unknowable' (p. 113).
10. Clarke is generally sceptical of all religions for their attempts to subdue the mysteries of the universe to their categories: see e.g. Clarke, *The City and the Stars*, pp. 131–2, 188, and *The Fountains of Paradise*, pp. 77–80. That does not however disallow the existence of a God – see *The Fountains of Paradise*, p. 150.
11. There has been a tendency in accounts of the book to see it only in satiric terms, as a belittling of man and a critique of homocentrism: see Peter Brigg, 'The Three Styles of Arthur C. Clarke: The Projector, the Wit and the Mystic', in Olander and Greenberg, pp. 43–5; George E. Slusser, *The Space Odysseys of Arthur C. Clarke*, p. 61; and Eric S. Rabkin, *Arthur C. Clarke*,

pp. 48–51, 68, who says that Rama 'show[s] the utter inconsequence of humanity in the cosmic scheme of things' (p. 48). Contrast, however, the reply of John Hollow, *Against the Night, the Stars: the Science Fiction of Arthur C. Clarke*, pp. 159–60.

12. Contrast Larry Niven's *Ringworld* (1970), where the gigantic artificial ring of worlds about a sun and the reasons for its (certain) dereliction, are given clear scientific explanation.

13. Rabkin, op. cit., sees the whole episode as a belittling of man's pride (p. 50); but Jimmy sees the occasion, not himself, as significant, and Rabkin misses out the part of the passage that pokes fun rather at the alien as animated garbage-truck.

14. Clarke uses this idea of *déjà vu* elsewhere in his fiction – see his *A Fall of Moondust*, p. 19; 'Maelstrom II' (1965), repr. in Clarke, *The Wind from the Sun*, pp. 24–5; and *Imperial Earth*, pp. 144, 146, 278–9. Except for pp. 278–9 of *Imperial Earth*, the mysterious sense is, as with Captain Norton and Jimmy Pak, given explanation in a specific event in the past: but there what Duncan experiences puts him 'in the presence of the transcendental [where he] . . . feels the sure foundations of his world and his philosophy trembling beneath his feet', for he sees 'that the recognition came not only from the past, but also from the future' (p. 279).

CHAPTER 9: CLIFFORD D. SIMAK

1. Simak has defended the pleasantness of his aliens by arguing that, since to come to Earth they would have to be so scientifically advanced as to have more in their power than Earth could offer, they would come only out of motives of interest or kindness. See Darrell Schweitzer, *Science Fiction Voices # 5: Interviews with American Science Fiction Writers of the Golden Age*, pp. 49–50. One striking exception, however, to this benign view can be found in the carnivorous aliens of Simak's *Our Children's Children* (1974).

2. Kingsley Amis, *New Maps of Hell*, p. 107. For more sympathetic general accounts, see Donald Wollheim, *The Universe Makers*, pp. 90–3; Thomas D. Clareson, 'Clifford D. Simak: The Inhabited Universe', in Clareson, ed., *Voices for the Future*, I, pp. 64–87; David Pringle, 'Aliens for Neighbours: a Reassessment of Clifford D. Simak', *Foundation: the Review of Science Fiction*, XI–XII, pp. 15–29; Mary S. Weinkauf, 'Simak', in Curtis C. Smith, ed., *Twentieth-Century Science-Fiction Writers*, pp. 495–7; Roald W. Tweet, 'Clifford D. Simak, 1904–'; in Bleiler, ed., *Science Fiction Writers*, pp. 513–8.

3. Simak earlier used the idea (derived from Heinlein's 'Universe', 1941) of such a thousand-year journey by colonising space-ship in 'Target Generation', repr. in his *Strangers in the Universe* (1958). The notion of a journey so long that one's stellar destination has already been reached by more advanced later modes of human transport while one is still in transit, Simak probably took from A. E. Van Vogt's 'Far Centaurus' (1943), repr. in Van Vogt, *Destination: Universe!* (1952). Also anticipative of *Shakespeare's Planet* is Simak's own *Destiny Doll* (1972), which has the motif of imprisonment on a far planet and discovery of how to break out, a bizarre

group of explorers (including a tentacled creature from another world and a robot, apart from a man and woman), and an isolated ancient explorer who lives in a hovel in a valley scattered with 'Grecian' villas and writes nonsense. See also Stapledon, *Star Maker* (1937), ch. 8, for ch. 1.

4. Simak, *Shakespeare's Planet* (London: Methuen, Magnum Books, 1978) p. 1. Page references in the text hereafter are to this edition.
5. An exception is the isolated Asher Sutton in *Time and Again* (1951).
6. See the conversation at p. 77 on the relative importance of names; Horton tells Elayne that she may call him by either or both of his names.
7. Concomitant with this is Simak's dislike of technology, which in his stories is continually either being abolished or humanized (as in his robots): perhaps the most interesting example is the perfect machines which are in effect anti-machines of *Ring Around the Sun* (1953).
8. Thus in 'earlier' novels (up to about 1970) things come to Earth or stay in one place on Earth – *City* (1952), *Ring Around the Sun, Time is the Simplest Thing* (1961), *They Walked Like Men* (1963), *Way Station* (1963), *All Flesh is Grass* (1965), *The Werewolf Principle* (1967), *Why Call Them Back from Heaven?* (1967), *The Goblin Reservation* (1968), *Out of their Minds* (1970); while in later ones the characters leave the Earth, set out on quests or journeys, or enter fantastic realms – *Destiny Doll* (1972), *Enchanted Pilgrimage* (1975), *Shakespeare's Planet* (1976), *A Heritage of Stars* (1977), *The Fellowship of the Talisman* (1978), *Project Pope* (1981), *Special Deliverance* (1982).

CHAPTER 10: A. A. ATTANASIO

1. Attanasio, *Radix* (London: Corgi Books (Transworld Publishers), 1982) p. 382. Page references hereafter are to this edition.
2. See also pp. 200, 229–30.
3. This emphasis on pain, as on the body and mutation, recalls Silverberg. Compare Burris in *Thorns* (1967), who says he loves his body because of the pain he endures: ' "It shows that I live" ' (London: New English Library edn, 1977) p. 157.

CHAPTER 11: GENE WOLFE

1. References are to the Arrow Books (Sidgwick & Jackson, London) editions of 1981, 1982, 1982 and 1983 respectively; cited hereafter as *ST, CC, SL*, and *CA*.
2. On whether the book is 'sword and sorcery' or 'science fiction', see the review by Colin Greenland of *ST* and *CC* in *Foundation: the Review of Science Fiction*, XXIV, pp. 82–5.
3. Compare the history of the human race given at *SL*, pp. 51–5, with the sheerly different one at *CA*, pp. 278–80.
4. Pamela Sargent, 'Gene Wolfe', in Curtis C. Smith, ed., *Twentieth Century Science Fiction Writers*, p. 595, quotes Wolfe on his liking for Proust, Chesterton, Dickens, Washington Irving, Carroll (all his work), Kipling,

Maugham, Wells, John Fowles, R. A. Lafferty, Le Guin, Kate Wilhelm, Borges, Tolkien and C. S. Lewis.

5. See also T. D. Clareson, ' "The Book of Gold": Gene Wolfe's *Book of the New Sun*', *Extrapolation*, XXIII, p. 271.
6. George MacDonald, *Lilith*, p. 13.
7. Wolfe's fondness for reversal can be seen elsewhere in his fiction, most notably in his three short stories, 'The Death of Doctor Island', 'The Island of Doctor Death' and 'The Doctor of Death Island'.
8. Perhaps the nearest writer to Wolfe in this breaking of boundaries between fiction and reality, one mind and another, or between life and death, is Philip K. Dick, in such works as *Eye in the Sky* (1957), *Ubik* (1969) or *Valis* (1981).
9. C. S. Lewis, *Perelandra*, p. 236; Lewis, *Surprised by Joy: the Shape of My Early Life*, p. 170.

CHAPTER 12: CONCLUSION

1. Compare Mark Rose, *Alien Encounters*, pp. 184–95, who derives this concern with identity in science fiction from 'self-alienation'. At p. 184 Rose says, 'The vision of the genre as a whole is the conviction of infinite human plasticity.'
2. See e.g. Patrick G. Hogan, Jr, 'The Philosophical Limitations of Science Fiction', in Thomas D. Clareson, ed., *Many Futures, Many Worlds*, pp. 260–77; Stephen W. Potts, 'Dialogues Concerning Human Understanding: Empirical Views of God from Locke to Lem', in George E. Slusser, *et al.*, eds, *Bridges to Science Fiction*, pp. 41–52; Nicholas D. Smith, ed., *Philosophers Look at Science Fiction*; Robert E. Myers, ed., *The Intersection of Science Fiction and Philosophy: Critical Studies*.
3. Rose, p. 191.
4. Compare on the last John Huntington, 'Science Fiction and the Future' (1975), repr. in Mark Rose, ed., *Science Fiction: a Collection of Critical Essays*, pp. 156–66. At pp. 159–61, Huntington says that the determinism comes from the 'science', the predictive element of science fiction, and the freedom from the 'fiction', the creative aspect.
5. Kurt Vonnegut, *God Bless You, Mr Rosewater, or Pearls Before Swine*, pp. 21–2.

Bibliography

Aldiss, Brian, ed., *Introducing SF: a Science Fiction Anthology* (London: Faber, 1964).

———, ed., *Yet More Penguin Science Fiction* (Harmondsworth, Middx.: Penguin Books, 1966).

———, *Hothouse* (London: Sphere Books, 1971).

———, *Billion Year Spree: the True History of Science Fiction* (London: Weidenfeld & Nicolson, 1973).

———, 'Magic and Bare Boards', in Aldiss and Harrison, eds, *Hell's Cartographers*, pp. 173–209.

———, *A Rude Awakening* (London: Weidenfeld & Nicolson, 1978).

———, *This World and Nearer Ones: Essays Exploring the Familiar* (London: Weidenfeld & Nicolson, 1979).

Aldiss, Brian, and Harrison, Harry, eds, *Hell's Cartographers: Some Personal Histories of Science Fiction Writers* (London: Weidenfeld & Nicolson, 1975).

Allen, L. David, *Herbert's 'Dune' and Other Works*, Cliff's Notes Series (Lincoln, Nebraska: Cliff's Notes Inc., 1975).

Allen, L. David, 'Isaac Asimov, 1920–', in Bleiler, ed., *Science Fiction Writers*, pp. 267–76.

Amis, Kingsley, *New Maps of Hell* (London: New English Library, 1969).

Ashley, Mike, *The History of the Science Fiction Magazine*, 3 vols (London: New English Library, 1974–76).

Asimov, Isaac, *Foundation* (London: Panther Books, 1969).

———, *Foundation and Empire* (London: Panther Books, 1968).

———, *Second Foundation* (London: Panther Books, 1969).

———, *Foundation's Edge* (London: Panther/Granada, 1984).

Attanasio, A. A., *Radix* (London: Corgi Books (Transworld Publishers), 1982).

Bleiler, Everett F., ed., *Science Fiction Writers: Critical Studies of the Major Authors from the Early Nineteenth Century to the Present Day* (New York: Scribner's, 1982).

Brigg, Peter, 'The Three Styles of Arthur C. Clarke: the Projector, the Wit and the Mystic', in Olander and Greenberg, eds, *Arthur C. Clarke*, pp. 15–51.

Brizzi, Mary T., *Philip José Farmer*, Starmont Reader's Guide, no. 3 (Mercer Island, Washington: Starmont House, 1980).

Cioffi, Frank, *Formula Fiction?: an Anatomy of American Science Fiction, 1930–1940*, Contributions to the Study of Science Fiction and Fantasy, no. 3 (Westport, Conn.: Greenwood Press, 1982).

Clareson, Thomas D., ed., *SF: The Other Side of Realism, Essays on Modern Fantasy and Science Fiction* (Bowling Green, Ohio: Bowling Green University Popular Press, 1971).

———, ed., *Voices for the Future: Essays on Major Science Fiction Writers*, 2 vols (Bowling Green, Ohio: Bowling Green University Popular Press, 1976–79).

Clareson, Thomas D., 'Clifford D. Simak: the Inhabited Universe', in Clareson, ed., *Voices for the Future*, I, pp. 64–87.
——, ed., *Many Futures, Many Worlds: Theme and Form in Science Fiction* (Kent, Ohio: Kent State University Press, 1977).
——, 'The Fictions of Robert Silverberg', in Clareson, ed., *Voices for the Future*, II, pp. 1–33.
——, ' "The Book of Gold": Gene Wolfe's *Book of the New Sun*', *Extrapolation*, XXIII, 3 (Fall 1982) pp. 270–4.
——, *Robert Silverberg*, Starmont Reader's Guide, no. 18 (Mercer Island, Washington: Starmont House, 1983).
Clarke, Arthur C., *Reach for Tomorrow* (New York: Ballantine Books, 1956).
——, *Imperial Earth* (London: Pan Books, 1977).
——, *The City and the Stars* (London: Corgi Books, 1979).
——, *A Fall of Moondust* (London: Pan Books, 1980).
——, *Rendezvous with Rama* (London: Pan Books, 1981).
——, *The Fountains of Paradise* (London: Pan Books, 1982).
——, *The Lion of Comarre and Against the Fall of Night* (London: Pan Books, 1982).
——, *The Wind from the Sun* (London: Pan Books, 1983).
Cooke, Monte, 'Who Inhabits Riverworld?', in Smith, Nicholas D., ed., *Philosophers Look at Science Fiction*, pp. 97–104.
Cowart, David, and Wymer, Thomas L., eds, *Twentieth-Century American Science-Fiction Writers*, 2 vols [*Dictionary of Literary Biography*, vol. 8] (Detroit: Gale Research Co., 1981).
Delany, Samuel, *The Jewel-Hinged Jaw: Notes on the Language of Science Fiction* (Elizabethtown, New York: Dragon Press, 1977).
Del Rey, Lester, 'A Variety of Excellence', in del Rey, ed., *The Best of Frederik Pohl*, pp. ix–xvi.
Edwards, Malcolm, 'Robert Silverberg, 1935–', in Bleiler, ed., *Science Fiction Writers*, pp. 505–11.
Elkins, Charles, 'Asimov's Foundation Novels: Historical Materialism Distorted into Cyclical Psycho-History', *Science-Fiction Studies*, III, 1 (March, 1976) pp. 26–35 [repr. in Olander and Greenberg, eds. *Isaac Asimov*, pp. 97–110].
Farmer, Philip José, *The Maker of Universes* (London: Sphere Books, 1978).
——, *To Your Scattered Bodies Go* (London: Panther/Granada, 1979).
——, *The Dark Design* (London: Panther/Granada, 1979).
——, *The Magic Labyrinth* (London: Panther/Granada, 1981).
——, *Inside Outside* (London: Corgi Books, 1982).
——, *The Book of Philip José Farmer* (London: Granada Publishing, 1983).
——, *River of Eternity* (Huntington Woods, Mich.: Phantasia Press, 1983).
——, *Gods of Riverworld* (London: Panther/Granada, 1984).
Fiedler, Leslie, 'Notes on Philip José Farmer', in Farmer, *The Book of Philip José Farmer*, pp. 311–18.
Franklin, H. Bruce, *Future Perfect: American Science Fiction of the Nineteenth Century* (New York: Oxford University Press, 1966).
Glicksohn, Susan, ' "A City of Which the Stars are Suburbs" ', in Clareson, ed., *SF: The Other Side of Realism*, pp. 334–47.
Greenland, Colin, Review of Gene Wolfe, *The Shadow of the Torturer* and *The Claw of the Conciliator*, in *Foundation: the Review of Science Fiction*, XXIV (Feb. 1982) pp. 82–5.

Greenland, Colin, *The Entropy Exhibition: Michael Moorcock and the British 'New Wave' in Science Fiction* (London: Routledge & Kegan Paul, 1983).

Griffin, Brian, and Wingrove, David, *Apertures: a Study of the Writings of Brian Aldiss*, Contributions to the Study of Science Fiction and Fantasy, no. 8 (Westport, Conn.: Greenwood Press, 1984).

Grigsby, John, 'Asimov's *Foundation* Trilogy and Herbert's *Dune* Trilogy: a Vision Reversed', *Science-Fiction Studies*, VIII, 2 (July, 1981) pp. 149–55.

Grigsby, John, 'Herbert's Reversal of Asimov's Vision Reassessed: *Foundation's Edge* and *God Emperor of Dune*', *Science-Fiction Studies*, XI, 2 (July 1984) pp. 174–80.

Gunn, James, *Isaac Asimov: the Foundations of Science Fiction* (Oxford University Press, 1982).

Hardesty, William H., '*Rendezvous with Rama*', in Magill, ed., *Survey of Science Fiction Literature*, IV, pp. 1759–63.

Harrison, Harry, '*The Long Afternoon of Earth*', in Magill, ed., *Survey of Science Fiction Literature*, III, pp. 1235–7.

Herbert, Frank, *Dune* (London: New English Library, 1969).

——, *Children of Dune* (London: New English Library, 1978).

——, *The Santaroga Barrier* (London: New English Library, 1981).

——, *Heretics of Dune* (London: Victor Gollancz, 1984).

Hogan, Patrick, G., Jr, 'The Philosophical Limitations of Science Fiction', in Clareson, ed., *Many Futures, Many Worlds*, pp. 260–77.

Hollow, John, *Against the Night, the Stars: the Science Fiction of Arthur C. Clarke* (New York: Harcourt Brace Jovanovich, 1983).

Hunt, Robert, 'Visionary States and the Search for Transcendence in Science Fiction', in Slusser, *et al.*, eds, *Bridges to Science Fiction*, pp. 64–77.

Huntington, John, 'Science Fiction and the Future', in Rose, ed., *Science Fiction: a Collection of Critical Essays*, pp. 156–66.

Ketterer, David, *New Worlds for Old: the Apocalyptic Imagination, Science Fiction, and American Literature* (Indiana University Press, 1974).

Le Guin, Ursula K., 'Introduction', *The Left Hand of Darkness* (New York: Ace Books, 1976).

Letson, Russell, 'The Faces of a Thousand Heroes: Philip José Farmer', *Science-Fiction Studies*, IV, 1 (Mar. 1977) pp. 35–41.

Letson, Russell, 'The Worlds of Philip José Farmer', *Extrapolation*, XVIII, 2 (May 1977) pp. 124–30.

Lewis, C. S., *Perelandra* (London: John Lane, 1943).

Lewis, C. S., *Surprised by Joy: the Shape of my Early Life* (London: Geoffrey Bles, 1955).

McLean, Susan, 'A Psychological Approach to Fantasy in the *Dune* Series', *Extrapolation*, XXIII, 2 (Summer 1982) pp. 150–8.

MacDonald, George, 'The Fantastic Imagination', *A Dish of Orts: Chiefly Papers on the Imagination, and on Shakspere* (London: Sampson Low, 1893) pp. 313–22.

MacDonald, George, *Lilith* (London: Chatto & Windus, 1895).

McNelly, Willis, and O'Reilly, Timothy, '*Dune*', in Magill, ed., *Survey of Science Fiction Literature*, II, 647–58.

Magill, Frank N., ed., *Survey of Science Fiction Literature*, 5 vols (Englewood Cliffs, N.J.: Salem Press, 1979).

Manlove, Colin N., 'On the Nature of Fantasy', in Schlobin, ed., *The Aesthetics of Fantasy Literature and Art*, pp. 16–35.

Mathews, Richard, *Aldiss Unbound: the Science Fiction of Brian W. Aldiss*, The Milford Series of Popular Writers of Today, no. 9 (San Bernardino, Calif.: The Borgo Press, 1977).

Miller, David M., *Frank Herbert*, Starmont Reader's Guide, no. 5 (Mercer Island, Washington: Starmont House, 1980).

Moore, Maxine, 'Asimov, Calvin and Moses', in Clareson, ed., *Voices for the Future*, I, pp. 88–103.

Moore, Maxine, 'The Use of Technical Metaphors in Asimov's Fiction', in Olander and Greenberg, eds, *Isaac Asimov*, pp. 59–96.

Moskowitz, Sam, *Seekers of Tomorrow: Masters of Modern Science Fiction* (Westport, Conn.: Hyperion Press, 1974).

Myers, Robert E., ed., *The Intersection of Science Fiction and Philosophy: Critical Studies* (Westport, Conn.: Greenwood Press, 1983).

Olander, Joseph D. and Greenberg, Martin Harry, eds, *Isaac Asimov*, Writers of the 21st Century Series (Edinburgh: Paul Harris Publishing, 1977).

Olander, Joseph D. and Greenberg, Martin Harry, eds, *Arthur C. Clarke*, Writers of the 21st Century Series (Edinburgh: Paul Harris Publishing, 1977).

O'Reilly, Timothy, *Frank Herbert* (New York: Frederick Ungar Publishing, 1981).

O'Reilly, Timothy, and McNelly, Willis. See under McNelly.

Ower, John, 'Idea and Imagery in Herbert's *Dune*', *Extrapolation*, XV, 2 (May 1974) pp. 129–39.

Parkinson, Robert C., '*Dune* – an Unfinished Tetralogy', *Extrapolation*, XIII, 1 (Dec. 1971) pp. 16–24.

Patrouch, Joseph, *The Science Fiction of Isaac Asimov* (London: Panther/Granada, 1976).

Patrouch, Joseph, 'Asimov's Most Recent Fiction', in Olander and Greenberg, eds, *Isaac Asimov*, pp. 159–73.

Pohl, Frederik, *Alternating Currents* (New York: Ballantine Books, 1956).

——, *Slave Ship* (London: New English Library, 1963).

——, *Day Million* (London: Pan Books, 1973).

——, *The Best of Frederik Pohl*, ed. Lester del Rey (London: Futura Publications, 1976).

——, 'Ragged Claws', in Aldiss and Harrison, eds, *Hell's Cartographers*, pp. 144–72.

Potts, Stephen W., 'Dialogues Concerning Human Understanding: Empirical Views of God from Locke to Lem', in Slusser, *et al.*, *Bridges to Science Fiction*, pp. 41–52.

Pringle, David, 'Aliens for Neighbours: a Reassessment of Clifford D. Simak', *Foundation: the Review of Science Fiction*, XI–XII (Mar. 1977) pp. 15–29.

Rabkin, Eric S., *Arthur C. Clarke*, Starmont Reader's Guide, no. 1, 2nd edn (Mercer Island, Washington: Starmont House, 1980).

Rabkin, Eric S. and Scholes, Robert. See under Scholes.

Rose, Mark, ed., *Science Fiction: a Collection of Critical Essays* (Englewood Cliffs, N.J.: Prentice-Hall, Inc., 1976).

Rose, Mark, *Alien Encounters: Anatomy of Science Fiction* (Cambridge, Mass.: Harvard University Press, 1981).

Rottensteiner, Franz, 'Playing Around with Creation: Philip José Farmer', *Science-Fiction Studies*, I, 2 (Fall 1973) pp. 94–8.

Samuelson, David N., *Visions of Tomorrow: Six Journeys from Outer to Inner Space* (New York: Arno Press, 1975).

Samuelson, David N., 'The Short Fiction of Frederik Pohl', in Magill, ed., *Survey of Science Fiction Literature*, IV, pp. 1948–53.

Sargent, Pamela, 'Gene Wolfe', in Smith (Curtis), ed., *Twentieth Century Science Fiction Writers*, pp. 595–6.

Schlobin, Roger C., ed., *The Aesthetics of Fantasy Literature and Art* (University of Notre Dame Press, 1982).

Scholes, Robert, and Rabkin, Eric S., *Science Fiction: History, Science, Vision* (Oxford University Press, 1977).

Schweitzer, Darrell, *Science Fiction Voices # 5: Interviews with American Science Fiction Writers of the Golden Age*, The Milford Series of Writers of Today, no. 35 (San Bernardino, Calif.: The Borgo Press, 1981).

Scicaj, Leonard M., '*Prana* and the Presbyterian Fixation: Ecology and Technology in Frank Herbert's *Dune* Tetralogy', *Extrapolation*, XXIV, 4 (Winter 1983) pp. 340–55.

Silverberg, Robert, 'Sounding Brass, Tinkling Cymbal', in Aldiss and Harrison, eds, *Hell's Cartographers*, pp. 7–45.

——, *Thorns* (London: New English Library, 1977).

——, *Nightwings* (London: Sphere Books, 1978).

——, *Shadrach in the Furnace* (London: Hodder & Stoughton, Coronet Books, 1981).

Simak, Clifford D., *Shakespeare's Planet* (London: Methuen, Magnum Books, 1978).

Slusser, George E., *The Space Odysseys of Arthur C. Clarke*, The Milford Series of Popular Writers of Today, no. 8 (San Bernardino, Calif.: The Borgo Press, 1978).

Slusser, George E., Guffey, George R., and Rose, Mark, eds, *Bridges to Science Fiction: Essays Prepared for the First Eaton Conference on Science Fiction and Fantasy Literature* (Carbondale and Edwardsville: Southern Illinois University Press, 1980).

Smith, Curtis C., ed., *Twentieth Century Science Fiction Writers* (London: Macmillan, 1981).

Smith, Nicholas D., ed., *Philosophers Look at Science Fiction* (Chicago: Nelson-Hall Inc., 1982).

Stableford, Brian, Review of Isaac Asimov, *Foundation's Edge*, in *The Science Fiction and Fantasy Book Review*, no. 15 (June 1983) p. 17.

Stableford, Brian, '*Nightwings*', in Magill, ed., *Survey of Science Fiction Literature*, III, pp. 1526–30.

Suvin, Darko, *Victorian Science Fiction in the U.K.: the Discourses of Knowledge and of Power* (Boston, Mass.: G. K. Hall, 1983).

Thron, E. Michael, 'The Outsider from Inside: Clarke's Aliens', in Olander and Greenberg, eds, *Arthur C. Clarke*, pp. 72–86.

Tuma, George, 'Robert Silverberg', in Cowart and Wymer, eds, *Twentieth-Century American Science-Fiction Writers*, II, pp. 106–19.

Tweet, Roald W., 'Clifford D. Simak, 1904–', in Bleiler, ed., *Science Fiction Writers*, pp. 513–18.

Vonnegut, Kurt, *God Bless You, Mr Rosewater, or Pearls Before Swine* (London: Panther Books, 1965).

Wagar, W. Warren, *Terminal Visions: the Literature of Last Things* (Indiana University Press, 1982).

Watt, Donald, 'A Galaxy Full of People: Characterisation in Asimov's Major Fiction', in Olander and Greenberg, eds, *Isaac Asimov*, pp. 135–58.

Weinkauf, Mary S., 'Simak', in Smith (Curtis), ed., *Twentieth Century Science Fiction Writers*, pp. 495–7.

Wingrove, David. See under Griffin, Brian, and Wingrove, David.

Wolfe, Gary, 'The Known and the Unknown: Structure and Image in Science Fiction', in Clareson, ed., *Many Futures, Many Worlds*, pp. 94–116.

Wolfe, Gene, *The Shadow of the Torturer* (London: Sidgwick & Jackson, Arrow Books, 1981).

——, *The Claw of the Conciliator* (London: Sidgwick & Jackson, Arrow Books, 1982).

——, *The Sword of the Lictor* (London: Sidgwick & Jackson, Arrow Books, 1982).

——, *The Citadel of the Autarch* (London: Sidgwick & Jackson, Arrow Books, 1983).

Wollheim, Donald A., *The Universe Makers: Science Fiction Today* (London: Gollancz, 1972).

Wymer, Thomas L., 'Philip José Farmer: The Trickster as Artist', in Clareson, ed., *Voices for the Future*, ii, pp. 34–55.

Wyntenbroek, Jaqueline, 'Science Fiction and Fantasy', *Extrapolation*, xxiii, 4 (Winter 1982) pp. 321–32.

Index

Aldiss, Brian, 3, 5, 9, 57–8, 229n.4; character of science fiction, 57; *An Age*, 10, 77, 229n.5; *Bow Down to Nul*, 77; *The Dark Light Years*, 77–8; *Earthworks*, 77; *Enemies of the System*, 78, 221; *Frankenstein Unbound*, 78; *Greybeard*, 58, 77; 'Helliconia' novels, 57; *Hothouse*, 3, 10, 13, 57–78, 80–3, 89, 90, 143, 181, 185, 198, 203, 217–24 *passim*: sources, 57–8; mental development in, 61–2; maturation theme in, 62–76; patterns of imagery in, 63–76; compared with other works, 77–8; *The Malacia Tapestry*, 9; *Moreau's Other Island*, 78; *Non-Stop*, 57, 77; *A Rude Awakening*, 229n.4; 'The Saliva Tree', 58

Amazing Stories, 7–8

Anthony, Piers, 'Cluster' series, 15

Asimov, Isaac, 3, 8, 9, 35, 227n.15; *The Currents of Space*, 34; *The End of Eternity*, 33; the *Foundation* trilogy, 3, 4, 7, 10, 11, 13, 15–34, 79, 83, 86, 88, 92, 104, 200, 201, 203, 217–24 *passim*, 226nn.5,10: control of history in, 15–19; duality in, 15–16, 19–21, 24–6; choice and determinism in, 21–4; ethic of dynamism in, 26–8; as scientific experiment, 28–9; limitations of, 31; *Foundation's Edge*, 31–4, 227n.15: as continuation of *Foundation* trilogy, 31–2; as expansion of earlier vision, 32–4; *Pebble in the Sky*, 34; 'robot' novels, 34; *The Stars, Like Dust*, 34

Astounding, 8

Attanasio, A. A., *Radix*, 3, 4, 10, 30, 181–97, 198, 217–24 *passim*, 219, 220, 221, 223: distinctive features, 181–2; as science fiction rather than fantasy, 182–3; plasticity of self in, 186–92; development of self in, 187–94; evolution and stasis in, 192–4; dual character of, 194–7

Ballard, J. G., 5, 9

Bangs, John Kendrick, *A Houseboat on the Styx*, 233–4n.6

Blake, W., *Songs of Innocence and of Experience*, 116

Blish, James, *A Case of Conscience*, 2; *Cities in Flight*, 12, 15

Borges, Jorge Luis, 198, 201

Burroughs, Edgar Rice, 15

Campbell, John W., 8, 29, 222, 226n.1, 227n.13

Čapek, Karel, *War with the Newts*, 12

Clarke, Arthur C., 3, 5, 235n.10, 236n.14; character of science fiction, 143–4; *Childhood's End*, 2, 143–4, 146, 147, 154; *The Deep Range*, 155; *The Fountains of Paradise*, 222; *A Fall of Moondust*, 235n.3, 236n.14; *Imperial Earth*, 222, 235n.3, 236n.14; 'Jupiter Five', 235n.14; *The Lion of Comarre*, 235n.8; 'Maelstrom II', 236n.14; *Rendezvous with Rama*, 3, 4, 10, 11, 143–60, 200, 203, 217–24 *passim*, 235nn.2,4; 236n.13: distinctive features of, 146–7; credibility of, 147–8; interplay of strange and familiar in, 147–54; critique of human perspective in, 154–60; uncertainty principle in, 157–60; *The City and the Stars*, 235n.3; *2001: A Space Odyssey*, 143, 144, 146, 147, 154

Tennyson, Alfred, Lord, 'Ulysses', 132

Tolkien, J. R. R., 223; *The Lord of the Rings*, 4, 9, 11, 12, 181, 183, 197

Twain, Mark, 'The Mysterious Stranger' or 'The Chronicle of Young Satan', 233–4n.6

Vance, Jack, *The Dying Earth*, 201

Van Vogt, A. E., 15, 166; 'Far Centaurus', 236n.3; 'The Monster', 228n.6; *The Voyage of the Space Beagle*, 7

Verne, Jules, *A Journey to the Centre of the Earth*, 6, 10, 11; *Twenty Thousand Leagues Under the Sea*, 6

Verrill, A. Hyatt, 'The World of the Giant Ants', 228n.7

Visiak, E. H., *Medusa*, 64

Vonnegut, Kurt, *God Bless You, Mr Rosewater*, quoted, 224

Watson, Ian, *The Gardens of Delight*, 9

Wells, H. G., 15; *The Invisible Man*, 5, 10; *The Island of Dr Moreau*, 5, 218, 221; 'The Star', 10; *The Time Machine*, 1, 3–4, 6, 10, 11, 59, 143; *The War of the Worlds*, 5, 10, 68

White, T. H., *The Once and Future King*, 11, 12

Williams, Charles, 197

Williamson, Jack, 35; *The Legion of Space*, 7; *The Legion of Time*, 7

Wolfe, Gene, 237–8n.4, 238nn.7,8; *The Book of the New Sun*, 3, 10, 11, 30, 198–216, 217–24 *passim*, 227n.11, 237n.3: character of, as science fiction, 198–9; refusal of explanation in, 199–201, 216; restriction of narrative drive in, 201–2; character of imagination in, 203–5; metaphysical ground of, 205–8; motif of reversal in, 208–10; absence of boundaries to identity, and inclusiveness in, 210–5; nature of meaning in, 215–6

Wyndham, John, 5, 8; *The Day of the Triffids*, 11, 66

Zelazny, Roger, *Damnation Alley*, 12